Welcome to New Zealand

Get ready for mammoth national parks, dynamic Māori culture, and world-class mountain biking, surfing and skiing. New Zealand can be mellow or action-packed, but it's always outstanding.

There are just 4.8 million New Zealanders, scattered across 268,021 sq km: bigger than the UK with one-fourteenth of the population. Plenty of room to explore – tackle one of the epic 'Great Walks' or spend a few hours wandering along a beach, paddling a canoe or mountain biking through some easily accessible wilderness.

Hungry yet? NZ chefs borrow influences from as far afield as South Pacific islands and Western Europe for creative takes on locally sourced lamb and seafood like abalone, oysters and scallops. Wash it down with craft beer and legendary cool-climate wines (sublime sauvignon blanc and pinot noir).

Next up, check out some indigenous culture: across NZ you can hear Māori language, watch Māori TV, join in a *hāngi* (Māori feast) or catch a cultural performance with song, dance and a blood-curdling *haka* (war dance).

But fear not: New Zealanders these days are far from warlike. This decent nation is a place where you can relax and enjoy (rather than endure) your holiday.

New Zealand can be mellow or action-packed, but it's always outstanding

Franz Josef Glacier (p194)
DAVIDTCLAY/SHUTTERSTOCK ©

Tasman
Sea

Ka

Op

A

Takaka○

Karamea○   Nels

B

Westport ○

Murchi

Punakaiki ○

Hokitika

Franz   ○ Arthur's Pass
Josef
Fox   ○ Glacier
Glacier ○

Aoraki/   Methven ○
Mt Cook
(3754m)   C
○ Haast   ▲   I

Haast   Ashburton
Pass

○ Wanaka   ○ Timaru

○ Waimate

○ Oamaru

○ Palmerston

Te Anau ○   ○ Palmerston

Lumsden   Dunedin
○

○ Gore ○ Balclutha

Tuatapere ○

○ Invercargill

Bluff ○

○ Oban

Waiheke Island (p42)
PONDERFUL PICTURES/SHUTTERSTOCK ©

Plan Your Trip
New Zealand's Top 12

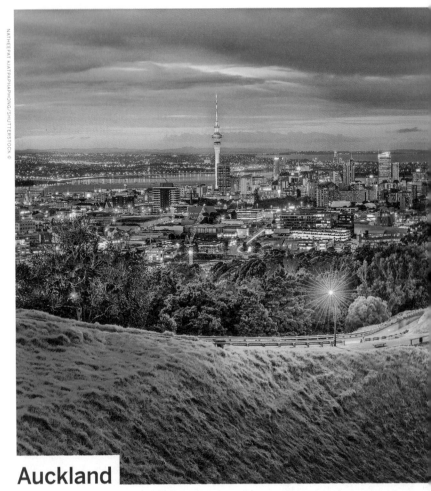

NATHEEPAT KIATPAPHAPHONG/SHUTTERSTOCK ©

Auckland

Hills, harbours and heady nightlife

Held in the embrace of two harbours and built on the peaks of long-extinct volcanoes, Auckland (p35) isn't your average metropolis. It's never going to challenge NYC or London in the excitement stakes, but this pretty city is blessed with fab beaches, museums and kickin' dining, drinking and live-music scenes. Cultural festivals are celebrated with gusto in the 'City of Sails', which has the biggest Polynesian population of any city in the world. From left: View over Auckland from the top of Mt Eden (p46); Sky Tower (p46)

1

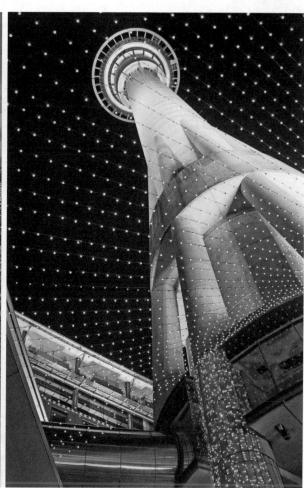

Wellington

The coolest little capital on the planet?

Windy Wellington (p131) lives up to the hype. It's long famed for
its buzzing arts and music scenes, fuelled by excellent espresso, a
crop of craft-beer bars, and more cafes and restaurants per capita
than New York City. Edgy yet sociable, colourful yet often dressed
in black, Wellington is big on the unexpected and unconventional.
A few gusts of wind only zest-up the experience...though it plays
havoc with all those hip haircuts. Top: Wellington Cable Car (p142); Bottom:
Bar in Wellington

I VIEWFINDER/SHUTTERSTOCK ©

Queenstown

Superb skiing, eating, drinking...and bungy jumping!

There's much more to Queenstown (p207) – the 'Adventure Capital of NZ' – than leaping off a bridge attached to a giant rubber band. The Remarkables mountain range provides a jagged indigo backdrop to days spent skiing, tramping and mountain biking, before dining in cosmopolitan restaurants or partying in some of NZ's best bars. Keep the adrenaline flowing with hang gliding, kayaking, rafting...or maybe a more sedate detour to the Gibbston Valley wineries. Kawarau Bridge bungy (p211)

3

4

Fiordland
Gorgeous fiords in NZ's deep south

On a clear Fiordland day, Milford Sound (p233) delivers an astounding collage of waterfalls, cliffs, peaks and dark cobalt waters. Drizzle is more likely than sunshine, but arguably more atmospheric, with the iconic profile of Mitre Peak revealing itself through the mist. Approaching via the Milford Track is an iconic NZ adventure, while further south, kayaking is a superb way to explore the silent shores of remote Doubtful Sound.

5

Marlborough
Sublime wine and wilderness

After a few days overindulging in Marlborough (p153) sauvignon blanc or Nelson craft beer made with locally grown hops, Abel Tasman National Park (pictured right) offers tramping, kayaking and swimming in golden sandy coves with gin-clear seas. The Marlborough Sounds are an impossibly photogenic wilderness, while seaside Kaikoura is the place to spy whales, seals and local bird life.

ALIZADA STUDIOS/SHUTTERSTOCK ©

Rotorua

Māori culture meets geothermal hullabaloo

Volcanic activity is what you're here for: gushing geysers, bubbling mud, stinky gas and boiling pools. Māori culture is also big business in Rotorua (p83) – book yourself in for a *hāngi* (feast) and a Māori concert, heavy on the *haka* (war dance). In true NZ style, there's also a slew of outdoor activities on offer here: ziplining, rafting, mountain biking... Or just stroll through the beautiful Redwoods Whakarewarewa Forest. Pōhutu geyser (p87)

Hawke's Bay

East Coast wine and architectural heritage

It's curious that more New Zealanders don't choose to live on the North Island's sunny East Coast. With a backdrop of chardonnay vines in the Hawke's Bay (p119) Wine Region and Napier's picture-perfect cache of art deco architecture, the living here is most definitely easy. You're the beneficiary: without the crowds there's plenty of room for you to venture out and enjoy your holiday. Craggy Range winery (p125)

7

Westland Tai Poutini National Park

Glaciers grind towards wild coastline

Hemmed in by the Tasman Sea and the Southern Alps, Westland Tai Poutini National Park (p191) is like nowhere else in New Zealand, and nowhere else on earth. Fed by upwards of 3m of annual rainfall, Franz Josef and Fox glaciers are truly awesome remnants from another time altogether. Book a helihike for an icy close encounter, or a scenic flight for an aerial assessment of their vast proportions.

JIMBOMCKIMBO/SHUTTERSTOCK ©

CHARLOTTE ROBINSON/SHUTTERSTOCK ©

CLOUDIA SPINNER/SHUTTERSTOCK ©

9

Bay of Islands
Photogenic coastline and history galore

Turquoise waters, empty bays, dolphins gliding gracefully by...chances are these are the kinds of images that drew you to NZ in the first place, and exactly the kinds of experiences the Bay of Islands (p65) delivers. There are myriad options to tempt you out on the water to explore the 150-odd islands that dot this beautiful bay. Back on dry land, uncover the history of modern NZ. From left: Bay views from Urupukapuka Island; Māori warrior carving

WINDAWAKE/SHUTTERSTOCK ©

Christchurch

Southern city on the rebound

It's fair to say that Christchurch (p175) – a city of 375,000 people that was rattled to the core by earthquakes in 2010 and 2011 – is a resilient kinda town. Exciting new buildings are opening at an astonishing pace, and most of the city's sights are open for business again – and despite all the hard work and heartache, the locals will be only too pleased to see you. Top: Historic tramway (p186); Bottom left: Chalice designed by Neil Dawson, Cathedral Square (p183); Bottom right: Transitional Cathedral windows (p179)

NAIRIS KRESLINS/SHUTTERSTOCK ©

Otago Peninsula

Go wild with the wildlife

With a constant backdrop of glorious coastal vistas, the Otago Peninsula (p255) offers some of NZ's best wildlife encounters. Dozens of little penguins achieve peak cuteness in their nightly beachside waddle, while their much rarer yellow-eyed cousin, the hoiho, can be glimpsed standing sentinel on deserted coves. Sea lions and seals laze on rocks while albatrosses from the world's only mainland colony soar above.

MARTIAN977/SHUTTERSTOCK ©

Taupo

Outdoor adventures and volcanic vistas

The heart of the North Island, hip little Taupo (p101) props on the doorstep of Tongariro National Park (pictured above) – an alien landscape of alpine desert punctuated by three smouldering volcanoes. The brilliant one-day Tongariro Alpine Crossing hike skirts past craters and iridescent lakes, with views across the vast Central Plateau. Lakeside Taupo itself offers hot springs, trout fishing, skydiving, mountain biking...and plenty of great places to wine and dine.

Plan Your Trip
Need to Know

When to Go

Auckland
GO Feb–Apr

Rotorua
GO Oct–Dec

Wellington
GO Dec–Feb

Christchurch
GO Jan–Mar

Queenstown
GO Jun–Aug

High Season (Dec–Feb)
○ Summer: busy beaches, festivals and sporting events.

○ Accommodation prices rise – book ahead.

○ High season in ski towns is winter (Jun–Aug).

Shoulder (Mar–Apr)
○ Prime travelling time: fine weather and warm(ish) ocean.

○ Queues are shorter and popular road-trip routes are clear.

○ Spring (Sep–Nov) is the end of snow season.

Low Season (May–Aug)
○ Brilliant skiing and snowboarding from mid-June.

○ Good accommodation deals; a seat in any restaurant.

○ Warm-weather beach towns may be half asleep.

Currency
New Zealand dollar ($)

Language
English, Māori

Visas
Citizens of 60 countries, including Australia, the UK, the US and most EU countries, don't need visas for New Zealand (length-of-stay allowances vary). See www.immigration.govt.nz.

Money
Credit cards are used for most purchases in NZ, and are accepted in most hotels and restaurants. ATMs widely available in cities and larger towns.

Mobile Phones
European phones should work on NZ's network, but most American or Japanese phones will not. Alternatively, if your phone is unlocked, buy a local SIM card and prepaid account.

Time
New Zealand is 12 hours ahead of GMT/UTC and two hours ahead of Australian Eastern Standard Time.

Daily Costs

Budget: Less than $150

○ Dorm beds or campsites: $25–40 per night

○ Main course in a budget eatery: less than $15

○ InterCity or Naked Bus pass: 15 hours or five trips $125–159

Midrange: $150–250

○ Double room in a midrange hotel/ motel: $110–200

○ Main course in a midrange restaurant: $15–32

○ Car rental: from $40 per day

Top End: More than $250

○ Double room in an upmarket hotel: from $200

○ Three-course meal in a classy restaurant: $80

○ Domestic flight Auckland to Christchurch: from $100

Useful Websites

100% Pure New Zealand (www.newzealand.com) Comprehensive official tourism site.
Department of Conservation (www.doc.govt.nz) DOC parks, trail conditions and camping info.
Lonely Planet (www.lonelyplanet.com/new-zealand) Destination information, hotel bookings, traveller forum and more.
Destination New Zealand (www.destination-nz.com) Event listings, and info from NZ history to fashion.
Te Ara (www.teara.govt.nz) Online encyclopaedia of NZ.

Opening Hours

Opening hours vary seasonally depending on where you are. Most places close on Christmas Day and Good Friday.

Banks 9am to 4.30pm Monday to Friday, some also 9am to noon Saturday
Cafes 7am to 4pm
Post Offices 8.30am to 5pm Monday to Friday; larger branches also 9.30am to noon Saturday
Pubs & Bars noon to late ('late' varies by region, and by day)
Restaurants noon to 2.30pm and 6.30pm to 9pm
Shops & Businesses 9am to 5.30pm Monday to Friday and 9am to noon or 5pm Saturday
Supermarkets 8am to 7pm, often 9pm or later in cities

Arriving in New Zealand

Auckland Airport Airbus Express buses run to the city every 10 to 30 minutes, 24 hourly. Door-to-door shuttle buses run 24 hours (from $35). A taxi costs $80 to $90 (45 minutes).
Wellington Airport Airport Flyer buses ($9) run to the city every 10 to 20 minutes, 7am to 9pm. Door-to-door shuttle buses run 24 hours. A taxi costs around $30 (20 minutes).
Christchurch Airport Christchurch Metro Purple Line runs to the city regularly, 7am to 11pm. Door-to-door shuttles run 24 hours (from $23). A taxi costs $45 to $65 (20 minutes).

Getting Around

New Zealand is long and skinny, with many narrow roads: getting from A to B requires some patience.

Car Travel at your own tempo, explore remote areas and visit regions with no public transport. Hire cars in major towns.

Bus Reliable, frequent services to most places (usually cheaper than flying).

Plane Fast-track your holiday with affordable, frequent, fast internal flights.

Train Reliable, regular services (if not fast or cheap) along specific routes on both islands.

For more on **getting around**, see p306

Plan Your Trip
Hotspots For...

Extreme Activities

Gravity getting you down? New Zealand is ripe with opportunities to defy it, not to mention caves to explore, airplanes to exit and rivers to rampage along.

SHAUN JEFFERS/SHUTTERSTOCK ©

Queenstown (p207)
Queenstown has built its rep on the back of extreme action: bungy jumping, rafting, skydiving...

Bungy! (p211)
Hurl yourself into the void on the Nevis Bungy.

Auckland (p35)
Auckland is awash with shopping and eating opps... but this buzzy city also packs an adrenaline punch.

Sky Tower (p46)
Check out SkyWalk and SkyJump.

Waitomo Caves (p78)
Waitomo's astonishing cave systems are ripe for adventure: abseiling, rafting, canyoning and more await.

Black-Water Rafting (p81)
Don a wetsuit and surge along an underground river.

Māori Culture

NZ's indigenous Māori culture is accessible and engaging. Museums around NZ are crammed with Māori artefacts, but this is a living culture: vibrant, potent and contemporary.

DPA PICTURE ALLIANCE/ALAMY ©

Rotorua (p83)
Catch a cultural performance featuring a *haka* (war dance) and a *hāngi* (Māori feast).

Te Puia (p87)
Dynamic performances in an active geothermal zone.

Westland Tai Poutini National Park (p191)
Glaciers, sure, but this part of the West Coast is also home to some masterful Māori carvers.

Hokitika (p201)
The primary source of NZ *pounamu* (greenstone).

Wellington (p131)
The NZ capital was where the famous *Ka Mate haka* (war dance) came into being.

Te Papa (p134)
Amazing carvings and a colourful *marae (meeting house)*.

Wine Regions

As the New Zealand wine industry goes from strength to strength, producers on both islands are expanding their cool-climate remit to embrace new varieties.

MILOSZ MASLANKA/SHUTTERSTOCK ©

Marlborough (p153)
The country's biggest wine region just keeps on turning out superb sauvignon blanc.

Blenheim Wineries (p158)
The hub of the Marlborough scene, with 35-plus wineries.

Auckland (p35)
The weekend playgrounds around Auckland produce amazing syrah, pinot gris and chardonnay.

Waiheke Island (p42)
The perfect climate for Bordeaux-style reds and rosés.

Hawke's Bay (p119)
Warm days shift into chardonnay nights on the sun-stroked East Coast.

Napier Wineries (p124)
Bike between vineyards around this art deco town.

Bars & Beer

The craft-beer scene in New Zealand has been booming for years now, and the results are spectacular (spectap-ular?). You'll find dedicated craft-beer bars right across the country.

IMAGE SUPPLIED BY THE GARAGE PROJECT ©

Wellington (p131)
There are 20-something craft-beer dens in the national capital (thirsty politicians?).

Garage Project (p137)
Drive-in craft beer by the gallon, with a little bar nearby.

Queenstown (p207)
The only place in NZ where you can head out for a big Monday night and not fly solo.

Zephyr (p230)
Not many mountain zephyrs waft into this brilliant bunker.

Taupo (p101)
New Zealand's booming craft-beer scene has even permeated the lofty Central Plateau.

Crafty Trout Brewing (p117)
There are 10 beers and ciders to mull over.

Plan Your Trip
Local Life

TIM CUFF/ALAMY ©

Activities

From mid-air adventures to deep dives, New Zealand is pure adrenaline. Inspired by NZ's rugged landscape, even the meekest travellers muster the courage to dangle on a bungy rope, skydive above mountains or thunder down river rapids. Hiking is a big deal here, too, with nine epic 'Great Walks' and myriad short hikes on offer – a rewarding way to delve into the country's abundant natural beauty and feast your eyes on mountain vistas, hidden water-falls and (if you're lucky) rare wildlife. NZ is also a premier southern-hemisphere destination for snow bunnies, where wintry pursuits span all levels: family-friendly ski areas, cross-country (Nordic) skiing, daredevil snowboarding terrain and pulse-quickening heliskiing. The NZ ski season varies between areas but it's generally mid-June through September, though it can run as late as mid-October.

Shopping

While shopping in New Zealand generally falls on the 'practical and necessary' side of the ledger, worthwhile souvenirs include Māori arts and crafts (including gorgeous hand-carved jewellery), and, if you're feeling flush, prints from one of NZ's world-class landscape photographers. But the best buys are edible: farmers markets are terrific places to stock up on local produce (such as kiwifruit jam and manuka honey), wine and beer.

Entertainment

You came for the landscape, but New Zealanders know how to entertain themselves on a rainy day (or night). Major touring acts crank up the decibels in Auckland and Wellington, while art-house cinemas, theatres and rockin' live-music rooms keep a buzz about big cities and towns. In smaller towns

you'll be limited to open-mic or a sports screening in the local pub. Check out local media to see what's happening.

Eating

New Zealand is a mighty fine place to wine and dine. From country pubs to chic restaurants, the emphasis is on home-grown ingredients like lamb, seafood and venison, with a thriving vegetarian and vegan food scene to cleanse the palate. Dining choices depend on the destination: you'll be spoilt for choice in Auckland while little seaside towns might have just a bakery and pub to pick from.

Drinking & Nightlife

New Zealanders love a drink. And if it's locally made, even better. Cool-climate wines do well here – like sauvignon blanc and pinot noir – and the craft-beer scene

★ **Best Bars**
Golding's Free Dive (p136)
Lovebucket (p58)
Emporium (p127)
Smash Palace (p188)
Blue Door (p228)

has caught fire. Most pubs have excellent local beers on tap or in the fridge.

Bars and pubs are great, but Kiwi clubs? Outside of Auckland, there's not a whole lotta shakin'. Nocturnal vibes are often geared towards quality drinks, tapas and conversation.

Above from left: Kawarau Zipride (p211), Queenstown; Bar in Auckland (p56)

Plan Your Trip
Month by Month

UMDMOS/SHUTTERSTOCK ©

January

Great weather, cricket season in full swing and happy holidays for the locals.

☆ World Buskers Festival

Christchurch hosts a gaggle of jugglers, musos, tricksters, puppeteers, mime artists and dancers throughout the 10-day summertime World Buskers Festival (www. worldbuskersfestival.com). Shoulder into the crowd, see who's making a scene in the middle and maybe leave a few dollars. Avoid if you're scared of audience participation...

February

The sun is shining, the kids are back at school and the sauv blanc is chillin' in the fridge: prime party time across NZ.

♣ Waitangi Day

On 6 February 1840 the Treaty of Waitangi was first signed between Māori and the British Crown. Waitangi Day remains a public holiday across NZ, but in Waitangi itself (the Bay of Islands) there's a lot happening: guided tours, concerts, market stalls and family entertainment.

♥ Marlborough Wine & Food Festival

New Zealand's biggest and best wine festival (www.wine-marlborough-festival. co.nz) features tastings from more than 40 Marlborough wineries, plus fine food and entertainment. The mandatory overindulgence usually happens on a Saturday early in the month. Keep quiet if you don't like sauvignon blanc...

♣ New Zealand Festival

Feeling artsy? This month-long spectacular (www.festival.co.nz) happens in Wellington in February to March every even-numbered year, and is sure to spark your imagination. NZ's cultural capital exudes artistic enthusiasm with theatre, dance, music, writing and visual arts. International acts aplenty.

♣ Fringe

Wellington simmers with music, theatre, comedy, dance, visual arts...but not the

PETER TITMUSS/SHUTTERSTOCK ©

mainstream acts gracing the stage at the New Zealand Festival. Fringe (https://fringe.co.nz/) shines the spotlight on unusual, emerging, controversial, low-budget and/or downright weird acts. In other words, the best stuff.

🎊 Art Deco Weekend

Napier, levelled by an earthquake in 1931 and rebuilt in high art deco style, celebrates its architectural heritage with this high-steppin' fiesta (p123), featuring music, food, wine, vintage cars and costumes over a long weekend in mid-February.

March

March brings a hint of autumn: expect long dusky evenings and plenty of festivals plumping out the calendar.

✕ Wildfoods Festival

Eat worms, baby octopi and 'mountain oysters' at Hokitika's comfort-zone-challenging food fest (www.wildfoods.co.nz). Local classics like whitebait patties

★ **Best Festivals**

Fringe

Marlborough Wine & Food Festival

Art Deco Weekend (p123)

Queenstown Winter Festival (p217)

Beervana (p24)

are represented too, if you aren't hungry for pork-blood casserole. Tip: avail yourself of quality NZ brews and wines to wash down taste-bud offenders.

🎊 Pasifika Festival

With upwards of 140,000 Māori and notable communities of Tongans, Samoans, Cook Islanders, Niueans, Fijians and other South Pacific Islanders, Auckland has the largest Polynesian community in the world. These vibrant island cultures come together at

Above from left: Waitangi Day celebrations; Art Deco Weekend (p123) in Napier

this annual fiesta (www.aucklandnz.com/pasifika) at Western Springs Park.

May

Party nights are over and a chilly winter beckons. Last chance to explore Fiordland in reasonable weather.

☆ New Zealand International Comedy Festival

Three-week laugh-fest (www.comedyfestival.co.nz) with venues across Auckland, Wellington and various regional centres: Whangarei to Invercargill with all the mid-sized cities in between. International gag-merchants (Arj Barker, Danny Bhoy, Bill Bailey) line up next to home-grown talent.

June

Time to head south: it's ski season! Queenstown and Wanaka hit their stride. For everyone else, head north: the Bay of Plenty is always sunny, and is it just us, or is Northland underrated?

🎊 Matariki

Māori New Year (www.teara.govt.nz/en/matariki-maori-new-year) is heralded by the rise of Matariki (aka Pleiades star cluster) in May and the sighting of June's new moon. Three days of remembrance, education, music, film, community days and tree planting take place, mainly around Auckland, Wellington and Northland.

July

Ski season slides on. If you want to avoid crowds, hit Mt Ruapehu on the North Island.

🎊 Queenstown Winter Festival

This southern snow-fest (p217) has been running since 1975, and now attracts more than 45,000 snow bunnies. It's a four-day party, with fireworks, live music, comedy, a community carnival, masquerade ball, and wacky ski and snowboard activities on the mountain slopes. Sometimes starts in late June.

August

Winter is almost spent, but tramping season is still a long way off. Music and art are your saviours.

☆ Bay of Islands Jazz & Blues Festival

You might think that the Bay of Islands is all about sunning yourself on a yacht while dolphins splash you with saltwater. And you'd be right. But in winter, this jazzy three-day festival (www.jazz-blues.co.nz) provides a toe-tapping alternative, showcasing over 45 acts from around NZ.

🍺 Beervana

Attain beery nirvana at this annual craft-beer guzzle fest (www.beervana.co.nz) in Wellington (it's freezing outside – what else is there to do?). Sample the best of NZ's booming beer scene. Not loving beer is heresy, but yes, it also has cider and wine.

September

Spring is sprung. The amazing and surprising World of WearableArt is always a hit.

🎊 World of WearableArt

A bizarre (in the best possible way) two-week Wellington event (www.worldof wearableart.com) featuring amazing hand-crafted garments. Entries from the show are displayed at the World of WearableArt & Classic Cars Museum in Nelson after the event (Cadillacs and corsetry?). Sometimes spills over into October.

October

October is 'shoulder season' – reasonable accommodation rates and minimal crowds.

✖ Kaikoura Seafest

Kaikoura is a town built on crayfish. Well, not literally, but there sure are plenty of crustaceans, many of which find themselves on plates during Seafest (www.seafest.co.nz). Also a great excuse to raise a few toasts and dance around to live music.

Plan Your Trip
Get Inspired

PHOTO COURTESY OF HOBBITON MOVIE SET TOURS ©

Read

The Luminaries (Eleanor Catton; 2013) Man Booker Prize winner: crime and intrigue on West Coast goldfields.

Mister Pip (Lloyd Jones; 2006) Tumult on Bougainville Island, intertwined with Dickens' *Great Expectations*.

Live Bodies (Maurice Gee; 1998) Post-WWII loss and redemption in New Zealand.

The 10pm Question (Kate De Goldi; 2009) Twelve-year-old Frankie grapples with life's big anxieties.

The Wish Child (Catherine Chidgey; 2016) Harrowing, heartbreaking WWII novel; NZ Book Awards winner.

Watch

Lord of the Rings trilogy (2001–03) Hobbits, dragons and magical rings – Tolkien's vision comes to life.

The Piano (1993) A piano and its owners arrive on a mid-19th-century West Coast beach.

Whale Rider (2002) Magical tale of family and heritage on the East Coast.

Once Were Warriors (1994) Brutal relationship dysfunction in South Auckland.

Boy (2010) Taika Waititi's bittersweet coming-of-age drama set in the Bay of Plenty.

Listen

Pure Heroine (Lorde; 2013) Soaring vocals, hypnotic electronica, and overnight an unknown teen became a superstar.

Submarine Bells (The Chills; 1990) Punkish energy and swoon-worthy soundscapes layered through a near-perfect indie-rock record.

True Colours (Split Enz; 1980) Urgent riffs, bittersweet lyrics and this NZ rock outfit's only number one single.

Woodface (Crowded House; 1991) Upbeat singalongs define the easy-going third album of this acclaimed NZ and Aussie pop-rock band.

Above: Hobbiton movie set (p62)

Plan Your Trip
Five-Day Itineraries

Auckland vs Wellington

Is there another 1.4-million-strong city with access to two oceans and vibrant Polynesian culture? Auckland is happening, but bohemian Wellington is arguably the hippest little city on the planet. Split five days between the two and decide who comes out on top.

Auckland (p35) Big-city essentials: Ponsonby Rd eating and drinking, Auckland Art Gallery and Auckland Museum. 🚢 40 mins to Waiheke Island

Waiheke Island (p42) Paradise found: wineries, cafes, beaches… Hello holiday! 🚢 40 mins to Auckland, ✈ 1 hr to Wellington

Wellington (p131) NZ's capital is raffish, arty and soulful. Hit the craft-beer bars, eat on Cuba St and plan your next novel.

FROM LEFT: TROY WEGMAN/SHUTTERSTOCK © IVO ANTONIE DE ROOIJ/SHUTTERSTOCK ©

Southern Scenic

Feeling less city, more pretty? Take a five-day jaunt across NZ's deep south for an eyeful of unforgettable mountain and seaside scenery. This is NZ at its most scenic – snowy peaks, dazzling coastline and bottomless fiords. And the wildlife down here is rampant!

Milford Sound (p240)
Rain, shine or misty drizzle, Milford Sound is an unbelievably atmospheric place to explore.

Queenstown (p207)
Scenic mountain biking or fine food and wine...maybe both.
🚗 3¾ hrs to Milford Sound

Otago Peninsula (p255)
Way down south, the wildlife-rich Otago Peninsula is pretty as a picture.
🚗 4 hrs to Queenstown

FROM LEFT: DANIELA CONSTANTINESCU/SHUTTERSTOCK ©, CHASH GAJANAYAKA/SHUTTERSTOCK ©

Plan Your Trip
10-Day Itinerary

Winter Wanderer

Yes, yes, we know – a whole bunch of you are here for one thing and one thing only: South Island snow! But there's plenty more to see and do on a 10-day tour around NZ's chilly southern zones.

Westland Tai Poutini National Park (p191)
Gargantuan Franz Josef Glacier and Fox Glacier are ice-age time-travellers. Take a helihike to assess their mass.

Christchurch (p175)
Spend a day or two finding your feet at upbeat bars and restaurants.
🚗 20 mins to Lyttelton

Lyttelton (p180)
Christchurch's harbour town is a soulful little enclave.
🚗 20 mins to Christchurch then ✈ 1 hr to Queenstown

Queenstown (p207)
Bungy? Jetboat? Skydive? As if there wasn't enough fun to be had skiing...
🚗 25 mins to Gibbston Valley

Gibbston Valley (p218)
Break from the snow to tour this nearby wine region.
🚗 4½ hrs to Westland Tai Poutini National Park

Plan Your Trip
Two-Week Itinerary

North & South

From the top of the north to halfway down the south, here's a playlist of New Zealand's greatest hits. Tune in to vibrant city scenes, bewitching islands, volcanic hubbub, eye-popping mountain scenery, sublime wine and lonesome wilderness – all the things NZ does best (other than rugby).

Auckland (p35) Hike up One Tree Hill (Maungakiekie) before drinks on K Rd.
🚗 3¼ hrs to Bay of Islands

Bay of Islands (p65) Show-stopping island scenery and a window into NZ's bicultural history.
🚗 6 hrs to Rotorua

Rotorua (p83) Geysers! Bubbling mud! Sulphurous gas! Rotorua is unique; Māori cultural performances equally so.
🚗 2 hrs to Tongariro National Park

Tongariro National Park (p104) Truck through progressive Taupo to hike amongst otherworldly peaks.
🚗 2 hrs to Napier

Napier (p126) Under the East Coast sun, little Napier is all artdeco facades and chardonnay.
🚗 4 hrs to Wellington

Marlborough Wine Region (p158) Tour the Blenheim wineries and sip some superb sauvignon blanc.
🚗 4 ¼ hrs to Christchurch

Wellington (p131) The hilly/windy NZ capital oozes charm and character.
⛴ 3¾ hrs to Picton then 🚗 30 mins to Marlborough Wine Region

Christchurch (p175) Swinging further south, cruise into 'ChCh' to enjoy some southern hospitality in a city of rapid reinvention.

Plan Your Trip
Family Travel

Planning

For all-round information and advice, check out Lonely Planet's *Travel with Children*. Plan ahead by browsing Kidz Go! (www.kidzgo.co.nz) or pick up a free copy of its booklet from tourism info centres in Queenstown, Wanaka and Fiordland.

When to Go

New Zealand is a winner during summer (December to February), but summer is peak season and school-holiday time. Accommodation will be pricey – book ahead. A better bet may be the shoulder months of March, April (sidestepping Easter) and November, when the weather is still good and there's less pressure on the tourism sector. Winter (June to August) is better again – chances are you'll have the whole place to yourselves! Except for the ski fields of course, most of which are fully geared towards family snow-fun.

Accommodation

Many B&Bs promote themselves as blissfully kid-free, but there are plenty of motels and holiday parks with playgrounds, games rooms and kids' DVDs, and often fenced swimming pools, trampolines and acres of grass (many have laundry facilities, too). Cots and high chairs aren't always available at budget and midrange accommodation, but top-end hotels supply them and some provide child-minding services.

Eating Out with Children

If you sidestep the flashier restaurants, children are generally welcome in NZ eateries. Cafes are kid-friendly, and you'll see families getting in early for dinner in pub dining rooms. Most places can supply high chairs. Dedicated kids' menus are common, but selections are usually uninspiring (pizza, fish fingers, chicken nuggets etc). If a restaurant doesn't have a kids' menu, find something on the regular menu and ask the

ROBERT CHG/SHUTTERSTOCK ©

kitchen to downsize it. It's usually fine to bring toddler food in with you. If the sun is shining, hit the farmers markets and find a picnic spot.

Getting Around

If your kids are little, check that your car-hire company can supply the right-sized car seat for your child, and that the seat will be properly fitted. Some companies legally require you to fit car seats yourself.

Most public transport – buses, trains, ferries etc – caters for young passengers, with discounted fares.

Consider hiring a campervan for the whole trip. These formidable beasts are everywhere in NZ, kitted out with beds, kitchens, even toilets and TVs.

Useful Websites

Kids Friendly Travel (www.kidsfriendlytravel. com) Directs you to baby equipment hire, accommodation listings and more.

★ Wildlife Encounters

Kiwi Birdlife Park (p224), Queenstown

West Coast Wildlife Centre (p197), Franz Josef

Zealandia (p142), Wellington

Royal Albatross Centre (p260), Otago Peninsula

Kelly Tarlton's Sea Life Aquarium (p47), Auckland

LetsGoKids (http://letsgokids.co.nz) Download the NZ edition for family travel inspiration and money-saving vouchers.

Kidspot (www.kidspot.co.nz) The 'Family Fun' section has suggestions for child-friendly activities, road trips and more.

Kids New Zealand (www.kidsnewzealand.com) Listings of family-friendly cafes and activities.

Above from left: Family picnic in Redwoods Whakare-warewa Forest (p93); Yellow-eyed penguins (p258)

Britomart (p55)

Viaduct Harbour (p58)

ASIATRAVEL/SHUTTERSTOCK ©

Arriving in Auckland

Auckland Airport (p60) New Zealand's main international gateway is 21km south of the city centre. Shuttles, dedicated SkyBus services and taxis run into the city.

SkyCity Coach Terminal (p60) The terminus for InterCity bus services. Other companies leave from 172 Quay St, opposite the Ferry Building.

Auckland Strand Station (p60) *Northern Explorer* trains depart for Wellington.

Sleeping

Auckland's city centre has plenty of luxury hotels, with several international chains catering to wandering business bods (and those who like predictability). There's plenty of budget accommodation in the city centre, too, but it can be noisy and shabby – you'll find better hostels in the inner suburbs. Historic Devonport is worth considering, if only for the fun ferry ride to/from the city. Check out our Where to Stay (p61) table for more.

Auckland Museum

One of Auckland's more distinctive buildings, the Auckland Museum sits proudly amid Auckland Domain. Auckland is the world's biggest Polynesian city: it follows that the museum's Pacific Island displays are compelling viewing.

This imposing neoclassical temple (1929), capped with an impressive copper-and-glass dome (2007), dominates the Auckland Domain and is a prominent part of the Auckland skyline, especially when viewed from the harbour. More importantly, Auckland Museum is culturally prominent – it's the repository of the city's stories and heritage, and occupies a special place in Aucklanders' hearts, minds and memories (just ask the colourful troupes of school kids as they shuffle through the front door).

The displays of Pacific Island and Māori artefacts on the museum's ground floor are essential viewing. Highlights include a 25m war canoe and an extant carved meeting house (remove your shoes before entering). There's also a fascinating display on Auckland's volcanic field, including an eruption simulation, and the upper floors

Great For...

☑ Don't Miss

The views across the harbour and central Auckland from the museum's entrance.

ⓘ Need to Know

Map p48; 📞09-309 0443; www.auckland museum.com; Auckland Domain, Parnell; adult/child $25/10; 🕙10am-5pm

✕ Take a Break

A cool cafe, Winona Forever (p55), patiently awaits in nearby Parnell.

★ Top Tip

Check the museum website for concerts, shows and events, often featuring local musicians.

showcase military displays, fulfilling the building's dual role as a war memorial. Auckland's main Anzac commemorations take place at dawn on 25 April at the cenotaph in the museum's forecourt.

Admission & Tours

Admission packages can be purchased, which incorporate a highlights tour and a Māori cultural performance ($45 to $55). Here's your chance to see twirling *poi* dances and a hair-raising *haka* (the Māori ceremonial war dance), and to meet and chat with the performers (the war stuff is all for show).

What's Nearby

Around 1.5km south of the museum, **Newmarket** is a buzzy retail district with some of Auckland's best fashion and designer shopping, especially around Teed and Nuffield Streets.

Karen Walker (Map p54; 📞09-522 4286; www.karenwalker.com; 6 Balm St, Newmarket; 🕙10am-6pm) is a world-renowned designer whose cool (pricey) threads have adorned the celebrity bods of Madonna and Kirsten Dunst; **Zambesi** (Map p54; 📞09-523 1000; www.zambesi.co.nz; 38 Osborne St, Newmarket; 🕙10am-6pm Mon-Fri, 11am-5pm Sat & Sun) is another iconic NZ label, much sought after by local and international celebs. For interesting art and design from a collective of 100 local artists, visit **Texan Art Schools** (Map p54; 📞09-529 1021; www.texanartschools. co.nz; 366 Broadway; 🕙9.30am-5.30pm Mon-Fri, 10am-5pm Sat & Sun).

Newmarket also offers good cafes and restaurants. At the **Teed St Larder** (Map p54; 📞09-524 8406; www.teedstreetlarder. co.nz; 7 Teed St, Newmarket; mains $14-23; 🕙7.30am-4pm Mon-Fri, 8am-4.30pm Sat & Sun) it's hard to go past the delicious sandwiches and tarts.

LUKEFRANKLINIMAGES/SHUTTERSTOCK ©

One Tree Hill

Auckland is a city of volcanoes, the ridges of lava flows forming thoroughfares and volcanic cones providing islands of green in the suburbs. And the most famous cone is One Tree Hill.

The volcanic cone of One Tree Hill was the isthmus' key *pā* (fortified village) and the greatest fortress in the country. A walk around the top proffers 360-degree views and the grave of John Logan Campbell, who gifted the land to the city in 1901 and requested that a memorial be built to the Māori people on the summit. Allow time to explore surrounding **Cornwall Park** with its mature trees and historic Acacia Cottage (1841).

The **Cornwall Park Information Centre** (Map p54; ☎09-630 8485; www.cornwallpark. co.nz; Huia Lodge, Michael Horton Dr; ⊗10am-4pm) has fascinating interactive displays illustrating what the *pā* would have looked like when 5000 people lived here. Near the excellent **children's playground**, the **Stardome** (Map p54; ☎09-624 1246; www. stardome.org.nz; 670 Manukau Rd; shows adult/

Great For...

☑ **Don't Miss**

Inspecting the stand of new native trees at the summit – which will be the 'one'?

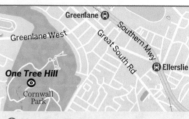

Greenlane

Greenlane West

Southern Mwy

Great South Rd

Ellerslie

One Tree Hill

Cornwall Park

ℹ Need to Know

Maungakiekie; Map p54

✕ Take a Break

There aren't many places to eat or drink around here. Pack a picnic and enjoy the view.

★ Top Tip

The view from One Tree Hill is good (182m), but from Mt Eden (p46) it's even better (196m).

child from $12/10; ☺10am-5pm Mon, to 9.30pm Tue-Thu, to 11pm Fri-Sun) **FREE** offers regular stargazing and planetarium shows that aren't dependent on Auckland's fickle weather (usually 7pm and 8pm Wednesday to Sunday, with extra shows on weekends).

Where's the Tree?

Looking at One Tree Hill, your first thought will probably be 'Where's the bloody tree?' Good question. Up until 2000 a Monterey pine stood at the top of the hill. This was a replacement for a sacred totara tree that was chopped down by British settlers in 1852. Māori activists first attacked the foreign usurper in 1994, finishing the job in 2000. The stump of this last 'one tree' is near John Logan Campbell's grave.

After much consultation with local Māori and tree experts, a grove of six pohutukawa and three totara was planted on the summit in mid-2016. In an arboreal version of the *X Factor,* the weaker-performing trees will be eliminated, with only one tree left standing by 2026.

No, It's Not a Joshua Tree

Auckland's most beloved landmark achieved international recognition in 1987 when U2 released the song 'One Tree Hill' on their acclaimed *The Joshua Tree* album. It was only released as a single in NZ, where it went to number one for six weeks.

Getting There

To get to One Tree Hill from the city, take a train to Greenlane and walk 1km along Green Lane West. By car, take the Greenlane exit off the Southern Motorway and turn right into Green Lane West.

DMITRI OGLEZNEV/SHUTTERSTOCK ©

Waiheke Island

World-class wineries, superb dining with sweeping ocean views and a few of the region's best beaches collude to make Waiheke Island a favourite weekender for city-weary Aucklanders.

Great For...

☑ Don't Miss

The ferry ride is part of the experience, with memorable views of the gulf, the city and Waiheke.

On the island's landward side, emerald waters lap at rocky bays, while its ocean flank has excellent sandy beaches. And indeed, beaches are Waiheke's biggest drawcard... but wine is a close second. There are around 30 boutique wineries scattered about here. The island also boasts plenty of quirky galleries and craft stores, a lasting legacy of its hippyish past.

Beaches

Waiheke's two best beaches are **Onetangi**, a long stretch of white sand at the centre of the island, and **Palm Beach**, a pretty little horseshoe bay between **Oneroa** and One-tangi. Both have nudist sections; head west just past some rocks in both cases. Oneroa and neighbouring **Little Oneroa** are also excellent, but you'll be sharing the waters with moored yachts in summer. Reached by

ℹ Need to Know

Waiheke is 40 minutes by ferry from downtown Auckland. Online, see www.tourismwaiheke.co.nz, www.waiheke.co.nz and www.aucklandnz.com.

✕ Take a Break

Dragonfired (📞021 922 289; www.dragonfired.co.nz; Little Oneroa Beach; mains $12-16; ⊙10am-8pm Dec-Feb, 11am-7pm Fri-Sun Mar-Nov; 🍴) is a pizza caravan by a beach – perfectly Waiheke!

★ Top Tip

Pick up the *Waiheke Art Map*, listing galleries and craft stores, from the **Tourist Information Booth** (Matiatia Wharf; ⊙9am-4pm).

---

an unsealed road through farmland, **Man O' War Bay** is a compact sheltered beach that's excellent for swimming.

Vineyard Restaurants

Many Waiheke wineries have tasting rooms, swanky restaurants and breathtaking views. Some of the best:

Cable Bay (📞09-372 5889; www.cablebay.co.nz; 12 Nick Johnstone Dr; meze $12-27, pizza $26-29, mains $42-45; ⊙11am-late; 🍴) Impressive mod architecture and beautiful views.

Shed at Te Motu (📞09-372 6884; www.temotu.co.nz/the-shed; 76 Onetangi Rd; shared plates small $16-21, large $29-42; ⊙11am-5pm daily, 6pm-late Fri & Sat Nov-Apr, reduced hours May-Oct) Rustic courtyard and shared plates.

Tantalus Estate (📞09-372 2625; www.tantalus.co.nz; 70-72 Onetangi Rd; mains $33-37; ⊙11am-4pm) 🍴 Waiheke's newest vineyard.

Walking

The island's beautiful coastal walks (ranging from one to three hours) include the 3km **Cross Island Walkway** (from Onetangi to Rocky Bay). Other tracks traverse **Whakanewha Regional Park**, a haven for rare coastal birds and geckos, and the Royal Forest & Bird Protection Society's three reserves: **Onetangi** (Waiheke Rd), **Te Haahi-Goodwin** (Orapiu Rd) and **Atawhai Whenua** (Ocean View Rd).

Te Ara Hura is a 100km network of connected trails taking in coastline, forests, vineyard stops and historic places. Route markers indicate the way ahead on the island. See www.aucklandcouncil.govt.nz for more info; search for 'Waiheke Island Walkways'.

City-Centre Ramble

This walk aims to show you some hidden nooks and architectural treats in Auckland's somewhat scrappy city centre – there's more here than meets the eye!

Start St Kevins Arcade, Karangahape Rd
Distance 4.5km
Duration Three hours

7 Finish your ramble at the vamped-up **Wynyard Quarter** (p58), via Viaduct Harbour's buzzy bars and cafes.

FINISH 7

Madden St

Viaduct Harbour

CITY CENTRE

Halsey St

Gaunt St

Viaduct Harbour Ave

Fanshawe St

Market Pl

Hobson St

Wyndham St

5 Head down Bowen Ave to the High St shops, then hang left into **Vulcan Lane**, lined with historic pubs.

Albert St

Aotea Sq

Queen St

2

2 Heading down Queen St, pass **Auckland Town Hall** (p59) and Aotea Sq, the city's civic heart.

Queen St

Scotia Pl

1 START

Karangahape Rd

1 Explore the shops in **St Kevins Arcade** (p51), then take the stairs down to Myers Park.

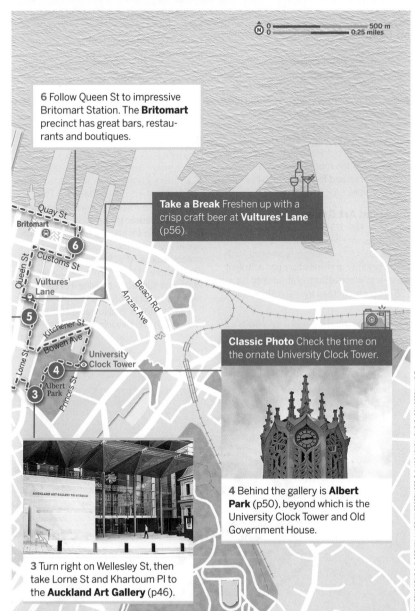

0 — 500 m
0 — 0.25 miles

6 Follow Queen St to impressive Britomart Station. The **Britomart** precinct has great bars, restaurants and boutiques.

Take a Break Freshen up with a crisp craft beer at **Vultures' Lane** (p56).

Quay St

Britomart

Customs St

Queen St

Vultures' Lane

Beach Rd

Anzac Ave

Kitchener St

Bowen Ave

Lorne St

Classic Photo Check the time on the ornate University Clock Tower.

University Clock Tower

Albert Park

Princes St

4 Behind the gallery is **Albert Park** (p50), beyond which is the University Clock Tower and Old Government House.

AUCKLAND ART GALLERY TOI O TĀMAKI

3 Turn right on Wellesley St, then take Lorne St and Khartoum Pl to the **Auckland Art Gallery** (p46).

Auckland Domain

2 CHAMELEONSEYE/SHUTTERSTOCK © 3 GEORGECLERK/GETTY IMAGES © 4 ONEWORLD PICTURE/ALAMY ©

◎ SIGHTS

Mt Eden
Volcano

(Maungawhau; Map p54; 250 Mt Eden Rd) From the top of Auckland's highest volcanic cone (196m) the entire isthmus and both harbours are laid bare. The symmetrical crater (50m deep) is known as Te Ipu Kai a Mataaho (the Food Bowl of Mataaho, the god of things hidden in the ground) and is considered highly *tapu* (sacred). Do not enter it, but feel free to explore the remainder of the mountain. The remains of *pā* terraces and food storage pits are clearly visible.

Auckland Art Gallery
Gallery

(Map p48; ✆09-379 1349; www.aucklandart gallery.com; cnr Kitchener & Wellesley Sts; adult/student/child $20/17/free; ⊙10am-5pm) Auckland's premier art repository has a striking glass-and-wood atrium grafted onto its 1887 French-chateau frame. It showcases

impossible-to-miss Sky Tower looks like a giant hypodermic giving a fix to the heavens

Sky Tower

the best of NZ art, along with important international works by Picasso, Cézanne, Gauguin and Matisse. Highlights include the intimate 19th-century portraits of tattooed Māori subjects by Charles Goldie, and the starkly dramatic text-scrawled canvases of Colin McCahon.

Free 60-minute tours depart from the foyer daily at 11.30am and 1.30pm.

Sky Tower
Tower

(Map p48; ✆09-363 6000; www.skycityauck land.co.nz; cnr Federal & Victoria Sts; adult/child $29/12; ⊙8.30am-10.30pm Sun-Thu, to 11.30pm Fri & Sat Nov-Apr, 9am-10pm May-Oct) The impossible-to-miss Sky Tower looks like a giant hypodermic giving a fix to the heavens. Spectacular lighting renders it space age at night and the colours change for special events. At 328m it is the southern hemisphere's tallest structure. Consider visiting at sunset and having a drink in the Sky Lounge Cafe & Bar.

The Sky Tower is also home to the Sky-Walk (p50) and SkyJump (p50).

Auckland Zoo
Zoo

(Map p54; ☎09-360 3805; www.auckland zoo.co.nz; Motions Rd; adult/child $28/12; ⊗9.30am-5pm, last entry 4.15pm) ✦ At this modern, spacious zoo, the big foreigners tend to steal the attention from the timid natives, but if you can wrestle the kids away from the tigers and orangutans, there's a well-presented NZ section.

Frequent buses (adult/child $5.50/3) run from 99 Albert St in the city to bus stop 8124 on Great North Rd, from where it is a 700m walk to the zoo's entrance.

Auckland Domain
Park

(Map p48; Domain Dr, Parnell; ⊗24hr) Covering about 80 hectares, this green swathe contains the Auckland Museum (p39), sports fields, interesting sculpture, formal gardens, wild corners and the **Wintergarden** (Map p48; Wintergarden Rd, Parnell; ⊗9am-5.30pm Mon-Sat, to 7.30pm Sun Nov-Mar, 9am-4.30pm Apr-Oct) **FREE**, with its fernery, tropical house, cool house, cute cat statue, coffee kiosk and neighbouring cafe.

Kelly Tarlton's
Sea Life Aquarium
Aquarium

(☎09-531 5065; www.kellytarltons.co.nz; 23 Tamaki Dr, Orakei; adult/child $39/22; ⊗9.30am-5pm) ✦ In this topsy-turvy aquarium sharks and stingrays swim over and around you in transparent tunnels that were once stormwater tanks. You can also enter the tanks in a shark cage with a snorkel ($124), or dive straight into the tanks ($265). Other attractions include the Penguin Discovery tour (10.30am Tuesday to Sunday, $199 per person).

A free shark-shaped shuttle bus departs from 172 Quay St (p60) hourly on the half-hour from 9.30am to 3.30pm.

New Zealand
Maritime Museum
Museum

(Map p48; ☎09-373 0800; www.maritime museum.co.nz; 149-159 Quay St; adult/child $20/10, incl harbour cruise $50/25; ⊗9am-5pm, free tours 10.30am & 1pm Mon-Fri) This museum traces NZ's seafaring history, from Māori voyaging canoes to the America's

 Tamaki Drive

This scenic, pohutukawa-lined road heads east from the city, hugging the waterfront. In summer it's a jogging/cycling/rollerblading blur.

A succession of child-friendly, peaceful swimming beaches starts at **Ohaku Bay**. Around the headland is **Mission Bay**, a popular beach with an electric-lit art deco fountain, historic mission house, restaurants and bars. Safe swimming beaches **Kohimarama** and **St Heliers** follow. **St Heliers Bay Bistro** (www.stheliersbaybistro.co.nz; 387 Tamaki Dr, St Heliers; brunch $16-27, dinner $27-34; ⊗7am-11pm) makes a classy lunch stop. Further east along Cliff Rd, the **Achilles Point Lookout** (Cliff Rd, St Heliers) offers panoramic views and Māori carvings. At its base is **Ladies Bay**, popular with nudists.

Buses 767 and 769 from behind Britomart station follow this route, while buses 745 to 757 go as far as Mission Bay.

GRACETHANG2/SHUTTERSTOCK ©

Cup. Recreations include a tilting 19th-century steerage-class cabin and a 1950s beach store and bach (holiday home).

Wallace Arts Centre
Gallery

(☎09-639 2010; www.tsbbankwallaceartscentre. org.nz; Pah Homestead, 72 Hillsborough Rd, Hillsborough; ⊗10am-3pm Tue-Fri, to 5pm Sat & Sun) **FREE** Housed in a gorgeous 1879 mansion with views to One Tree Hill (p41) and the Manukau Harbour, this arts centre is

City Centre & Ponsonby

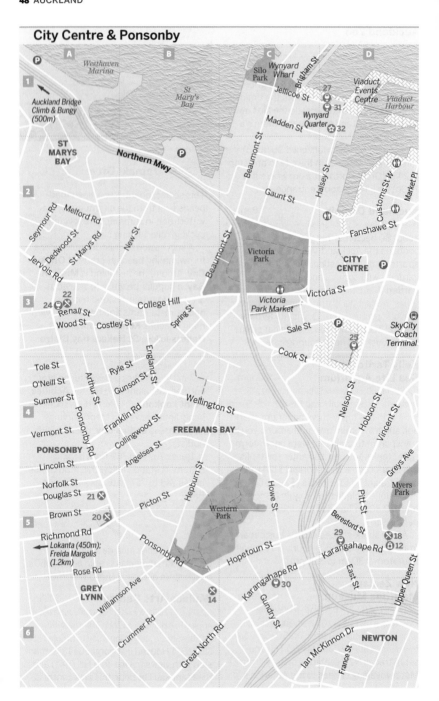

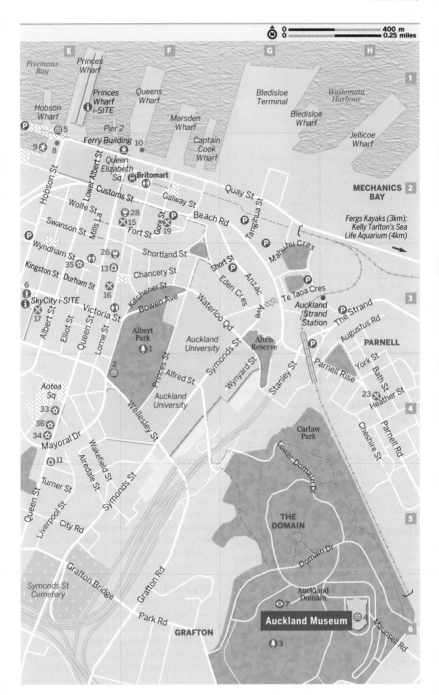

City Centre & Ponsonby

endowed with contemporary New Zealand art from an extensive private collection, which is changed every four to six weeks. Have lunch on the veranda at the excellent **Homestead Cafe** and wander among the magnificent trees in the surrounding park. The art is also very accessible, ranging from a life-size skeletal rugby ruck to a vibrant Ziggy Stardust painted on glass.

Bus 299 (Lynfield) departs every 15 minutes from Queen St (outside the Civic Theatre) and heads to Hillsborough Rd ($5.50, 40 minutes).

Albert Park   Park
(Map p48; Princes St) Hugging the hill on the city's eastern flank, Albert Park is a charming Victorian formal garden overrun by students from the neighbouring University of Auckland during term time. The park was once part of the Albert Barracks (1847), a fortification that enclosed 9 hectares during the New Zealand Wars. A portion of the original barracks wall survives at the centre of the university campus.

✪ ACTIVITIES

Auckland Bridge
Climb & Bungy   Adventure Sports
(☎09-360 7748; www.bungy.co.nz; 105 Curran St, Westhaven; adult/child climb $125/85, bungy $160/130) ✐ Climb up or jump off the Auckland Harbour Bridge.

SkyWalk   Adventure Sports
(Map p48; ☎0800 759 925; www.skywalk.co.nz; Sky Tower, cnr Federal & Victoria Sts; adult/child $145/115; ☺10am-4.30pm) The SkyWalk involves circling the 192m-high, 1.2m-wide outside halo of the Sky Tower (p46) without rails or a balcony. Don't worry, it's not completely crazy – there is a safety harness.

SkyJump   Adventure Sports
(Map p48; ☎0800 759 586; www.skyjump.co.nz; Sky Tower, cnr Federal & Victoria Sts; adult/child $225/175; ☺10am-5.15pm) This thrilling 11-second, 85km/h base wire leap from the observation deck of the Sky Tower (p46) is more like a parachute jump than a bungy.

Combine it with the SkyWalk in the Look & Leap package ($290).

Explore
Boating

(Map p48; ☑0800 397 567; www.exploregroup. co.nz; Viaduct Harbour) 🏄 Shoot the breeze for two hours on a genuine America's Cup yacht (adult/child $170/120), take a 90-minute cruise on a glamorous large yacht (adult/child $85/55) or tuck into a 2½-hour Harbour Dinner Cruise ($130/85).

Fergs Kayaks
Kayaking

(☑09-529 2230; www.fergskayaks.co.nz; 12 Tamaki Dr, Orakei; ☺9am-5pm) Hires kayaks (per hour from $25), paddle boards ($30), bikes ($20) and in-line skates ($20). Guided kayak trips head to Devonport ($100, 8km, three hours) or Rangitoto ($160, 13km, six hours).

Fullers
Cruise

(Map p48; ☑09-367 9111; www.fullers.co.nz; adult/child $42/21; ☺10.30am & 1.30pm) Twice-daily 1½-hour harbour cruises, including Rangitoto and a free return ticket to Devonport.

⊖ TOURS

Big Foody Food Tour
Tours

(☑021 481 177, 0800 366 386; www.thebigfoody. com; per person $125-185) Small-group city tours, including visits to markets and artisan producers, and lots of tastings. A recent addition are hop-fuelled explorations of Auckland's burgeoning craft-beer scene.

Tāmaki Hikoi
Cultural

(☑021 146 9593; www.tamakihikoi.co.nz; 1/3hr $50/95) Guides from the Ngāti Whātua *iwi* (tribe) lead various Māori cultural tours, including walking and interpretation of sites such as Mt Eden (p46) and the Auckland Domain (p47).

Toru Tours
Bus

(☑027 457 0011; www.torutours.com; per person $79) The three-hour Express Tour will depart with just one booking – ideal for solo travellers.

Auckland Hop On, Hop Off Explorer
Bus

(Map p48; ☑0800 439 756; www.explorerbus. co.nz; adult/child per day $45/20) Two services – the red or blue route – take in the best of the waterfront, including attractions along Tamaki Drive (p47), or highlights including Mt Eden (p46) and the Auckland Zoo (p47). Red route buses depart from near Princes Wharf hourly from 10am to 3pm (more frequently in summer), and it's possible to link to the blue route at the Auckland Museum (p39).

🛍 SHOPPING

Dedicated followers of fashion should head to the Britomart precinct, Newmarket's Teed and Nuffield Sts, and Ponsonby Rd. For vintage clothing and secondhand boutiques, try Karangahape Rd (K Rd) or Ponsonby Rd.

Real Groovy
Music

(Map p48; ☑09-302 3940; www.realgroovy. co.nz; 369 Queen St; ☺9am-7pm) Masses of new, secondhand and rare releases in vinyl and CD format, as well as concert tickets, giant posters, DVDs, books, magazines and clothes.

St Kevins Arcade
Shopping Centre

(Map p48; www.stkevinsarcade.co.nz; 183 Karangahape Rd) Built in 1924, this historic, renovated shopping arcade has interesting stores selling vintage clothing and organic and sustainable goods. The arcade also has excellent cafes and restaurants.

Unity Books
Books

(Map p48; ☑09-307 0731; www.unitybooks. co.nz; 19 High St; ☺8.30am-7pm Mon-Sat, 10am-6pm Sun) The inner city's best independent bookshop.

Royal Jewellery Studio
Jewellery

(Map p54; ☑09-846 0200; www.royaljewellery studio.com; 486 New North Rd, Kingsland; ☺10am-4pm Tue-Sun) Work by local artisans, including beautiful Māori designs and authentic *pounamu* (greenstone) jewellery.

From left: Giapo ice cream; Bars and restaurants along Jellicoe St, Wynyard Quarter (p58); St Kevins Arcade (p51)

Otara Flea Market
Market

(☎09-274 0830; www.otarafleamarket.co.nz; Newbury St; ⊗6am-noon Sat) Held in the car park between the Manukau Polytech and the Otara town centre, this market has a palpable Polynesian atmosphere and is good for South Pacific food, music and fashion. Catch a train on the southern line to Papatoetoe and then switch to a bus to Otara.

EATING

Because of its size and ethnic diversity, Auckland tops the country when it comes to dining options and quality. Lively eateries have sprung up to cater to the many Asian students, and offer inexpensive Japanese, Chinese and Korean staples. If you're on a budget, you'll fall in love with the city's food halls.

City Centre

Chuffed
Cafe $

(Map p48; ☎09-367 6801; www.chuffedcoffee. com; 43 High St; mains $6.50-18; ⊗7am-4pm

Mon-Wed, 7am-10pm Thu & Fri, 9am-10pm Sat, 9am-4pm Sun) Concealed in a light well at the rear of a building, this hip place, liberally coated in street art, is a definite contender for the inner city's best cafe. Grab a seat on the indoor-outdoor terrace and tuck into cooked breakfasts, Wagyu burgers, lamb shanks or surprisingly flavour-packed toasted sandwiches. From Thursday to Saturday nights, cocktails and craft beers also feature.

Giapo
Ice Cream $$

(Map p48; ☎09-550 3677; www.giapo.com; 12 Gore St; ice cream $10-22; ⊗noon-10.30pm Sun-Thu, to 11.30pm Fri & Sat; ☝) ✔ That there are queues outside this boutique ice-cream shop even in the middle of winter says a lot about the magical confections that it conjures up. Expect elaborate constructions of ice-cream art topped with all manner of goodies, as Giapo's extreme culinary creativity and experimentation combines with the science of gastronomy to produce quite possibly the planet's best ice-cream extravaganzas.

RAFAEL BEN ARI/ALAMY ©

Depot
Modern NZ $$

(Map p48; 🗹09-363 7048; www.eatatdepot.
co.nz; 86 Federal St; dishes $16-38; ⊙7am-
late) TV chef Al Brown's popular eatery
offers first-rate comfort food in informal
surrounds (communal tables, butcher tiles
and a constant buzz). Dishes are designed
to be shared, and a pair of clever shuck-
ers prepare the city's freshest clams and
oysters. No bookings.

Federal Delicatessen
American $$

(Map p48; 🗹09-363 7184; www.thefed.co.nz; 86
Federal St; mains $11-26; ⊙7am-late) Celebrity
chef Al Brown's take on a New York Jewish
deli serves up simple stuff like bagels and
sandwiches, matzo ball soup and lots of
delicious comfort food to share (turkey
meatloaf, spit-roasted chicken, New York
strip steak). White butcher tiles, vinyl booth
seating and waitstaff in 1950s uniforms
add to the illusion.

Cassia
Indian $$$

(Map p48; 🗹09-379 9702; www.cassia
restaurant.co.nz; 5 Fort Lane; mains $32-40;
⊙noon-3pm Wed-Fri, 5.30pm-late Tue-Sat)
Occupying a moodily lit basement, Cassia

serves modern Indian food with punch and
panache. Start with a *pani puri,* a bite-sized
crispy shell bursting with flavour, before
devouring a decadently rich curry. The
Delhi duck is excellent, as is the Goan-style
snapper. Artisan gins and NZ craft beer are
other highlights.

✖ Ponsonby & Grey Lynn

Azabu
Japanese, Peruvian $$

(Map p48; 🗹09-320 5292; www.azabupon
sonby.co.nz; 26 Ponsonby Rd; mains & shared
plates $16-35; ⊙noon-late Wed-Sun, from 5pm
Mon & Tue) Nikkei cuisine, an exciting blend
of Japanese and Peruvian influences, is the
focus at Azabu. Amid a dramatic interior
enlivened by striking images of Tokyo,
standout dishes include the tuna sashi-
mi tostada, Japanese tacos with wasabi
avocado, and king prawns with a jalapeño
and ponzu dressing. Arrive early and enjoy
a basil- and chilli-infused cachaça cocktail
at Azabu's Roji bar.

Saan
Thai $$

(Map p48; 🗹09-320 4237; www.saan.co.nz;
160 Ponsonby Rd, Ponsonby; dishes $14-32;

Mt Eden, Newmarket & One Tree Hill

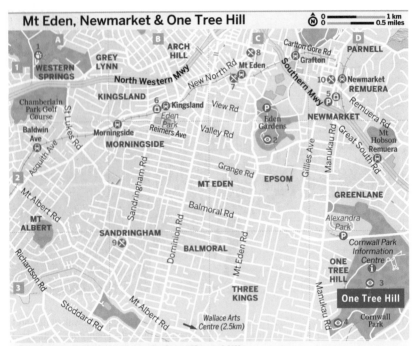

Mt Eden, Newmarket & One Tree Hill

⊘4pm-late Mon & Tue, noon-late Wed-Fri, 11am-late Sat & Sun) Hot in both senses of the word, this super-fashionable restaurant focuses on the fiery cuisine of the Isaan and Lanna regions of northern Thailand. The menu is conveniently sorted from least to most spicy and split into smaller and larger dishes for sharing. Be sure to order the soft-shell crab.

Ponsonby Central   Cafe $$
(Map p48; www.ponsonbycentral.co.nz; 136-138 Ponsonby Rd, Ponsonby; mains $15-35;

⊘7am-10.30pm Sun-Wed, to midnight Thu-Sat) Restaurants, cafes, bars and gourmet food shops fill this upmarket former warehouse space offering everything from Auckland's best pizza and Argentinean barbecue to Indo-Burmese curries partnered with zingy cocktails. If you're after the city's best gourmet burgers, look no further.

Lokanta   Greek, Turkish $$
(⊘09-360 6355; www.lokanta.nz; 137a Richmond Rd; meze $7-19, mains $25-33; ⊘4pm-late Tue-Sun) Featuring the cuisine of the eastern

Mediterranean, unpretentious Lokanta is a laid-back alternative to the more trendy eateries along nearby Ponsonby Rd. Greek and Turkish flavours happily coexist, and robust Greek wines partner well with hearty dishes including char-grilled octopus and roast goat with a barley risotto.

Sidart   Modern NZ $$$

(Map p48; ☑09-360 2122; www.sidart.co.nz; Three Lamps Plaza, 283 Ponsonby Rd, Ponsonby; 5-course lunch $65, 7-course dinner $145; ☻noon-2.30pm Fri, 6-11pm Tue-Sat) No one in Auckland produces creative degustations quite like Sid Sahrawat. It's food as art, food as science but, more importantly, food to fire up your taste buds, delight the brain, satisfy the stomach and put a smile on your face.

Parnell

Winona Forever   Cafe $$

(Map p48; ☑09-974 2796; www.facebook.com/winonaforevercafe; 100 Parnell Rd; mains $13-21; ☻7am-4.30pm Mon-Fri, 8am-4pm Sat & Sun) Some of Auckland's best counter food – including stonking cream doughnuts – partners with innovative cafe culture at this always-busy eatery near good shopping and art galleries along Parnell Rd. Local residents crowd in with travellers for coffee, craft beer and wine, and one of the cafe's signature dishes – the Ladyboy, a Thai-influenced eggs Benedict with grilled prawns.

Mt Eden

Brothers Juke
Joint BBQ   Barbecue $

(Map p54; ☑09-638 7592; www.jukejoint.co.nz; 5 Akiraho St, Mt Eden; snacks & mains $10-15; ☻11.30am-10pm Tue-Sat, to 8pm Sun; ☝) A spin-off from central Auckland's excellent Brothers Beer (p56) craft-beer bar, Juke Joint BBQ serves up Southern US–style barbecue in a hip renovated warehouse. Retro 1960s furniture underpins the decor and the compact kids' play area is popular with local families on weekend afternoons.

¶◯¶ Foodie Enclaves

The city's hippest new foodie enclaves are Britomart (the blocks above the train station) and Federal St (under the Sky Tower), and recent openings have resurrected and reinforced the culinary reputation of Ponsonby (p53), which has its own website: www.iloveponsonby.co.nz. The Wynyard Quarter and the former City Works Depot on the corner of Wellesley and Nelson Sts are also up-and-coming areas. Easily reached by train, Orakei Bay Village in the city's eastern suburbs is another emerging precinct.

Britomart
CORNERS74/SHUTTERSTOCK ©

⊗ Newton

Gemmayze St   Lebanese $$

(Map p48; ☑09-600 1545; www.facebook.com/gemmayzest; St Kevins Arcade, 15/183 Karangahape Rd; meze & mains $18-34; ☻6-11.30pm Tue-Sat, noon-3pm Thu & Fri; ☝) Located amid the restored heritage architecture of St Kevins Arcade, Gemmayze St presents a modern and stylish update on traditional Lebanese cuisine. Delicate mint, orange blossom and rosewater cocktails are prepared at the beaten-copper bar, while shared tables encourage lots of sociable dining on meze and expertly grilled meats. The $18 lunchtime selection of five meze is excellent value.

French Cafe   French $$$

(Map p54; ☑09-377 1911; www.thefrenchcafe.co.nz; 210 Symonds St; 3/4/7 courses $110/135/160;

Auckland's Multicultural Menu

Around 30% of New Zealanders live in Auckland, and the country's biggest city is also the most ethnically diverse. With immigration – especially from Asia – has come a cosmopolitan restaurant scene, and savvy Auckland foodies (and a few of the city's top chefs) keenly explore central fringe neighbourhoods for authentic tastes of the city's multicultural present and future.

Head to Dominion Rd in Balmoral (catch bus 267 from stop 7058 near the intersection of Queen and Wellesley Sts and get off at stop 8418) to be surrounded by Auckland's best Chinese food.

A few blocks west (catch bus 249 from stop 7022 in Victoria St East to stop 8316 on Sandringham Rd) are some of the city's best Indian and Sri Lankan restaurants. Our favourite is **Paradise** (Map p54; 09-845 1144; www.paradiseindianfood. co.nz; 591 Sandringham Rd, Sandringham; mains $12-18; ⊘11.30am-9.30pm; 🖍), specialising in the Mughlai cuisine you'd find on the streets of Hyderabad.

At the city's bustling night markets – held in a different suburban car park each night of the week – scores of stalls serve food from a diverse range of countries, from Argentina and Samoa, to Hungary and Turkey. Most convenient for travellers is the Thursday **Henderson Night Market** (www.aucklandnight market.co.nz; Waitakere Mega Centre, under Kmart; ⊘5.30-11pm Thu). Catch a western-line train from Britomart to Henderson and walk 650m to underneath the Kmart department store.

If you're in town around late March or early April, the **Auckland International Cultural Festival** (www.facebook.com/ culturalfestival; Mt Roskill War Memorial Park; ⊘late Mar/early Apr) offers a very tasty peek into the city's ethnically diverse future. Online, Cheap Eats (www.cheap eats.co.nz) scours Auckland for the city's best food for under $20.

⊘noon-3pm Fri, 6pm-late Tue-Sat) The legendary French Cafe has been rated as one of Auckland's top restaurants for more than 20 years and it still continues to excel. The cuisine is nominally French-influenced, but chef Simon Wright sneaks in lots of tasty Asian and Pacific Rim touches. The service is impeccable.

DRINKING & NIGHTLIFE

Auckland's nightlife is quiet during the week – for some vital signs, head to Ponsonby Rd, Britomart or the Viaduct. Karangahape Rd (K Rd) wakes up late on Friday and Saturday; don't even bother staggering this way before 11pm.

City Centre

Brothers Beer   Craft Beer
(Map p48; 🖉09-366 6100; www.brothersbeer. co.nz; City Works Depot, 90 Wellesley St; ⊘noon-10pm) This beer bar combines quirky decor with 18 taps crammed with Brothers' own brews and guest beers from NZ and further afield. Hundreds more bottled beers await chilling in the fridges, and bar food includes pizza. There are occasional movie and comedy nights, and beers are available for takeout purchase. The adjacent City Works Depot has other good eating options.

Gin Room   Bar
(Map p48; www.ginroom.co.nz; Level 1, 12 Vulcan Lane; ⊘5pm-midnight Tue & Wed, 5pm-2am Thu, 4pm-4am Fri, 6pm-4am Sat) There's a slightly dishevelled colonial charm to this bar, discreetly tucked away above Auckland's oldest pub, which is completely in keeping with its latest incarnation as a gin palace. There are at least 50 ways to ruin mother here – ask the bar staff for advice – and that's not even counting the juniper-sozzled cocktails.

Vultures' Lane   Pub
(Map p48; 🖉09-300 7117; www.vultureslane. co.nz; 10 Vulcan Lane; ⊘11.30am-late) With 22 taps, over 75 bottled beers and sports on the TV, this pleasantly grungy historic pub

is popular with the savviest of Auckland's craft-beer fans. Check the website for what's currently on tap, and also for news of regular tap takeovers from some of New Zealand's best brewers.

Jefferson   Bar

(Map p48; www.thejefferson.co.nz; basement, Imperial Bldg, Fort Lane; ☺4pm-1am Mon-Thu, to 3am Fri & Sat) Lit by the golden glow of close to 600 different whisky bottles, this subterranean den is a sophisticated spot for a nightcap. There's no list – talk to the knowledgeable bar staff about the kind of thing you're after (peaty, smooth, smoky, not-too-damaging-to-the-wallet) and they'll suggest something.

Ponsonby & Grey Lynn

Freida Margolis   Bar

(☎09-378 6625; www.facebook.com/freida margolis; 440 Richmond Rd; ☺4-11pm Sun-Wed, to 2am Thu-Sat) Formerly a butchers – look for the Westlynn Organic Meats sign – this corner location is now a great little neighbourhood bar with a backstreets of

Bogotá ambience. Loyal locals sit outside with their well-behaved dogs, supping on sangria, wine and craft beer, and enjoying eclectic sounds from the owner's big vinyl collection.

Annabel's   Wine Bar

(Map p48; www.annabelswinebar.com; 277 Ponsonby Rd; ☺3-11pm) A self-described 'neighbourhood bar', Annabel's would also be right at home in the backstreets of Bordeaux or Barcelona. Cheese and charcuterie platters combine with a Euro-centric wine list, while Spanish beers and classic Negroni cocktails also help turn the South Pacific into the south of France. A thoroughly unpretentious affair; worth a stop before or after dining along Ponsonby Rd.

Newton

Galbraith's Alehouse   Brewery

(Map p54; ☎09-379 3557; http://alehouse.co.nz; 2 Mt Eden Rd; ☺noon-11pm) Brewing real ales and lagers on-site, this cosy English-style pub in a grand heritage building offers bliss on tap. There are always more craft beers

Bars on Vulcan Lane

from around NZ and the world on the guest taps, and the food's also very good. From April to September, Galbraith's Sunday roast is one of Auckland's best.

Lovebucket
Cocktail Bar, Craft Beer

(Map p48; ☑09-869 2469; www.lovebucket. co.nz; K'Road Food Workshop, 309 Karangahape Rd; ☺4pm-late Tue-Sun) Lovebucket is a more sophisticated alternative to K Rd's often youthful after-dark vibe. Courtesy of shared ownership with the Hallertau Brewery in West Auckland, Lovebucket's craft-beer selection is one of Auckland's best – including barrel-aged and sour beers. Quirky cocktails and a well-informed wine list join interesting bar snacks like cheeses, charcuterie and gourmet toasted sandwiches.

Madame George
Bar

(Map p48; ☑09-308 9039; www.facebook. com/madamegeorgenz; 490 Karangahape Rd; ☺5pm-late Tue-Sat) Two patron saints of cool – Elvis Presley and Al Pacino – look down in this compact space along Karangahape Rd. Shoot the breeze with the friendly bar staff over a craft beer or Auckland's best tatucocktails, or grab a shared table out front and watch the passing theatre of K Rd. It's just like hanging at your hippest mate's place.

🍸 Viaduct Harbour & Wynyard Quarter

Sixteen Tun
Craft Beer

(Map p48; ☑09-368 7712; www.16tun.co.nz; 10-26 Jellicoe St, Wynyard Quarter; tasting 4/6/8 beers $12/18/24; ☺11.30am-late) The glister of burnished copper perfectly complements the liquid amber on offer here in the form of dozens of NZ craft beers by the bottle and a score on tap. If you can't decide, go for a good-value tasting 'crate' of 200mL serves.

Jack Tar
Pub

(Map p48; ☑09-303 1002; www.jacktar.co.nz; North Wharf, 34-37 Jellicoe St, Wynyard Quarter; ☺8am-late) A top spot for a late-afternoon/ early-evening beer or wine and pub grub amid the relaxed vibe of the waterfront Wynyard Quarter.

Al fresco bar in Viaduct Harbour

⭐ ENTERTAINMENT

Whammy Bar   Live Music
(Map p48; www.facebook.com/thewhammybar;
183 Karangahape Rd, Newton; ⊗8.30pm-4am
Wed-Sat) Small, but a stalwart on the live
indie music scene nonetheless.

Q Theatre   Theatre
(Map p48; ☏09-309 9771; www.qtheatre.co.nz;
305 Queen St) Theatre by various companies
and intimate live music. Silo Theatre (www.
silotheatre.co.nz) often performs here.

Auckland Town Hall   Classical Music
(Map p48; ☏09-309 2677; www.aucklandlive.
co.nz; 305 Queen St) This elegant Edwardian venue (1911) hosts the NZ Symphony
Orchestra (www.nzso.co.nz) and Auckland
Philharmonia (www.apo.co.nz), among
others.

Classic Comedy Club   Comedy
(Map p48; ☏09-373 4321; www.comedy.co.nz;
321 Queen St; ⊗6.30pm-late) Stand-up
performances most nights, with legendary late-night shows during the annual
Comedy Festival (www.comedyfestival.co.nz;
⊗Apr-May).

ASB Waterfront Theatre   Theatre
(Map p48; ☏box office 0800 282 849; www.asb
waterfronttheatre.co.nz; 138 Halsey St, Wynyard
Quarter) The new ASB Waterfront Theatre
is used by the Auckland Theatre Company
and also for occasional one-off shows and
concerts. There's a good selection of bars
and restaurants in close proximity.

Ding Dong Lounge   Live Music
(Map p48; ☏09-377 4712; www.dingdong
loungenz.com; 26 Wyndham St; ⊗6pm-4am Wed-
Fri, 8pm-4am Sat) Rock, indie and alternative
sounds from live bands and DJs, washed
down with craft beer.

ℹ️ INFORMATION

Auckland International Airport i-SITE (p403)

Princes Wharf i-SITE (p403) Auckland's main
official information centre.

 **Auckland
Volcanic Field**

Some cities think they're tough just
by living in the shadow of a volcano.
Auckland's built on 50 of them and, no,
they're not all extinct. The last one to
erupt was Rangitoto about 600 years
ago and no one can predict when the
next eruption will occur. Auckland's
quite literally a hotspot – with a reser-
voir of magma 100km below, waiting
to bubble to the surface. But relax: this
has only happened 19 times in the last
20,000 years.

Some of Auckland's volcanoes are
cones, some are filled with water and
some have been completely quarried
away. Moves are afoot to register
the field as a World Heritage site and
protect what remains. Most of the
surviving cones show evidence of
terracing from when they formed a
formidable series of Māori pā (fortified villages). The most interesting to
explore are Mt Eden (p46), One Tree
Hill (p40), **North Head** (Maungauika;
Takarunga Rd, Devonport; ⊗6am-10pm) and
Rangitoto, but **Mt Victoria** (Takarunga;
Victoria Rd, Devonport), Mt Wellington
(Maungarei), Mt Albert (Owairaka), Mt
Roskill (Puketāpapa), Lake Pupuke, Mt
Mangere and Mt Hobson (Remuera) are
all also worth a visit.

Mt Eden (p46)
SORANG/SHUTTERSTOCK ©

SkyCity i-SITE (Map p48; ☏09-365 9918; www.
aucklandnz.com; SkyCity Atrium, cnr Victoria &
Federal Sts; ⊗9am-5pm)

 **Devonport Detour**

With well-preserved Victorian and Edwardian buildings and loads of cafes, Devonport is an extremely pleasant place to visit and only a short ferry trip from the city. There are also two volcanic cones to climb and easy access to the first of the North Shore's beaches.

For a self-guided tour of historic buildings, pick up the *Old Devonport Walk* pamphlet from the **Visit Devonport** (www.visitdevonport.co.nz; Victoria Rd; ⊙9am-5pm Mon-Fri; 🛜) information centre. Bikes can be hired from the ferry terminal.

Ferries to Devonport (adult/child return $12/6.50, 12 minutes) depart from the Ferry Building at least every 30 minutes from 6.15am to 11.30pm (until 1am Friday and Saturday), and from 7.15am to 10pm on Sundays and public holidays. Some Waiheke Island and Rangitoto ferries also stop here.

CHAMELEONSEYE/SHUTTERSTOCK ©

ⓘ GETTING THERE & AWAY

AIR
Auckland Airport (AKL; ☏09-275 0789; www.aucklandairport.co.nz; Ray Emery Dr, Mangere) is 21km south of the city centre. It has separate international and domestic terminals, a 10-minute walk apart from each other via a signposted footpath; a free shuttle service operates every 15 minutes (5am to 10.30pm).

BUS
Coaches depart from 172 Quay St, opposite the **Ferry Building** (Map p48; 99 Quay St), except for InterCity services, which depart from **SkyCity Coach Terminal** (Map p48; 102 Hobson St). Many southbound services also stop at the airport.

TRAIN
Northern Explorer (☏0800 872 467; www.greatjourneysofnz.co.nz) 🍴 trains leave from **Auckland Strand Station** (Map p48; Ngaoho Pl), bound for Wellington.

ⓘ GETTING AROUND

The most useful bus services are the environmentally friendly Link Buses that loop in both directions around three routes (taking in many of the major sights) from 7am to 11pm:

City Link (adult/child $1/50c, every seven to 10 minutes) Wynyard Quarter, Britomart, Queen St, Karangahape Rd.

Inner Link (adult/child $3.50/2, every 10 to 15 minutes) Queen St, SkyCity, Victoria Park, Ponsonby Rd, Karangahape Rd, Museum, Newmarket, Parnell and Britomart.

Outer Link (maximum $5.50, every 15 minutes) Art Gallery, Ponsonby, Herne Bay, Westmere, MOTAT 2, Pt Chevalier, Mt Albert, St Lukes Mall, Mt Eden, Newmarket, Museum, Parnell and University.

Where to Stay

Befitting a burgeoning international city, Auckland has a wide range of accommodation. Booking ahead can secure better deals. Keep an eye out for when international concerts and big rugby games are scheduled as accommodation around the city can fill up.

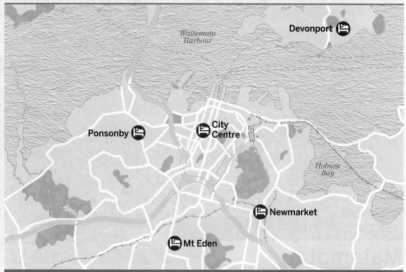

Neighbourhood	Atmosphere
City Centre	The CBD features luxury hotels, international chains and hostels of varying repute. Convenient but lacking character.
Ponsonby	Near to good restaurants and bars with a good selection of B&Bs and hostels. A short distance from central Auckland.
Mt Eden	A leafy suburb on the fringe of the city with good hostels and B&Bs. Good transport links to the CBD and harbour ferries.
Devonport	A seaside suburb reached by ferry from downtown Auckland with beautiful Edwardian B&Bs.
Newmarket	Good-value motels along Great South Rd and near to good shopping. An easy bus ride into central Auckland.

Matamata

Rolling green hills, a pretty lake and well-kept gardens around compact Hobbit holes all make it very easy to suspend reality in Matamata's make-believe Middle-earth world of Hobbiton.

Matamata was just one of those pleasant, horsey country towns you drove through until Peter Jackson's epic film trilogy *The Lord of the Rings* put it on the map. During filming, 300 locals got work as extras (hairy feet weren't a prerequisite).

Following the subsequent filming of *The Hobbit*, the town has now ardently embraced its Middle-earth credentials, including a spooky statue of Gollum, and given the local information centre an appropriate extreme makeover.

Most tourists who come to Matamata are dedicated Hobbit-botherers. For everyone else there's a great cafe and bar, avenues of mature trees and undulating green hills.

Great For...

☑ Don't Miss

Slurping an Oakbarton Brew or Sackville Cider at Hobbiton's Green Dragon Inn.

Hobbiton Movie Set & Tours

Due to copyright, all the movie sets around NZ were dismantled after the filming of *The*

Hobbiton

Lord of the Rings, but Hobbiton's owners
negotiated to keep their hobbit holes,
which were then rebuilt for the filming of
The Hobbit. Tours include a drink at the
wonderful Green Dragon Inn. Free transfers
leave from the Matamata i-SITE – check
timings on the Hobbiton website. Booking
ahead is strongly recommended. The popular Evening Banquet Tours on Wednesday
and Sunday include a banquet dinner.

To get to Hobbiton with your own
transport, head towards Cambridge from
Matamata, turn right into Puketutu Rd and
then left into Buckland Rd, stopping at the
Shire's Rest Cafe.

Non-Hobbit Stuff

Firth Tower   Museum, Historic Building
(📞07-888 8369; www.firthtower.co.nz; Tower
Rd; grounds free, buildings adult/child $10/5;
⊙grounds 10am-4pm daily, buildings 10am-4pm
Thu-Mon) Firth Tower was built by Auckland
businessman Josiah Firth in 1882. The 18m
concrete tower was then a fashionable
status symbol; now it's filled with Māori and
pioneer artefacts. It's 3km east of town.

Wairere Falls   Waterfall
About 15km northeast of Matamata are the
spectacular 153m Wairere Falls, the highest
on the North Island. From the car park it's
a 45-minute walk through native bush to
the lookout or a steep 1½-hour climb to the
summit.

Getting There & Away

Matamata is on SH27, 160km south of
Auckland. **InterCity** (📞09-583 5780; www.
intercity.co.nz) runs here from Auckland
($31, 3¼ hours, at least three daily) usually
via Hamilton; and Rotorua ($28, one hour,
two daily). **Naked Bus** (📞09-979 1616;
https://nakedbus.com) also runs a bus to/
from Auckland ($17, 3½ hours, two daily).

BAY OF ISLANDS

Bay of Islands at a Glance...

With turquoise waters and 150 undeveloped islands, the Bay of Islands ranks as one of New Zealand's top summertime destinations. Most of the action is out on the water: yachting, fishing, kayaking, diving or spying whales and dolphins.

It's also a place of enormous historical significance. Māori knew it as Pēwhairangi and settled here early in their migrations. It's also the site of NZ's first permanent British settlement, at Russell. It was here that the Treaty of Waitangi was drawn up and first signed in 1840; the treaty remains the linchpin of race relations in NZ today.

Bay of Islands in Two Days

Check out historic **Russell** (p72) in the morning, then ferry across to Paihia and spend the afternoon understanding the impact of the Treaty of Waitangi at the **Waitangi Treaty Grounds** (p69). Head to dinner at **Provenir** (p76) in Paihia, and the following morning hook up with an exciting **boat trip** (p70) exploring the Bay of Islands. After your marine excursion, relax with absolute waterfront drinks at **Alongside** (p77).

Bay of Islands in Three Days

Kick off the following morning with great coffee and a breakfast burrito at **El Cafe** (p75) in Paihia, before continuing the history theme with a trip to nearby Kerikeri to have a wander around **Kerikeri Mission Station** (p77) and nearby **Kororipo Pā** (p77). Duck back to Paihia then ferry over to Russell for an excellent end-of-bay dinner at **Gables** (p73).

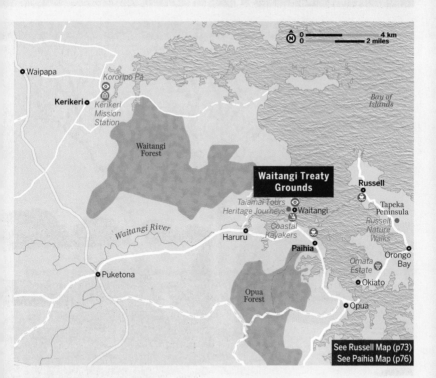

Arriving in the Bay of Islands

Bay of Islands (Kerikeri) Airport (KKE; ☏09-407 6133; www.bayofislandsairport.co.nz; 218 Wiroa Rd) The airport is 8km southwest of Kerikeri. The only scheduled flights are Air New Zealand services from Auckland. Super Shuttle connects you to Kerikeri and Paihia.

Bus Services InterCity and Mana Bus travellers de-bus at Paihia. InterCity continues to Kerikeri.

Ferry Car and passenger ferry from Paihia to Russell.

Sleeping

Sleepy after the drive from Auckland? There's a wide range of accommodation available up here in the Bay of Islands. Motels and backpacker hostels are clustered in Paihia, while Russell and Kerikeri have a solid range of bed and breakfast accommodation and drive-in motels.

VERONIKA HANZLIKOVA/SHUTTERSTOCK ©

Waitangi Treaty Grounds

Occupying a lawn-draped headland, this is NZ's most significant historic site. Here, on 6 February 1840, the first 43 Māori chiefs signed the Treaty of Waitangi with the British Crown; eventually, over 500 chiefs would sign it.

Great For...

☑ Don't Miss

The beautiful carvings and *tukutuku* (woven panels) at Waitangi's Whare Rūnanga (meeting house).

Te Kōngahu Museum of Waitangi

Opened in 2016, Te Kōngahu Museum of Waitangi is a modern and comprehensive showcase of the role of the treaty in the past, present and future of Aotearoa New Zealand. It provides a warts-and-all look at the early interactions between Māori and Europeans, the events leading up to the treaty's signing, the long litany of treaty breaches by the Crown, the wars and land confiscations that followed, and the protest movement that led to the current process of redress for historic injustices. Many *taonga* (treasures) associated with Waitangi were previously scattered around NZ, and this excellent museum is now a safe haven for a number of key historical items. One room is devoted to facsimiles of all the key documents, while another screens

Ngātokimatawhaorua's canoe house

❶ Need to Know

📞09-402 7437; www.waitangi.org.nz; 1 Tau Henare Dr, Waitangi; adult/child $50/free; ⊙9am-5pm; ✐

✕ Take a Break

Overlooking the Treaty Grounds, the **Whare Waka** (📞09-402 7437; www. waitangi.org.nz; Waitangi Treaty Grounds, 1 Tau Henare Dr, Waitangi; mains $13-19; ⊙8am-4pm) offers good cafe fare.

★ Top Tip

Experience a *hāngi* dinner and concert at Whare Waka; Tuesday, Thursday and Sunday evenings, December to March.

a fascinating short film dramatising the events of the initial treaty signing.

Treaty House

The Treaty House was shipped over as a kit-set from Australia and erected in 1834 as the four-room home of the official British Resident James Busby. It's now preserved as a memorial and museum containing displays about the house and the people who lived here.

Whare Rūnanga

Across the lawn, the magnificently detailed Whare Rūnanga was completed in 1940 to mark the centenary of the treaty. The fine carvings represent the major Māori tribes. It's here that the cultural performances take place, starting with a *haka pōwhiri*

(challenge and welcome) and then heading inside for *waiata* (songs) and spine-tingling *haka* (war dances).

Ngātokimatawhaorua

Near the cove is the 35m, 6-tonne *waka taua* (war canoe) *Ngātokimatawhaorua*, also built for the centenary. A photographic exhibit details how it was fashioned from gigantic kauri logs. There's also an excellent gift shop selling Māori art and design, with a carving studio attached.

Tours & Admission

Tours leave on the hour from 10am to 3pm. Admission is discounted to $25 for NZ residents upon presentation of a passport or drivers licence. Admission incorporates a guided tour and spirited cultural performance, and entry to the Museum of Waitangi, the Whare Rūnanga and the historic Treaty House.

JON SPARKS/ALAMY ©

Marine Adventures

Getting out onto the water is the best way to experience the Bay of Islands. There are myriad opportunities here for kayaking, sailing, cruising, jetboating, sea kayaking and marine mammal-watching amid the bay's eye-popping scenery.

Great For...

☑ Don't Miss

Subtropical diving on the wreck of the *Rainbow Warrior*, an hour north of Paihia by boat.

Boat tours leave from either Paihia or Russell, calling into the other town as their first stop.

Out on the bay, one of the most striking islands is Piercy Island (Motukokako) off Cape Brett, at the bay's eastern edge. This steep-walled rock fortress features a vast natural arch – the famous Hole in the Rock. If conditions are right, most boat tours pass right through the heart of the island. En route it's likely you'll encounter bottlenose and common dolphins, and you may see orcas, other whales and penguins.

A fabulous way to explore the bay is under sail. Either help crew the boat (no experience required), or sit back and spend the afternoon island-hopping, swimming and snorkelling.

Boat at the Hole in the Rock

Tours

Phantom — Boating

(📞0800 224 421; www.yachtphantom.com; day sail $110) A fast 50ft racing sloop, known for its wonderful food. BYO (bring your own) beer and wine is allowed.

R Tucker Thompson — Boating

(📞09-402 8430; www.tucker.co.nz; ⊙Nov-Mar) The *Tucker* is a majestic tall ship offering day sails (adult/child $149/75, including a barbecue lunch) and late-afternoon cruises (adult/child $65/33).

Explore NZ — Cruise

(📞09-402 8234; www.exploregroup.co.nz; cnr Marsden & Williams Rds, Paihia) 🍃 Explore's four-hour Discover the Bay cruise (adult/child $149/90 including barbecue lunch)

🛈 Need to Know

The Bay of Islands i-SITE (p77) at Paihia can help you book your water-based adventures.

✖ Take a Break

Hell Hole (p72) in Russell brews hellishly good coffee.

★ Top Tip

Booking a few days ahead is highly rec-ommended, especially during summer and school holidays.

heads to the Hole in the Rock and stops at Urupukapuka Island.

Carino — Cruise

(📞09-402 8040; www.sailingdolphins.co.nz; Paihia Wharf; adult/child $124/80) 🍃 This 50ft catamaran offers day cruises with an island stopover and snorkelling; a barbecue lunch is available for $6.

Fullers Great Sights — Cruise

(📞09-402 7421; www.dolphincruises.co.nz; Maritime Bldg, Marsden Rd, Paihia) 🍃 The four-hour Hole in the Rock Cruise (adult/child $107/54) heads out to the famous sea arch and stops at Urupukapuka Island on the way back.

Coastal Kayakers — Kayaking

(📞0800 334 661; www.coastalkayakers.co.nz; Te Karuwha Pde, Paihia) Runs guided tours (half-/full day $89/139, minimum two people) and multiday adventures. Kayaks (half-/full day $40/60) can also be rented for independent exploration.

Russell

Although it was once known as the 'Hell-hole of the Pacific', those coming to Russell for debauchery will be sadly disappointed: they've missed the orgies on the beach by 180 years. Instead they'll find a historic town with gift shops and B&Bs, and, in summer, you can rent kayaks and dinghies along the Strand.

◎ SIGHTS

Pompallier Mission
Historic Building

(☑09-403 9015; www.pompallier.co.nz; 5 The Strand; adult/child $10/free; ⊙10am-4pm) Built in 1842 to house the Catholic mission's printing press, this rammed-earth building is the mission's last remaining building in the western Pacific and NZ's oldest factory. Over its seven years of operation, a staggering 40,000 books were printed here in Māori. Admission includes extremely interesting hands-on tours which lead you through the entire bookmaking process, from the icky business of tanning animal hides for the covers, to setting the type and stitching together the final books.

Christ Church
Church

(www.oldchurch.org.nz; Church St) English naturalist Charles Darwin made a donation towards the cost of building what is now the country's oldest surviving church (1836). The graveyard's biggest memorial commemorates Tamati Waka Nene, a powerful Ngāpuhi chief from the Hokianga who sided against Hōne Heke in the Northland War. The church's wooden exterior has musket and cannonball holes dating from the 1845 battle.

Omata Estate
Winery

(☑09-403 8007; www.omata.co.nz; 212 Aucks Rd; ⊙11am-6pm Oct-May, by appointment Jun-Sep) With a growing reputation for red wines – especially its old-growth syrah – Omata Estate is one of Northland's finest wineries. To complement the tastings and sea views, shared platters ($40) are availa-

ble. The winery is on the road from Russell to the car ferry at Okiato.

Long Beach
Beach

(Oneroa; Long Beach Rd) About 1.5km behind Russell (an easy walk or cycle) is this placid, child-friendly beach. Turn left (facing the sea) to visit **Donkey Bay**, a small cove that is an unofficial nudist beach.

◎ TOURS

Russell Nature Walks
Ecotour

(☑027 908 2334; www.russellnaturewalks.co.nz; 6080 Russell Whakapara Rd; adult/child from $55/25) ✦ Located in privately owned native forest 2.5km south of Russell, guided day and night tours provide the opportunity to see native birds, including the weka and tui, and insects such as the weta. Glowworms softly illuminate night tours, and after dark there's the opportunity to hear (and very occasionally see) kiwi. Walks last 1½ to two hours.

Russell Mini Tours
Bus

(☑09-403 7866; www.russellminitours.com; cnr The Strand & Cass St; adult/child $30/15; ⊙tours 11am, noon, 1pm & 2pm year-round, also 10am, 3pm & 4pm Oct-Apr) Minibus tour around historic Russell with commentary.

◎ EATING & DRINKING

Hell Hole
Cafe $

(☑022 175 7847; www.facebook.com/hellhole coffee; 19 York St; snacks $6-12; ⊙7am-5pm Jan & Feb, 8am-3pm Mar, Apr, Nov & Dec) Bagels, baguettes and croissants all feature with the best coffee in town at this compact spot one block back from the waterfront. Beans are locally roasted and organic soft drinks and artisan ice blocks all combine to make Hell Hole a hugely popular place.

Newport Chocolates
Cafe $

(☑09-403 8888; www.newportchocolates.co.nz; 1 Cass St; chocolates around $3; ⊙10am-6pm Tue-Thu, 10am-7.30pm Fri & Sat) The delicious artisan chocolates are all handmade on-site, with flavours including raspberry, lime

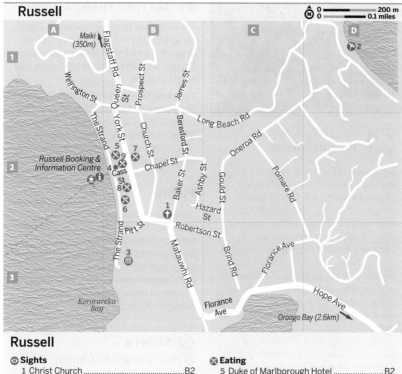

Russell

⊙ Sights

⊙ Activities, Courses & Tours

⊙ Eating

and chilli, and, our favourite, caramel and sea salt. It's also a top spot for divinely decadent hot chocolate and refreshing frappés.

Gables   Contemporary $$

(☏09-403 7670; www.thegablesrestaurant.co.nz; 19 The Strand; mains lunch $22-28, dinner $27-35; ⊙noon-3pm & 5.30-10pm Wed-Mon) Serving an imaginative take on Kiwi classics (lamb, beef, seafood), the Gables occupies an 1847 building on the waterfront built using whale vertebrae for foundations. Ask for a table by the windows for maritime views and look forward to top-notch local produce, including oysters and cheese.

Duke of Marlborough Hotel   Pub Food $$

(☏09-403 7829; www.theduke.co.nz; 35 The Strand; mains lunch $20-32, dinner $25-37; ⊙11.30am-9pm) There's no better spot in Russell to while away a few hours, glass in hand, than the Duke's sunny deck. Thankfully the upmarket bistro food matches the views, plus there's an excellent wine list and a great selection of NZ craft beers.

Hōne's Garden   Pizza $$

(☏022 466 3710; www.facebook.com/hones garden; 10 York St; pizza $18-25; ⊙noon-10pm Wed-Mon Nov-Apr) Head out to Hōne's pebbled courtyard for wood-fired pizza

 Historic Russell

Before it was known as a hellhole, or even as Russell, this was Kororāreka (Sweet Penguin), a fortified Ngāpuhi village. In the early 19th century the tribe permitted it to become Aotearoa's first European settlement. It quickly became a magnet for rough elements, such as fleeing convicts, whalers and drunken sailors. By the 1830s dozens of whaling ships at a time were anchored in the harbour. In 1839 Charles Darwin described it as full of 'the very refuse of society'.

After the signing of the Treaty of Waitangi in 1840, Okiato (where the car ferry now leaves from) was the residence of the governor and New Zealand's temporary capital. The capital was officially moved to Auckland in 1841 and Okiato, which was by then known as Russell, was eventually abandoned. The name Russell ultimately replaced Kororāreka.

ROBIN BUSH/GETTY IMAGES ©

(with 11 different varieties), cold craft beer on tap and a thoroughly easy-going Kiwi vibe. An expanded menu features tasty wraps and healthy salads. Antipasto platters are good for groups and indecisive diners.

❶ INFORMATION

Russell Booking & Information Centre (☎09-403 8020; www.russellinfo.co.nz; Russell Wharf; ⊗8am-5pm, extended hours summer)

❶ GETTING THERE & AWAY

The Russell **car ferry** (car/motorcycle/passenger $13/5.50/1) runs every 10 minutes from Opua (5km from Paihia) to Okiato (8km from Russell), between 6.50am and 10pm. Buy your tickets on board.

On foot, the easiest way to reach Russell is on a **passenger ferry** from Paihia (adult/child return $12/6). They run from 7am to 9pm (until 10pm October to May), generally every 30 minutes, but hourly in the evenings. Buy your tickets on board or at the i-SITE (p77) in Paihia.

Paihia

Joined to Waitangi by a bridge, and to Russell by a passenger ferry across the harbour, Paihia is the most central base from which to explore the Bay of Islands. Many boat trips and other marine excursions depart from its main jetty, and it has a healthy crop of restaurants, bars and accommodation.

◎ SIGHTS

St Paul's Anglican Church   Church
(36 Marsden Rd) The characterful St Paul's was constructed of Kawakawa stone in 1925, and stands on the site of the original mission church, a simple *raupo* (bulrush) hut erected in 1823. Look for the native birds in the stained glass above the altar – the kotare (kingfisher) represents Jesus (the king plus 'fisher of men'), while the tui (parson bird) and kereru (wood pigeon) portray the personalities of the Williams brothers (one scholarly, one forceful), who set up the mission station here.

Opua Forest   Forest
(www.doc.govt.nz) Just behind Paihia, this regenerating forest has walking trails ranging from 10 minutes to five hours. A few large trees have escaped axe and fire, including some big kauri. Information on Opua Forest walks is available from the i-SITE (p77), including the 1.5km **Paihia School Road Track** (about 30 minutes each way) leading to a lookout. You can also drive into

the forest by taking Oromahoe Rd west from Opua.

🚴 ACTIVITIES

Bay Beach Hire   Kayaking, Boating
(☎09-402 6078; www.baybeachhire.co.nz; Marsden Rd; ⊗9am-5pm) Hires kayaks (from $15 per hour), sailing catamarans ($50 first hour, $40 per additional hour), mountain bikes ($75 per day), boogie boards ($10/25 per hour/day), stand-up paddleboards ($25 per hour), fishing rods (from $10 per day), wetsuits and snorkelling gear (both $20 per day). Kayaking tours are also offered, including a twilight paddle ($69).

Paihia Dive   Diving
(☎09-402 7551; www.divenz.com; 7 Williams Rd; dives from $249; ⊗7.45am-5.30pm daily Oct-May, 8.30am-5pm Mon-Fri, to 1.30pm Sat Jun-Sep) This PADI five-star dive crew offers combined reef and wreck trips to either the *Canterbury* or the *Rainbow Warrior*. They also sell fishing gear and snorkelling sets.

Taiamai Tours Heritage Journeys   Cultural, Canoeing
(☎09-405 9990; www.taiamaitours.co.nz; 2½hr tour $135; ⊗departs 9am Tue, Thu, Sat & Sun Oct-Apr) 🛶 Paddle a traditional 12m carved *waka* (canoe) from the Waitangi bridge to the Haruru Falls. The Ngāpuhi hosts wear traditional garb, and perform the proper *karakia* (incantations) and share stories. The price includes admission to the Waitangi Treaty Grounds (p69).

Tango Jet Ski Tours   Boating
(☎0800 253 8754; www.tangojetskitours.co.nz; Paihia Wharf, Marsden Rd; tours $160-460) Zip around the bay led by a guide on your own jet ski; longer trips go all the way to the Hole in the Rock.

🍴 EATING

El Cafe   Latin American $
(☎09-402 7637; www.facebook.com/elcafe paihia; 2 Kings Rd; mains $11-15; ⊗8am-4pm; 🛜) This excellent Chilean-owned cafe has the best coffee in town and terrific breakfast burritos, tacos and baked-egg dishes, such

Boats and kayaks in Paihia

RIEKEPHOTOS/SHUTTERSTOCK ©

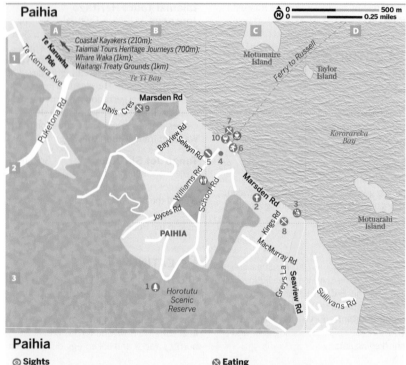

Paihia

as spicy *huevos rancheros*. The Cuban pulled-pork sandwich is truly a wonderful thing. The fruit smoothies are also great on a warm Bay of Islands day.

Charlotte's Kitchen
Contemporary $$

(☎09-402 8296; www.charlotteskitchen.co.nz; Paihia Wharf, 69 Marsden Rd; mains lunch $16-27, dinner $20-35; ⊕11.30am-late Mon-Fri, 8am-late Sat & Sun) Named after an escaped Australian convict who was NZ's first white

female settler, this hip restaurant/bar occupies a cheeky perch on the main pier. Bits of Kiwiana decorate the walls, while the menu takes a swashbuckling journey around the world, including steamed pork buns, quesadillas, Cubano sandwiches and a particularly delicious Asian-style broth with pork dumplings.

Provenir
Contemporary $$$

(☎09-402 0111; www.paihiabeach.co.nz; Paihia Beach Resort, 130 Marsden Rd; mains $30-40;

⊗8-10am & 6pm-late) A concise seasonal menu of main dishes showcases regional NZ produce and local seafood (including plump oysters from nearby Orongo Bay), underpinned by subtle Asian influences and one of Northland's best wine lists. Desserts are extraordinarily creative and well worth leaving room for.

🍷 DRINKING & NIGHTLIFE

Alongside   Bar
(☎09-402 6220; www.alongside35.co.nz; 69 Marsden Rd; ⊗8am-10pm) Quite possibly the biggest deck in all of Northland extends over the water, and a versatile approach to entertaining begins with coffee and bagels for breakfast before the inevitable transformation of Alongside into a very enjoyable bar. There are bar snacks and meals on offer, and lots of comfy lounges ready for conversations fuelled by cocktails or cold beer.

Kings Road Bar & Brasserie   Bar
(☎09-402 6080; 14 Kings Rd; ⊗11.30am-midnight; 🛜) Slink into this low-lit bar for a cosy beverage on one of the couches or a crack at the free pool table.

ℹ️ INFORMATION

Bay of Islands i-SITE (☎09-402 7345; www.northlandnz.com; 69 Marsden Rd; ⊗8am-5pm Mar-Dec, to 7pm Jan & Feb) Information and bookings.

ℹ️ GETTING THERE & AWAY

All **buses** serving Paihia stop at the Maritime Building by the wharf.

Ferries (Paihia Wharf) depart regularly for Russell, and there are seasonal services to Urupukapuka Island.

ℹ️ GETTING AROUND

For bike rental, visit Bay Beach Hire (p75).

🡢 Kerikeri Detour

Kerikeri, a quick 23km jaunt northwest of Paihia, is famous for its oranges...but it also offers a snapshot of early Māori and Pākehā interaction.

Two of the nation's most significant buildings nestle side-by-side at **Kerikeri Mission Station** (☎09-407 9236; www.historic.org.nz; 246 Kerikeri Rd; museum $8, house tour $8, combined $10; ⊗10am-4pm). Start at the **Stone Store**, NZ's oldest stone building (1836). Upstairs there's an interesting little museum while downstairs the shop sells the type of goods that used to be stocked here in the 19th century. Tours of neighbouring **Kemp House** depart from here. Built by the missionaries in 1822, this humble yet pretty wooden Georgian-style house is NZ's oldest building. In summer, the Honey House Cafe operates from a neighbouring cottage.

Just up the hill from the Mission Station is a marked historical walk, which leads to the site of Hongi Hika's **Kororipo Pā** (Kerikeri Rd) 𝗙𝗥𝗘𝗘 (fortress) and village. Little remains aside from the terracing which once supported wooden palisades. Huge war parties once departed from here, terrorising much of the North Island and slaughtering thousands during the Musket Wars. The role of missionaries in arming Ngāpuhi remains controversial. The walk emerges near the cute wooden St James Anglican Church (1878).

Stone Store

Ruakuri Cave (p80)

Waitomo Caves

Even if damp, dark tunnels are your idea of hell, head to Waitomo anyway. The limestone caves and glowing bugs here are one of the North Island's premier attractions.

Great For...

Otorohanga

Waitomo Caves

Hangatiki

Oparure

Te Kuiti

ⓘ Need to Know

Naked Bus (📞0900 625 33; https://naked bus.com) runs one bus daily to Waitomo Caves village from Otorohanga at 5pm ($13, 20 minutes). Other departures include Hamilton ($16, one hour) and New Plymouth ($22, 3¼ hours).

★ **Top Tip**

There's no petrol in town, but there's an ATM at **Kiwi Paka** (📞07-878 3395; www.waitomokiwipaka.co.nz; Hotel Access Rd; dm/s/d $35/65/75, chalet s/d/tw/q $95/100/110/150; @🛜). Stock up on cash, groceries and petrol in Te Kuiti or Otorohanga.

The name Waitomo comes from *wai* (water) and *tomo* (hole or shaft): dotted across this region are numerous shafts dropping into underground cave systems and streams. There are 300-plus mapped caves in the area: the three main caves – Glowworm, Ruakuri and Aranui – have been bewitching visitors for over 100 years.

Caves

Book tours for the three main caves at the **Waitomo Caves Visitor Centre** (⏱0800 456 922; www.waitomo.com; Waitomo Caves Rd; ⏰9am-5pm).

Glowworm Cave

The guided tour of the **Glowworm Cave** (⏱0800 456 922; www.waitomo.com/waitomo-glowworm-caves; adult/child $51/23; ⏰45min tours half-hourly 9am-5pm), behind the visitor

centre, leads past impressive stalactites and stalagmites into the large Cathedral cavern. At the tour's end you board a boat and float along beneath a Milky Way of little lights – these are the glowworms. The acoustics are so good that Dame Kiri Te Kanawa and the Vienna Boys' Choir have given concerts here.

Ruakuri Cave

Ruakuri Cave (⏱0800 782 587, 07-878 6219; www.waitomo.com/ruakuri-cave; adult/child $74/29; ⏰2hr tours 9am, 10am, 11am, 12.30pm, 1.30pm, 2.30pm & 3.30pm) has an impressive 15m-high spiral staircase, bypassing a Māori burial site at the cave entrance. Tours lead through 1.6km of the 7.5km system, taking in caverns with glowworms, subterranean streams and waterfalls, and intricate limestone structures. Some claim

Ruakuri Cave

the cave is haunted – it's customary to wash your hands when leaving to remove the *tapu* (taboo).

Aranui Cave

Three kilometres west from the Glowworm Cave is **Aranui Cave** (📞0800 456 922; www.waitomo.com/aranui-cave; adult/child $50/23; ⏰1hr tours 9am-4pm). This cave is dry (hence no glowworms) but compensates with an incredible array of limestone formations. Thousands of tiny 'straw' stalactites hang from the ceiling. There is transport to the

cave entrance from the visitor centre. A 15-minute bush walk is also included.

Going Underground

Waitomo excels with challenging and unique ways to explore the area's subterranean wonders. Recommended operators:

Legendary Black Water Rafting Company (📞0800 782 5874; www.waitomo.com/black-water-rafting; 585 Waitomo Caves Rd) The Black Labyrinth tour ($142, three hours) involves floating in a wetsuit on an inner tube down a river through Ruakuri Cave. Leap off a waterfall then float through a long, glowworm-covered passage. The trip ends with showers, soup and bagels in the cafe. There's also the more adventurous Black Abyss tour ($246, five hours).

CaveWorld (📞0800 228 338, 07-878 6577; www.caveworld.co.nz; cnr Waitomo Caves Rd & Hotel Access Rd) The Tube It black-water rafting trip ($139, two hours) heads through glowworm-filled Te Anaroa. Also available is the Footwhistle Glowworm Cave Tour ($59, one hour), incorporating a stop in a forest shelter for a mug of restorative kawakawa tea.

Waitomo Adventures (📞0800 924 866, 07-878 7788; www.waitomo.co.nz; 654 Waitomo Caves Rd) The Lost World trip ($405/580, four/seven hours) combines a 100m abseil with walking, rock climbing, wading and swimming. Haggas Honking Holes ($275, four hours) includes three waterfall abseils, rock climbing and a subterranean river.

FOTO5593/SHUTTERSTOCK ©

ROTORUA

Rotorua at a Glance...

A whiff of Rotorua's sulphurous airs will probably be your first encounter with New Zealand's most dynamic thermal area, home to spurting geysers, steaming hot springs and exploding mud pools. Māori revered this place; today 35% of the population is indigenous, and their cultural performances and traditional hāngi (feasts) are hugely popular. Beyond the mud and Māori culture, Rotorua also delivers some of the best mountain biking in the country, plus a raft of adrenaline-charged outdoor activities. The town itself is fairly touristy and isn't much to look at, but the lake it presides over is gorgeous!

Rotorua in Two Days

Explore Rotorua's geothermal landscape at **Te Puia** (p87) and **Whakarewarewa** (p86) before a **Māori concert** (p90) and *hāngi* in the evening. Kick off day two with breakfast at **Artisan Cafe** (p96) before launching into the **Redwoods Treewalk** (p93) or some mountain biking in the **Redwoods Whakarewarewa Forest** (p93). Recount your adventures over dinner at **Sabroso** (p96) and drinks at **Ponsonby Rd** (p98).

Rotorua in Three Days

Have a walk around the lakefront then fuel up on some crêpes at **Le Café de Paris** (p96) before further outdoor action. Dangle from a forest zipline with **Rotorua Canopy Tours** (p93), roll downhill in a giant plastic bubble with **Zorb** (p95), or defy gravity at **Agroventures** (p94), before a pure Italian dinner at **Leonardo's Pure Italian** (p97).

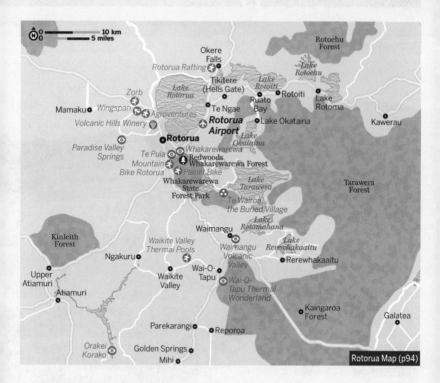

Rotorua Map (p94)

Arriving in Rotorua

Rotorua Airport (p99) The airport is 9km northeast of town. Super Shuttle offers door-to-door service; Baybus route 10 stops at the airport hourly. A taxi to/from town costs about $30.

Bus Long-haul InterCity and Mana Bus services stop outside the i-SITE.

Sleeping

Rotorua has plenty of motels (especially along Fenton St, which is something of a motel alley), plus some great holiday parks, big chain hotels and an ever-changing backpacker scene. If you're looking for some peace and quiet, Ngongotaha, 7km northwest of the town centre, has some good B&Bs in its rural hinterland.

FILED IMAGE / SHUTTERSTOCK ©

Geothermal Rotorua

Rotorua's main drawcard is Whakarewarewa (pronounced 'fah-kah-reh-wah-reh-wah'), a geothermal reserve 3km south of the city centre. Local Māori have lived on this bubbling and steaming terrain for hundreds of years.

Great For...

☑ Don't Miss

A tour with Māori guides at Whaka-rewarewa, many descended from the area's first families.

Whakarewarewa Village

Whakarewarewa Village (🕿 07-349 3463; www.whakarewarewa.com; 17 Tyron St; adult/child $40/18, incl hāngi $70/40; ⏰8.30am-5pm) is a living community where the local Tūhourangi/Ngāti Wāhiao people have resided for centuries. Villagers lead the tours (hourly, 9am to 4pm) amid steamy bubbling pools, silica terraces and geysers.

Admission includes a **cultural performance** (11.15am and 2pm daily; additional show 12.30pm November to March) and a self-guided nature trail. Village shops sell authentic arts and crafts, and you can learn more about Māori traditions such as flax weaving, carving and *tā moko* (tattooing). Buttery sweetcorn ($2) is pulled straight out of a boiling mineral pool.

Wai-O-Tapu Thermal Wonderland

Te Puia

Te Puia (☎07-348 9047; www.tepuia.com; Hemo Rd, Whakarewarewa; adult/child $54/29, incl performance $69/35, Te Pō $125/63; ⊙8am-5pm) dials up the heat on *Māoritanga* (things Māori) with explosive cultural performances and **Pōhutu** (Big Splash), the famous geyser which erupts 20 times a day, spurting hot water 30m skyward. The adjacent **Prince of Wales' Feathers** geyser starts up shortly before Pōhutu blows its top. Also here is the **National Carving School** and the **National Weaving School**.

Daytime visits *(Te Rā)* feature a guided tour (hourly), which includes a *wharenui* (carved meeting house), a recreated pre-colonial village, a nocturnal kiwi enclosure, three major geysers and a huge

pool of boiling mud. **Cultural performances** (10.15am, 12.15pm and 3.15pm), incorporate a traditional welcome into the *wharenui* and a 45-minute *kapa haka* (traditional song and dance) concert.

The three-hour *Te Pō* (night) experience (6pm) includes a cultural show and a *hāngi*, followed by a tour through the thermal zone.

Kuirau Park

Just west of central Rotorua is **Kuirau Park** (Ranolf St), a volcanic area you can explore for free. Steam hisses from fenced-off sections, while occasional eruptions smother the park in mud, thwarting the gardeners' best efforts. Keep your toddlers on a tight rein.

Nearby

Ask at the Rotorua i-SITE about visiting the region's other big-ticket geothermal attractions, including the amazing **Wai-O-Tapu Thermal Wonderland** (☎07-366 6333; www.waiotapu.co.nz; 201 Waiotapu Loop Rd; adult/child $33/11; ⊙8.30am-5pm) and **Waimangu Volcanic Valley** (☎07-366 6137; www.waimangu.co.nz; 587 Waimangu Rd; adult/child walk $39/12, cruise $45/12; ⊙8.30am-5pm, last admission 3pm), both south of Rotorua en route to the lakeside town of Taupo.

FERDINAND WAGNER/SHUTTERSTOCK ©

Mountain Biking

Welcome to one of the southern hemisphere's finest destinations for mountain biking, offering a range of experiences for everyone from families and beginners, through to gung-ho two-wheeled downhill lunatics.

Great For...

☑ Don't Miss

Catching the gondola up Mt Ngongotaha then hurtling along downhill tracks.

Redwoods Whakarewarewa Forest

On the edge of town is the Redwoods Whakarewarewa Forest (p93), home to some of the best mountain-bike trails in the country. There are close to 100km of tracks to keep bikers of all skill levels happy for days on end. Note that not all tracks in the forest are designated for bikers, so adhere to the signposts. Pick up a trail map at the forest visitor centre. At the time of research, a professional-standard BMX track was also being constructed in the park.

Skyline Rotorua MTB Gravity Park

More evidence of Rotorua's status as a world-class mountain-biking destination is the **Skyline Rotorua MTB Gravity**

Redwoods Whakarewarewa Forest

Bike Hire & Tours

Mountain Bike Rotorua (☎07-348 4295; www.mtbrotorua.co.nz; Waipa State Mill Rd, Whakarewarewa; hire per 2hr/day from $35/60, guided rides from $130; ⏱9am-5pm) hires out bikes at the Waipa Mill car park entrance to the Redwoods forest. Its new central **Rotorua adventure hub** (☎07-348 4290; www.mtbrotorua.co.nz; 1128 Hinemoa St; ⏱9am-5pm) offers rentals, info and a cool cafe.

Planet Bike (☎07-346 1717; www.planet bike.co.nz; 8 Waipa Bypass Rd, Whakarewarewa; hire per 2hr/day from $35/60) offers bike hire and guided mountain-bike rides (from $150) in Redwoods Whakarewarewa Forest.

Bike Barn (☎07-347 1151; www.bikebarn. co.nz; 1109 Eruera St; bikes per half-/full day from $35/50; ⏱8.30am-5.30pm Mon-Fri, 10am-3pm Sat & Sun) provides bike hire (hardtail and full suspension) and repairs.

Park (☎07-347 0027; www.skyline.co.nz; 178 Fairy Springs Rd, Fairy Springs; 1/15/40 gondola uplifts with bike $30/59/110; ⏱9am-5.30pm), a network of 11 MTB tracks coursing down Mt Ngongotaha. There are options for riders of all experience levels, and access to the top of the park is provided by the Skyline gondola (p95). Bike rental is available on-site.

Te Ara Ahi (Thermal by Bike)

The two-day, 48km Te Ara Ahi (Thermal by Bike) trail starts in Rotorua and heads south via various geothermal attractions to the **Waikite Valley Thermal Pools** (☎07-333 1861; www.hotpools.co.nz; 648 Waikite Valley Rd; adult/child $17/9, private pools 40min per person $20; ⏱10am-9pm) ⦿ 35km away. This intermediate-level route is designated as one of the New Zealand Cycle Trail's 'Great Rides' (www.nzcycletrail.com).

BOB HILSCHER/SHUTTERSTOCK ©

Māori Rotorua

Māori culture is a big-ticket item in Rotorua and, although the experiences are largely commercialised and packaged up neatly for visitor consumption, they're still a great introduction to authentic Māori traditions.

Great For...

☑ Don't Miss

The heavenly scents of meat-and-veg, cooked in an *umu* (earth oven).

Haka & Hāngi

Rotorua's Māori cultural experiences focus on two big activities: *kapa haka* (traditional performing arts) concerts and earth-cooked *hāngi* (feasts), often packaged together in an evening's entertainment featuring a *pōwhiri* (welcoming ceremony), the famous *haka* (war dance), *waiata* (songs) and *poi* dances, where women showcase their dexterity by twirling balls of flax.

Tamaki Māori Village (☎07-349 2999; www.tamakimaorivillage.co.nz; booking office 1220 Hinemaru St; adult/child $130/70) is an established favourite, offering a 3½-hour twilight Māori cultural experience starting with free transfers from Rotorua to its recreated pre-colonial village, 15km south of town. The concert is followed by a *hāngi*.

Family-run **Mitai Māori Village** (☎07-343 9132; www.mitai.co.nz; 196 Fairy Springs Rd, Fairy

Tamaki Mãori performers

❶ Need to Know

Transfers to/from Mãori cultural experiences beyond the city centre (Mitai, Tamaki) are available.

✕ Take a Break

Most of Rotorua's Mãori cultural experiences involve plenty of food – you won't go hungry!

★ Top Tip

Both Whakarewarewa (p86) and Te Puia (p87) offer cultural performances along with geothermal action.

Copthorne Hotel Mãori Concert & Feast (☏07-348 0199; www.millenniumhotels.co.nz; 328 Fenton St, Glenholme; per person $47)
Millennium Hotel Feast & Revue (☏07-347 1234; www.millenniumrotorua.co.nz; 1270 Hinemaru St; adult/child $70/35)

Ohinemutu is a lakeside Mãori village that is home to around 260 people. Highlights include the 1905 **Tama-te-Kapua Meeting House** (not open to visitors), many steaming volcanic vents, and the wonderful Mãori–British mash-up that is **St Faith's Anglican Church** (☏07-348 2393; Korokai St, Ohinemutu; admission by donation; ⊙8am-6pm, services 9am Sun & 10am Wed). Be respectful if you visit the village: the residents don't appreciate loud, nosy tourists wandering around taking photos of their private property.

Springs; adult $116, child $23-58; ⊙6.30pm) offers a popular three-hour evening event with a concert, *hãngi* and glowworm bushwalk. The experience starts with the arrival of a *waka taua* (war canoe) and can be combined with a nighttime tour of Rainbow Springs (p93) next door, including a walk through the kiwi enclosure. Pick-ups and a concert-only option are available.

Te Puia (p87) and Whakarewarewa (p86) offer the added thrill of being situated within an active geothermal zone. Both stage daytime shows; Te Puia also has an evening *hãngi*-and-show package while Whakarewarewa serves *hãngi*-cooked lunches.

Many of the big hotels also offer packages (less atmosphere, but less expense): **Matariki** (☏07-346 3888; www.novotelrotorua.co.nz; 11 Tutanekai St; concerts adult/child $35/18, incl hãngi $69/35) At the Novotel.

⊙ SIGHTS

Rotorua Museum   Notable Building
(☏07-350 1814; www.rotoruamuseum.co.nz; Oru-awhata Dr; adult/child $20/8) Constructed in a striking faux-Tudor style, Rotorua's most magnificent building opened in 1908 as an elegant spa retreat called the Bath House. In 1969 it was converted into a museum, with an art gallery added later. Sadly it was closed in November 2016 after cracks were spotted following the major earthquake in Kaikoura, 650km away. Seismic strengthening was being planned at the time of research, but the work is expected to take years to complete.

Lake Rotorua   Lake
Lake Rotorua is the largest of the district's 18 lakes and is – underneath all that water – a spent volcano. Near the centre of the lake is **Mokoia Island**, which has for centuries been occupied by various subtribes

Rotorua's most magnificent building opened in 1908 as an elegant spa retreat

of the area. The lake can be explored by boat, with several operators situated at the lakefront.

Wingspan   Bird Sanctuary
(☏07-357 4469; www.wingspan.co.nz; 1164 Paradise Valley Rd, Ngongotaha Valley; adult/child $25/10; ⊙9am-3pm) The Wingspan National Bird of Prey Centre is dedicated to conserving threatened NZ raptors, particularly the karearea (NZ falcon). Learn about the birds in the museum display, then take a sneaky peek into the incubation area before walking through the all-weather aviary. Make sure you're here by 1.30pm for the 2pm flying display.

Paradise Valley Springs   Nature Centre
(☏07-348 9667; www.paradisevalleysprings. co.nz; 467 Paradise Valley Rd, Ngongotaha Valley; adult/child $30/15; ⊙8am-dusk, last entry 5pm) ✐ At the foot of Mt Ngongotaha, 8km from Rotorua, this 6-hectare park has trout springs, big slippery eels, native birds and various land-dwelling animals such as deer, alpacas, possums and a pride of lions (fed

Rotorua Museum

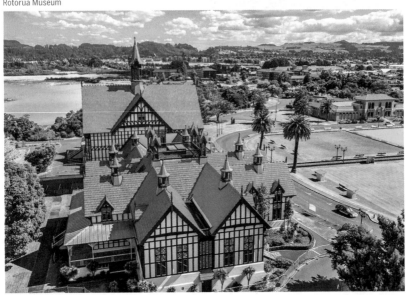

at 2.30pm). There's also a coffee shop and an elevated treetop walkway.

Rainbow Springs   Nature Centre

(☑07-350 0440; www.rainbowsprings.co.nz; 192 Fairy Springs Rd, Fairy Springs; 24hr passes adult/ child/family $40/20/99; ◷8.30am-10pm) ✎ The natural springs here are home to wild trout and eels, which you can peer at through an underwater viewer. There are interpretive walkways, a 'Big Splash' water ride and plenty of animals, including tuatara (a native reptile) and native birds. The **Kiwi Encounter** offers a rare peek into the lives of these birds: excellent 30-minute tours (an extra $10 per person) have you tiptoeing through incubator and hatchery areas. There's also a free-flight exotic bird show at 11.30am.

Rainbow Springs is around 3km north of central Rotorua.

Government Gardens   Gardens

(Hinemaru St) The manicured Government Gardens surrounding the Rotorua Museum are a wonderful example of the blending of English (rose gardens, croquet lawns and bowling greens) and Māori traditions (carvings at the entrance and subtly blended into the buildings). Being Rotorua there are steaming thermal pools scattered about, and it's well worth taking a walk along the active geothermal area at the lake's edge.

ACTIVITIES

Rotorua
Canopy Tours   Adventure Sports

(☑07-343 1001; www.canopytours.co.nz; 147 Fairy Springs Rd, Fairy Springs; 3hr tours adult/ child $149/119; ◷8am-8pm Oct-Apr, to 6pm May-Sep) Explore a 1.2km web of bridges, flying foxes, ziplines and platforms, 22m high in a lush native forest canopy 10 minutes out of town (they say that rimu tree is 1000 years old!), with plenty of native birds to keep you company. All trips depart from its office opposite the gondola.

Rotorua Rafting   Rafting

(☑0800 772 384; www.rotorua-rafting.co.nz; 761 SH33, Okere Falls; rafting $85-90) The

Redwoods Whakarewarewa Forest

This magical forest **park** (☑07-350 0110; www.redwoods.co.nz; Long Mile Rd, Whakarewarewa) is 3km southeast of town on Tarawera Rd. From 1899, 170 tree species were planted here to see which could be grown successfully for timber. Mighty Californian redwoods (up to 72m high) give the park its grandeur today. Walking tracks range from a half-hour wander through the Redwood Grove to a whole-day route to the Blue and Green Lakes. Several walks start from the Redwoods i-SITE (p99), where you'll also find the spectacular Redwoods Treewalk.

Aside from walking, the forest is great for picnics, and is acclaimed for its accessible mountain biking (p88).

CHAMELEONSEYE/SHUTTERSTOCK ©

minimum age for rafting the Grade V-rated Kaituna River is 13, but 10-year-olds are allowed on the Grade III–rated section of the river. Transfers from central Rotorua are included in the price.

Redwoods Treewalk   Walking

(☑07-350 0110; www.treewalk.co.nz; Long Mile Rd, Whakarewarewa; adult/child $25/15; ◷8.30am-9.30pm) ✎ More than 500m is traversed on this walkway combining 23 bouncy wooden bridges suspended between century-old redwood trees. Most of the pathway is around 6m off the forest floor, but it ascends to 20m in some parts. It's at its most impressive at night when it's

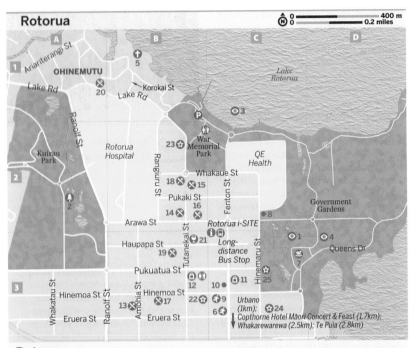

Rotorua

lit by striking wooden lanterns, hung from the trees.

Agroventures   Adventure Sports

(☎07-357 4747; www.agroventures.co.nz; 1335 Paradise Valley Rd, Ngongotaha; 1/2/4 rides $49/85/129, bungy $129; ⊙9am-5pm)
Agroventures is a hive of action, 9km north of Rotorua (free shuttles available). Start off with the 43m **bungy** and the **Swoop**, a 130km/h swing. The **Freefall Xtreme**

simulates skydiving, and also here is the **Shweeb**, a monorail velodrome from which you hang in a clear capsule and pedal yourself along at speeds of up to 50km/h.

Alongside is the **Agrojet**, one of NZ's fastest jetboats, splashing and weaving around a very tight 1km course. Plus there's a **BMX** airbag and ramps for practising your jumps (two hours $30, BYO bike).

Skyline Rotorua   Cable Car
(☑07-347 0027; www.skyline.co.nz; 178 Fairy Springs Rd, Fairy Springs; adult/child gondola $30/15; ☺9am-10pm) The cable car ride up the side of Mt Ngongotaha is only a teaser for the thrills on offer at the top. Most popular is the **luge**, which shoots along three different tracks (one/three/five/seven rides $14/28/38/45). For even speedier antics, try the **Sky Swing** (adult/child $89/74), the **Zoom Zipline** ($95/85) or the mountain-bike Gravity Park (p88). The summit also offers a restaurant, wine tasting at the **Volcanic Hills Winery** (☑07-282 2018; www.volcanichills.co.nz; 176 Fairy Springs Rd, Fairy Springs; tastings 3/5 wines $9.50/15; ☺11am-5.30pm), a nature trail and stargazing sessions (adult/child $93/49).

Note the Sky Swing and Zipline prices include the gondola and five luge rides. A baffling array of combination tickets is available.

Zorb   Adventure Sports
(☑07-357 5100; www.zorb.com; 149 Western Rd, Ngongotaha; 1-/2-/3-person ride $45/70/90; ☺9am-5pm, to 7pm Jan) The Zorb is 9km north of Rotorua on SH5 – look for the grassy hillside with large, clear, people-filled spheres rolling down it. There are three courses: 150m straight, 180m zigzag or 250m 'Drop'. Do your zorb strapped in and dry, or freestyle with water thrown in. And you can even rattle around with up to two friends inside.

Blue Baths   Swimming
(☑07-350 2119; www.bluebaths.co.nz; Queens Dr; adult/child $11/6; ☺10am-6pm) The gorgeous Spanish Mission–style Blue Baths opened in 1933 (and, amazingly, were closed from 1982 to 1999) and they now regularly host special events (performances, weddings etc). If you feel like taking a dip, the pool is a fraction of the price of the nearby Polynesian Spa, but note that while it's geothermically heated, it's not mineral water.

⊙ TOURS

Elite Adventures   Tours
(☑07-347 8282; www.eliteadventures.co.nz; half-/full day from $155/290) Small-group tours covering a selection of Rotorua's major cultural and natural highlights.

Happy Ewe Tours   Cycling
(☑022 622 9252; www.happyewetours.com; departs 1148 Hinemaru St; adult/child $60/30; ☺10am & 2pm) Saddle-up for a three-hour, small-group bike tour of Rotorua, wheeling past 27 sights around the city. It's all flat and slow-paced, so you don't need to be at your physical peak (you're on holiday after all).

Rotorua Duck Tours   Tours
(☑07-345 6522; www.rotoruaducktours.co.nz; 1241 Fenton St; adult/child $69/45; ☺tours 11am, 1pm & 3.30pm Oct-Apr, 11am & 2.15pm May-Sep) Ninety-minute trips in an amphibious biofuelled vehicle take in the major sites around town and head out onto three lakes (Rotorua, Okareka and Tikitapu/Blue).

⋒ SHOPPING

South of town, Te Puia and Whakarewarewa Village have excellent selections of genuine Māori-made arts.

Rākai Jade   Arts & Crafts
(☑027 443 9295; www.rakaijade.co.nz; 1234 Fenton St; ☺9am-5pm Mon-Sat) In addition to purchasing off-the-shelf *pounamu* (greenstone, jade) pieces, you can work with Rākai's on-site team of local Māori carvers to design and carve your own pendant or jewellery. A day's notice for 'Carve Your Own' experiences ($150) is preferred if possible; allow a full day.

 Hinemoa & Tūtānekai

Hinemoa was a young woman of a *hapū* (subtribe) that lived on the eastern shore of Lake Rotorua, while Tūtānekai was a young man of a Mokoia Island *hapū*. The pair met and fell in love during a regular tribal meeting. While both were of high birth, Tūtānekai was illegitimate, so marriage between the two was forbidden.

Home on Mokoia, the lovesick Tūtānekai played his flute for his love, the wind carrying the melody across the water. Hinemoa heard his declaration, but her people took to tying up the canoes at night to ensure she wouldn't go to him.

Finally, Tūtānekai's music won her over. Hinemoa undressed and swam the long distance from the shore to the island. When she arrived on Mokoia, Hinemoa found herself in a quandary. Having shed her clothing in order to swim, she could hardly walk into Tūtānekai's village naked. She hopped into a hot pool to think about her next move.

Eventually, Tūtānekai found Hinemoa in the pool and secreted her into his hut. Next morning, after a suspiciously long lie-in, a slave reported that someone was in Tūtānekai's bed. The lovers were busted, but when Hinemoa's superhuman efforts to reach Tūtānekai were revealed, their union was celebrated.

Descendants of Hinemoa and Tūtānekai still live around Rotorua today.

Lake Rotorua (p92)
ISTOCK/GETTY IMAGES PLUS/GETTY IMAGES ©

Rotorua Night Market Market

(www.rotoruanightmarket.co.nz; Tutanekai St; ⏱5pm-late Thu) Tutanekai St is closed off on Thursday nights between Haupapa and Hinemoa Sts to allow this market to spread its wings. Expect local arts and crafts, souvenirs, cheesy buskers, coffee, wine and plenty of ethnically diverse food stalls for dinner.

EATING

The lake end of Tutanekai St – known as 'Eat Streat' – is a car-free strip of eateries beneath a canopy roof.

Le Café de Paris Cafe $

(☏07-348 1210; www.facebook.com/cafede parisrotorua; 1206 Hinemoa St; mains $10-18; ⏱7.30am-4pm Tue-Sat; 🛜) The greeting is *très français* but this little cafe walks a fine line between a traditional *crêperie* and the kind of cafe that Kiwi retirees gravitate to. *Galettes* (savoury crêpes) are cooked to order and served alongside toasted sandwiches and jam scones. The coffee's good too.

Sabroso Latin American $$

(☏07-349 0591; www.sabroso.co.nz; 1184 Hau-papa St; mains $21-25; ⏱5-9pm Wed-Sun) This modest Latin American cantina – adorned with sombreros, guitars and salt-and-pepper shakers made from Corona bottles – serves zingy south-of-the-border fare. The black-bean chilli and the seafood tacos are excellent, as are the zesty margaritas. Booking ahead is highly recommended as Sabroso is *muy popular.* Buy a bottle of the owners' hot sauce to enliven your next Kiwi barbecue.

Artisan Cafe Cafe $$

(☏07-348 0057; www.artisancaferotorua.com; 1149 Tutanekai St; mains $11-24; ⏱7am-4pm; 🛜) A spinning wheel and a Mary Poppins–type bicycle lend a folksy feel to Rotorua's best cafe. Yet there's nothing old-fashioned about the food, which includes cooked breakfasts, burgers, salads and a couple of vegan options. Even hardened blokes should consider ordering the Little Miss Bene, an eggs Benedict of agreeably modest proportions.

Atticus Finch International $$

(📞07-460 0400; www.atticusfinch.co.nz; Eat Streat, 1106 Tutanekai St; lunch $16-20, shared plates $7.50-34; ⊘noon-2.30pm & 5pm-late; 🖊) Named after the righteous lawyer in *To Kill a Mockingbird*, the hippest spot on Eat Streat follows through with a Harper Lee cocktail and a Scout Sangria. Beyond the literary references, the menu of shared plates channels Asia and the Mediterranean rather than the American South, and a concise menu of NZ beer and wine imparts a local flavour.

Third Place Cafe $$

(📞07-349 4852; www.thirdplacecafe.co.nz; 35 Lake Rd, Ohinemutu; mains $15-20; ⊘7.30am-4pm; 🖭) This super-friendly cafe is away from the hubbub and has awesome lake views. All-day breakfast/brunch sidesteps neatly between fish and chips, and a 'mumble jumble' of crushed kumara (sweet potato), green tomatoes and spicy chorizo

topped with a poached egg and hollandaise sauce. Hangover? What hangover? Slide into a red-leather couch or score a window seat overlooking Ohinemutu.

Leonardo's
Pure Italian Italian $$

(📞07-347 7084; www.leonardospure.co.nz; Eat Streat, 1099 Tutanekai St; mains $22-36; ⊘5pm-late; 🖊) Although it looks cavernous from the outside, Leonardo's is surprisingly pleasant inside, with dark wood, soft lighting and welcoming service. Sometimes the simple things are the best, and that's certainly the case with its traditional (ie creamless) *tagliatelle alla carbonara*. The desserts are more hit and miss.

Abracadabra
Cafe Bar Mediterranean, Mexican $$

(📞07-348 3883; www.abracadabracafe.com; 1263 Amohia St; mains $26-32, tapas $11-15; ⊘10.30am-11pm Tue-Sat, to 3pm Sun; 🖭🖭) Channelling Spain, Mexico and North Africa, Abracadabra is a magical cave of spicy delights, from beef-and-apricot tagine to chicken enchiladas. There's an attractive

Rotorua Night Market

Fat Dog

front deck and a great beer terrace out the back – perfect for sharing some tapas over a few local craft brews.

Fat Dog   Cafe $$

(☎07-347 7586; www.fatdogcafe.co.nz; 1161 Arawa St; mains breakfast $13-19, lunch & dinner $19-26; ⊙7am-9pm; 🛜🚼) With paw prints and silly poems painted on the walls, this is the town's friskiest and most child-friendly cafe. During the day it dishes up burgers (try the Dogs Bollox), nachos, salads and massive sandwiches; in the evening it's candlelit lamb shanks and venison. Fine craft brews are also served.

Urbano   Bistro $$

(☎07-349 3770; www.urbanobistro.co.nz; 289 Fenton St, Glenholme; mains brunch $15-25, dinner $26-44; ⊙9am-11pm Mon-Sat, to 3pm Sun) This hip suburban diner, with a darkened interior and streetside tables, offers casual cafe-style dining by day (cooked breakfasts, salads, burgers, curry-of-the-day) and a more ritzy bistro vibe at night. Coffee comes in bucket-like proportions.

🍸 DRINKING & NIGHTLIFE

Brew   Craft Beer

(☎07-346 0976; www.brewpub.co.nz; Eat Streat, 1103 Tutanekai St; ⊙11am-1am) Run by the lads from Croucher Brewing Co, Rotorua's best microbrewers, Brew sits in a sunny spot on 'Eat Streat'. Thirteen taps showcase the best of Croucher's brews as well as guest beers from NZ and overseas. Try the hoppy Sulfur City Pilsner with pizza or a burger. There's regular live music, too.

Ponsonby Rd   Cocktail Bar

(☎021 151 2036; www.ponsonbyrd.co.nz; Eat Streat, 1109 Tutanekai St; ⊙4pm-3am Tue-Sat; 🛜) Former TV weatherman turned Labour MP Tamati Coffey has introduced an approximation of flashy big-city style to Rotorua – the bar's name is a pretentious nod to an Auckland eating strip. Drenched in red light and trimmed with velvet, the decor is certainly vibrant, while the front terrace is perfect for cocktail sipping and people watching. Look forward to live music most weekends.

Pig & Whistle — Pub

(📞07-347 3025; www.pigandwhistle.co.nz; 1182 Tutanekai St; ⊙11am-late; 📶) Inside an art deco former police station (look for the Māori motifs on the facade), this busy pub serves up frosty lager, big-screen TVs, a beer garden, live music and solid pub grub. The menu runs the gamut from harissa-spiced chicken salad to hearty burgers and fish and chips.

ENTERTAINMENT

Basement Cinema — Cinema

(📞07-350 1400; www.basementcinema.co.nz; 1140 Hinemoa St; adult/child $15/12; ⊙sessions vary) Oddly combined with a rock-climbing facility and a hostel, Basement offers off-beat, foreign-language and art-house flicks. Tickets are just $10 on Tuesdays.

❶ INFORMATION

Redwoods i-SITE (📞07-350 0110; www.redwoods.co.nz; Long Mile Rd, Whakareware-wa; ⊙8.30am-9.30pm) Sells tickets for the Redwoods Treewalk, and provides information on Whakarewarewa Forest and all of Rotorua.

Rotorua i-SITE (📞07-348 5179; www.rotoruanz.com; 1167 Fenton St; ⊙7.30am-6pm; 📶) The hub for travel information and bookings, including DOC walks.

❶ GETTING THERE & AWAY

AIR

Rotorua Airport (ROT; 📞07-345 8800; www.rotorua-airport.co.nz; SH30) is 9km northeast of town.

Air New Zealand (📞0800 737 000; www.airnewzealand.co.nz) flies to/from Auckland, Wellington and Christchurch.

BUS

All of the **long-distance buses** (Fenton St) stop outside the Rotorua i-SITE.

InterCity (📞07-348 0366; www.intercity.co.nz) destinations include Auckland (from $21, four hours, six daily), Taupo (from $13, one hour, four daily), Napier ($20, four hours, daily) and Wellington (from $26, 7½ hours, three daily).

Mana Bus (📞09-367 9140; www.manabus.com) destinations include Auckland (from $21, four hours, five daily), Taupo ($23, one hour, two daily), Napier ($23, 3¼ hours, daily) and Wellington (from $25, 7¼ hours, two daily).

❶ GETTING AROUND

Baybus (📞0800 422 928; www.baybus.co.nz) has local buses to Ngongotaha via Rainbow Springs/Skyline gondola, the Redwoods, the airport and Whakarewarewa.

Rotorua Taxis (📞07-348 1111; www.rotoruataxis.co.nz) Well-established Rotorua taxi company.

TAUPO

Taupo at a Glance...

Travelling into Taupo on a clear day along the northeastern shores of Lake Taupo is breathtaking: beyond the trout-filled lake, which is the size of Singapore, you can see the snowcapped peaks of Tongariro National Park.

With an abundance of adrenaline-pumping activities, world-famous hikes, thermally heated waters and some wonderful places to eat, Taupo now rivals Rotorua as the North Island's premier resort town. Yet it remains a laid-back sort of place, at ease with itself in the high Central Plateau air.

Taupo in Two Days

Take a boat trip to the **Māori rock carvings** (p112) on Lake Taupo before checking out the excellent **Taupo Museum** (p112) in the afternoon. Have a local Lakeman beer at the **Lakehouse** (p116) – with views of the peaks of Tongariro National Park – to prep yourself for the **Tongariro Alpine Crossing** (p105) the next day, arguably the best day walk in NZ (oh, how they argue...). Celebrate afterwards with a meal at **Bistro** (p115).

Taupo in Three Days

Charge-up with a big breakfast at **Storehouse** (p116), then explore the amazing terraces and geysers at **Orakei Korako** (p112) geothermal area, a half-hour north of town. Alternatively, dangle a line in the lake and see if the **trout** are biting. Back in town, eat some meat at **Southern Meat Kitchen** (p115), sluiced down with craft beers from **Crafty Trout Brewing** (p117).

Taupo Map (p114)

Arriving in Taupo

Taupo Airport (p117) The airport is 8km south of town. Air New Zealand flies to/from Auckland thrice daily; Sounds Air flies to/from Wellington once daily Thursday to Monday.

Bus InterCity, Mana Bus and Naked Bus services grind to a halt outside the Taupo i-SITE.

Sleeping

Taupo has plenty of good accommodation – hotels, motels, B&Bs, holiday parks and hostels – all of which is in hot demand during late December and January, and during major sporting events like the Lake Taupo Cycle Challenge (November) and Ironman New Zealand (March); book ahead.

MARTIAN9277/SHUTTERSTOCK ©

Tongariro National Park

Even before you arrive in Tongariro National Park its three mighty volcanoes – Ruapehu, Ngauruhoe and Tongariro – steal your breath from the horizon. Get closer via ski fields and the other-worldly, day-long Tongariro Alpine Crossing.

Great For...

☑ **Don't Miss**

Descending scoria slopes on the Tongariro Alpine Crossing, from the Red Crater to the Blue Lake.

Tongariro National Park – New Zealand's first – was gifted by local Tuwharetoa Māori more than a century ago. Long before it was granted dual Unesco World Heritage status for its volcanic landscape and deep cultural importance, Māori believed that the mountains were strong warriors who fought among each other. In the process, they created the landscape that attracts more than 200,000 visitors each year. Visit once and you'll understand why it was worth fighting for.

Volcanoes

At 2797m, **Mt Ruapehu** (www.mtruapehu. com) is the highest mountain in the North Island. It is also one of the world's most active volcanoes. One eruption began in March 1945 and continued for almost a year, spreading lava over Crater Lake

Mt Ngauruhoe

❶ Need to Know

Whakapapa Visitor Centre; ☑07-892 3729; www.doc.govt.nz/tongarirovisitorcentre; Bruce Rd; ⊙8am-5pm last weekend Oct-Apr, 8.30am-4.30pm May-last Fri Oct

✘ Take a Break

It's tea and scones by the fire at **Chateau Tongariro** (☑0800 242 832; www.chateau.co.nz/chateau-high-tea; Bruce Rd; high tea $32; ⊙11am-5pm) in Whakapapa Village.

★ Top Tip

Sun can soon turn to snow on the Tongariro Alpine Crossing. Be prepared for anything.

and sending huge, dark ash clouds as far away as Wellington. No wonder, then, that the mountain's name translates to 'pit of sound'.

Ruapehu rumbled in 1969, 1973 and most recently in 2007, but its worst disaster was on Christmas Eve 1953, when a crater-lake lip collapsed. An enormous lahar (volcanic mudflow) swept down the mountainside, destroying everything in its path, including a railway bridge. As a result, a crowded train plunged into the river, killing 151 people; it was one of NZ's worst tragedies.

Ongoing rumbles are reminders that the volcanoes in Tongariro National Park are very much in the land of the living. The last major event was in 2012 when **Mt Tongariro** (www.visitruapehu.com/explore/tongariro-national-park) – the northernmost and lowest peak in the park (1967m) – gave a couple of good blasts from its northern craters, causing a nine-month partial closure of the famous Tongariro Alpine Crossing track. (To see video of the 2012 eruptions, visit www.doc.govt.nz/eruption.)

Northeast of Mt Ruapehu is **Mt Ngauruhoe** (☑07-892 3729; www.visitruapehu.com/explore/tongariro-national-park/volcanoes) (2287m), the youngest of Tongariro National Park's three volcanoes. Its first eruptions are thought to have occurred 2500 years ago. Until 1975 Ngauruhoe had erupted at least every nine years, including a 1954 eruption that lasted 11 months and disgorged 6 million cu metres of lava. Its perfectly symmetrical slopes are the reason that it was chosen to star as Mt Doom in Peter Jackson's *Lord of the Rings*.

Tongariro Alpine Crossing

This popular **crossing** (www.tongarirocrossing.org.nz) is lauded as one of NZ's finest one-day walks, with more than 100,000 trampers finishing it yearly. It takes between six to eight hours to complete the 19.4km mixed-terrain walk amid steaming vents and springs, stunning rock formations, peculiar moonscape basins, impossible scree slopes and vast views – the most iconic across the Emerald Lakes.

The crossing starts at Mangatepopo Rd car park, off SH47, and finishes at Ketetahi Rd, off SH46. As of late 2017, a four-hour parking restriction at the Mangatepopo Road car park has been implemented to resolve overcrowding. Those undertaking the crossing need to organise shuttle transport; often your accommodation can provide a recommendation. Shuttle services operate from Whakapapa Village, National Park Village, Turangi, Taupo, Ohakune and Raetihi.

Safety Considerations

This is a fair-weather tramp. In poor conditions it is little more than an arduous up-and-down, with only orange-tipped poles to mark the passing of the day. Strong winds see trampers crawl along the ridge of Red Crater, the high point of the trek, and can blow people off their feet. A sunny day could still be a gusty day, so check in with your nearest information centre.

This is an alpine crossing, and it needs to be treated with respect. You need a reasonable level of fitness and you should be prepared for all types of weather. Shockingly ill-equipped trampers are legendary on this route – stupid shoes, no rain jackets, blue jeans soaked to the skin – we've seen it all. As well as proper gear, you'll need to stock up on water and snacks. If you're keen to undertake a guided tramp, contact **Adrift Guided Out-**

Whakapapa resort

door **Adventures** (☏07-892 2751; www.adriftnz.
co.nz; 53 Carroll St; ☺by appt) or **Adventure
Outdoors** (☏0800 386 925, 027 242 7209; www.
adventureoutdoors.co.nz; 60 Carroll St; ☺by appt).

When to Go

The most crowded times on the track are
the first nice days after Christmas and
Easter, when there can easily be more than
1000 people strung out between the two
road ends.

Ski Tongariro

The linked **Whakapapa** (☏07-892 4000;
www.mtruapehu.com/winter/whakapapa; Bruce
Rd; daily lift pass adult/child $119/69) and
Turoa (☏06-385 8456; www.mtruapehu.com/
winter/Turoa; Ohakune Mountain Rd; daily lift
pass adult/child $119/69) resorts straddle
either side of Mt Ruapehu and are New

Zealand's two largest ski areas. Each offers
similar skiing at an analogous altitude
(around 2300m), with areas to suit every
level of experience – from beginners'
slopes to black-diamond runs for the pros.
The same lift passes cover both ski areas.

The only accommodation at the Whakapapa ski field is in private lodges (mainly
owned by ski clubs), so – if you're not
journeying here from Taupo – most visitors
stay at Whakapaka or National Park Village.
Turoa is only 16km from Ohakune, which
has the best après-ski scene.

Club-operated **Tukino** (☏0800 885 466,
06-387 6294; www.tukino.org; Tukino Access Rd;
day pass adult/child $65/35) is on Mt Ruape-
hu's east, 46km from Turangi and 35km
from Waiouru. It's quite remote, 7km down
a gravel road from the sealed Desert Rd
(SH1), and you need a 4WD vehicle to get in
(or call ahead to book a return shuttle from
the 2WD car park, adult/child $20/10). It
offers uncrowded, backcountry runs, mostly beginner and intermediate.

Getting There & Away

Passing National Park Village and Ohakune
are buses run by **InterCity** (☏09-583 5780;
www.intercity.co.nz) and Naked Bus (www.
nakedbus.com/nz), and the *Northern Explorer* train run by **KiwiRail Scenic** (☏04-
495 0775, 0800 872 467; www.kiwirailscenic.
co.nz) stops at National Park Village.

The main gateway into Tongariro National Park is Whakapapa Village, which also
leads to Whakapapa Ski Area on SH48, but
the park is also bounded by roads: SH1
(called the Desert Rd) to the east, SH4 to
the west, SH46 and SH47 to the north, and
SH49 to the south.

Ohakune Mountain Rd leads up to the
Turoa Ski Area from Ohakune. The Desert
Rd is regularly closed when the weather
is bad; detours will be in force. Likewise,
Ohakune Mountain Rd and Bruce Rd are
subject to closures, and access beyond
certain points may be restricted to 4WDs
or cars with snow chains.

Ask your hotel or call the Tongariro
National Park Visitor Centre (p105) in
Whakapapa Village if you're uncertain.

RAFAEL BEN-ARI/ALAMY ©

Adventure Sports

Taupo is known as the 'Skydiving Capital of NZ'. Hurl yourself out of a plane if you must, but also on offer here are jetboating, white-water rafting, bungy jumping, parasailing, mountain biking...

Great For...

☑ **Don't Miss**

The view of Lake Taupo from a *looong* way above it (and getting rapidly closer).

Skydiving

More than 30,000 jumps a year are made over Taupo, which makes it the skydiving capital of the world (not just NZ!). With the deep-blue lake and snowcapped volcanic peaks of Tongariro National Park as a backdrop, it's certainly a picturesque place to do it. Just remember to keep your eyes open. Companies provide free transport to Taupo Airport (p117).

Skydive Taupo   Skydiving
(☎07-378 4662, 0800 586 766; www.skydivetaupo.co.nz; Anzac Memorial Dr; 12,000/15,000ft jump from $279/359) Packages available (from $458), including a reduced-price second jump for altitude junkies.

Tandem skydiving over Lake Taupo

❶ Need to Know

Taupo i-SITE (p117) can help with bookings.

✕ Take a Break

You're going to need some fuel: try Spoon & Paddle (p116) cafe.

★ Top Tip

For mega discounts, try booking activities through www.bookme.co.nz or www.grabone.co.nz/rotorua-taupo.

Craters MTB Park Mountain Biking
(www.biketaupo.org.nz; Karapiti Rd; ⊘24hr)
FREE For 50km of exciting off-road mountain-biking trails for all abilities, head to the Craters MTB Park, around 10 minutes' drive north of Taupo in the Wairakei Forest.

Big Sky Parasail Adventure Sports
(☑0800 724 4759; www.bigskyparasail.co.nz;
Taupo Boat Harbour, Redoubt St; tandem/solo
$95/115; ⊘9am-6pm mid-Oct–May) Lofty parasailing flights from the lakefront. Choose from 1000ft or 500ft.

**Rafting NZ
Adventure Centre** Adventure Sports
(Adventure Centre; ☑0508 238 3688, 07-378
8482; www.theadventurecentre.co.nz; 47 Ruapehu St; ⊘9am-5pm Dec-May, 10am-5pm Jun-Nov)
This well-run operation can hook you up with everything from rafting on the Tongariro River through to skydiving, jetboating and bungy jumping.

Taupo Tandem Skydiving Skydiving
(☑0800 826 336; www.taupotandemskydiving.
com; Anzac Memorial Dr; 12,000/15,000ft jump
$279/359) Various packages that include
DVDs, photos, T-shirts etc ($418 to $659);
bungy combo available.

Other Stuff

Taupo Bungy Bungy Jumping
(☑0800 888 408; www.taupobungy.co.nz; 202
Spa Rd; solo/tandem jump $169/338; ⊘9.30am-
5pm) On a cliff high above the Waikato
River, this picturesque bungy site is the
North Island's most popular. The courageous throw themselves off the edge of
a platform, jutting 34m out over the cliff,
for a heart-stopping 47m plunge. The 11m
Cliffhanger swing is just as terrifying (solo/
tandem swing $145/290).

CHAMELEONSEYE/SHUTTERSTOCK ©

Trout Fishing

Famed around the world, the stellar trout fishing scene around Taupo is also a super-scenic chance for some holiday downtime, knee-deep in Lake Taupo or the mountain-fed rivers of Tongariro National Park.

Great For...

☑ Don't Miss

Arcing your line across misty-still Lake Taupo before most folks are out of bed.

Early European settlers who wanted to improve New Zealand's farming, hunting and fishing opportunities are responsible for the introduction of such ghastly wreckers as possums and rabbits. But one of their more benign introductions was that of trout – brown and rainbow – released into NZ rivers in the second half of the 19th century.

Today they are prized by sports anglers, who you'll find thigh-deep in limpid rivers and on the edge of deep green pools. Celebrities have also tried their luck in these North Island waters, including ex-US president Jimmy Carter, Michael Keaton, Harrison Ford and Liam Neeson, all of whom have stayed at the exclusive **Tongariro Lodge** (☏07-386 7946; www.tongariro lodge.co.nz; 83 Grace Rd; 1-bedroom chalet $175, 2-/5-bedroom villas $269-750; 🛜) on the Tongariro River.

Fishing in the Tongariro River

Tall tales boast of Taupo trout weighing more than a sack of spuds and measuring the length of a surfboard. Truth be told, more than 28,000 legal trout are bagged annually, by both domestic and international fishing enthusiasts.

Trout fishing is highly regulated, with plenty of rules regarding where and how they're to be fished. Licences are required and can be bought online at www.doc.govt.nz or www.fishandgame.org.nz. Our advice is to seek out a guide. Most are based in Taupo or Turangi, and offer flexible trips, with $300 for a half-day a ballpark figure. Operators:

Taupo Rod & Tackle (☑07-378 5337; www.tauporodandtackle.co.nz; 7 Tongariro St; full-day gear rental $20-35; ⊗8am-5pm Mon-Fri, 7am-4pm Sat, 8am-4pm Sun Dec-May, 8am-5pm Mon-Fri, to 4pm Sat & Sun Jun-Nov) One-stop-shop

ℹ Need to Know

Turangi i-SITE (☑0800 288 726, 07-386 8999; www.greatlaketaupo.com; 1 Ngawaka Pl, Turangi; ⊗9am-4.30pm summer, 8.30am-4pm winter; @ ☎) is a good stop for information on trout fishing and Tongariro National Park. It issues fishing licences.

✕ Take a Break

Recharge with a kickin' coffee from Taupo institution Replete Cafe & Store (p115).

★ Top Tip

You'll need a fishing licence before you cast your first fly ($20 per day from outdoors shops).

for gear hire, licences and advice on guides and boat charters.

Taupo Troutcatcher (☑0800 376 882; www.taupotroutcatcher.co.nz; Taupo Marina, Ferry Rd; per hour from $110; ⊗9am-9pm, weather dependent) Just what the name implies! Two decades of experience.

Flyfishtaupo (☑027 4450 223, 07-377 8054; www.flyfishtaupo.com) Turangi-based guide Brent Pirie offers a range of fishing excursions.

Fish Cruise Taupo (Launch Office; ☑07-378 3444; www.fishcruisetaupo.co.nz; Taupo Boat Harbour, 65 Redoubt St; ⊗9am-5pm Oct-Mar, 9.30am-3pm Apr-Sep) Booking office for 13 local fishing boat operators.

Chris Jolly Outdoors (☑07-378 0623, 0800 252 628; www.chrisjolly.co.nz; Taupo Boat Harbour, Ferry Rd; ⊗adult/child $46/18) Fishing trips and cruises, ex-Taupo.

◎ SIGHTS

Taupo Museum   Museum

(📞07-376 0414; www.taupodc.govt.nz; 4 Story Pl; adult/child $5/free; ⏲10am-4.30pm) With an excellent Māori gallery and quirky displays, which include a 1960s caravan set up as if the occupants have just popped down to the lake, this little museum makes an interesting rainy-day diversion. The centrepiece is an elaborately carved Māori meeting house, Te Aroha o Rongoheikume. Historical displays cover local industries, volcanic activity and a mock-up of a 19th-century shop.

Māori Rock Carvings   Historic Site

Accessible only by boat, these 10m-high carvings were etched into the cliffs near Mine Bay by master carver Matahi Whakataka-Brightwell in the late 1970s. They depict Ngātoro-i-rangi, the visionary Māori navigator who guided the Tūwharetoa and Te Arawa tribes to the Taupo area a thousand years ago. Go bright and early or take a sunset cruise.

Huka Falls   Waterfall

(www.greatlaketaupo.com; Huka Falls Rd) Clearly signposted and with a car park and kiosk, these falls mark where NZ's longest river, the Waikato, is slammed into a narrow chasm, making a dramatic 11m drop into a surging crystal-blue pool at 220,000 litres per second.

Orakei Korako   Natural Feature

(📞07-378 3131; www.orakeikorako.co.nz; 494 Orakei Korako Rd; adult/child $36/15; ⏲8am-4.30pm; 👶) A little off the beaten track, Orakei Korako gets fewer visitors than other thermal areas. But since the destruction of the Pink and White Terraces, it's arguably the best thermal area left in NZ, with active geysers, stunning terraces, bubbling rainbow land and NZ's only geothermal cave.

It's about 30 minutes' drive to Orakei Korako from Taupo. You can also arrive via the **New Zealand River Jet** (📞0800 748 375, 07-333 7111; www.riverjet.co.nz; Mihi Bridge, SH5; adult/child $179/99, incl entry to Orakei Korako).

Wairakei Terraces & Thermal Health Spa   Hot Springs

(📞07-378 0913; www.wairakeiterraces.co.nz; Wairakei Rd; thermal walk adult/child $15/7.50, pools $25, massage from $85; ⏲8.30am-9pm Oct-Mar, to 8.30pm Apr-Sep, closes 7pm Thu) 🍃 Mineral-laden waters from the Wairakei geothermal steamfield cascade over silica terraces into pools (open to those 14 years and older) nestled in native gardens. Spending a few hours soaking in the therapeutic waters is well worthwhile.

Craters of the Moon   Natural Feature

(📞027 6564 684; www.cratersofthemoon. co.nz; Karapiti Rd; adult/child/family $8/4/20; ⏲8.30am-5pm) This geothermal area sprang to life when hydroelectric tinkering around the power station caused water levels to fall. The pressure shifted, creating new steam vents and bubbling mud pools. The 2.7km perimeter loop walk takes about 45 minutes and affords great views down to the lake and mountains beyond. There's a kiosk at the entrance, staffed by volunteers who keep an eye on the car park.

More active from June through August when it's cold and wet (from December through February, summer can dry everything out), it's signposted from SH1 about 5km north of Taupo.

⊕ ACTIVITIES

Canoe & Kayak   Canoeing, Kayaking

(📞07-378 1003; www.canoeandkayak.co.nz/ taupo; 54 Spa Rd; ⏲9am-5pm Mon-Fri, to 3pm Sat & Sun Nov-Mar, closed Sun Apr-Oct) Guided tours, including a two-hour trip on the Waikato River ($59) and a half-day visit to the Māori rock carvings for $99.

Great Lake Trail   Walking, Cycling

(www.greatlaketrail.com) A purpose-built 71km track from Whakaipo Bay to Waihaha in the remote northwestern reaches of the lake. The **W2K** section between Whakaipo and Kinloch has splendid views across the lake to Tongariro National Park.

Māori Rock Carvings

Hukafalls Jet   Adventure Sports
(☎07-374 8572, 0800 485 253; www.hukafallsjet.
com; 200 Karetoto Rd; adult/child $129/89)
This 30-minute thrill ride takes you up the
river to the spray-filled foot of the Huka
Falls and down to the Aratiatia Dam, all the
while dodging daringly and doing acrobatic
360-degree turns.

Rock'n Ropes   Outdoors
(☎0800 244 508, 07-374 8111; www.rockn-
ropes.co.nz; 65 Karetoto Rd; per person $20-70;
☺weather dependent) With high-flying
bridges, a trapeze, zipline and a giant
swing, you might be tempted to stay on the
ground – but know that everyone from four
to 86 years of age has given it a go. Feeling
brave? Check out the latest addition: the
only five-storey free fall in the country.

Spa Thermal
Park Hot Spring   Hot Springs
(Country Ave; ☺7am-8pm) **FREE** The hot thermal waters of the Otumuheke Stream meet
the bracing Waikato River at this pleasant
and well-worn spot under a bridge, creating
a free spa bath with natural nooks.

⊙ TOURS
Sail Barbary   Boating
(☎07-378 5879; www.sailbarbary.com; Taupo
Boat Harbour, Redoubt St; adult/child $49-
54/29-54; ☺10.30am & 2pm, plus 5pm Dec-Feb)
🚢 A classic 1926 yacht offering 2½-hour
cruises to the Māori rock carvings daily.
The evening cruises include buffet pizza
and a drink.

Taupo Kayaking
Adventures   Kayaking
(☎0274 801 231; www.tka.co.nz; 2/876 Acacia
Bay Rd, Acacia Bay; tours from $60) Runs guid-
ed kayaking trips from its base in Acacia
Bay to the Māori rock carvings, with the
return trip taking around four hours ($100,
including refreshments).

Taupo's Floatplane   Scenic Flights
(☎07-378 7500; www.tauposfloatplane.co.nz;
Taupo Boat Harbour, Ferry Rd; flights $109-955)
Located near the marina, the floatplane offers a variety of trips, including quick flights
over the lake and longer forays over Mt
Ruapehu. The three-hour 'Taupo Trifecta'

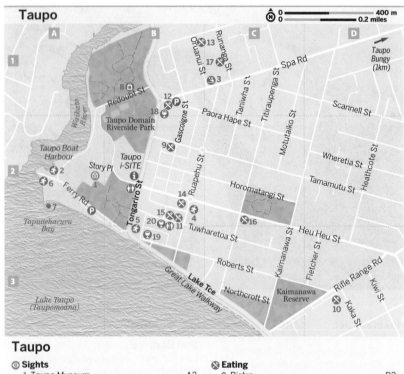

Taupo

combines a scenic flight, visit to Orakei Korako (p112) and jetboat ride ($645).

 **SHOPPING**

Taupo Market   Food, Crafts
(☏027 306 6167, 07-3782 980; www.taupo market.kiwi.nz; Redoubt St; ⊙9am-1pm Sat)

Plenty of food stalls and trucks, local souvenirs, arts and crafts and a scattering of produce are all good reasons to make your first coffee of the day an al fresco espresso at this popular weekend market.

Kura Gallery   Art
(☏07-377 4068; www.kura.co.nz; 47a Heu Heu St; ⊙10am-5pm Mon-Fri, to 4pm Sat & Sun) This

compact gallery represents more than 70 artists from around NZ. Works for sale include weaving, carving, painting and jewellery. Many items are imbued with a Māori or Pasifika influence.

Lava Glass
Arts & Crafts

(☎07-374 8400; www.lavaglass.co.nz; 165 SH5; glass-blowing display/garden entry/combo $5/7.50/10; ☉10am-5pm) More than 600 unique glass sculptures fill the garden and surroundings of this gallery, around 10km north of Taupo on SH5. Glass-blowing displays and an excellent **cafe** (open 9am-4pm) provide great reasons to linger while you're considering what to purchase in the Lava Glass shop. All items can be carefully shipped anywhere in the world (free when you spend more than $200).

Huka Falls Chocolate
Chocolate

(☎0274 883 286; www.hukafallschocolate.co.nz; 703 Karetoto Rd; sweet treats $2-7; ☉Tue-Sun 10am-5pm; 🖻) On-site at **Shooters Golf Range** (☎07-374 8416; www.shootersgolfrange. com; 703 Karetoto Rd; driving range/archery/ bubble soccer from $12/20/20; ☉10am-6pm Tue-Wed, to 7.30pm Thu-Sun; 🖻), this hidden gem roasts coffee, sells Belgian hot chocolate and makes truffles using Barry Callebaut chocolate and local NZ ingredients. Family operated, Paul is a chocolatier, but wife Jane is a chef and makes the cakes. If you ask nicely, little chocolate lovers can see the 50-plus-year-old burnt-orange chocolate machine from France.

 EATING

Pauly's Diner
Burgers $

(☎07-378 4315; www.paulysdiner.nz; 3 Paora Hape St; burgers $12-15; ☉11.30am-8.30pm Wed-Sun & alternating Mon) Two brothers from Auckland set up this popular burger joint in an old fish and chipper, and it seems they've got the formula just right (selling out isn't uncommon). The shop only seats about a dozen, plus a few more outside, and specials are posted on Instagram (Dorito chip-fried chicken is a thing). Shakes and deep-fried goodies also available.

Raw Balance
Health Food $

(☎021 138 2066; www.facebook.com/raw balancenz; 45 Oruanui St; smoothies $8, mains $8-12, raw sweets $2-7; ☉8am-5pm Mon-Fri, Sat 9am-3pm; 🖻) 🖉 This is heaven for vegans, the gluten-free inclined, health conscious and environmentally aware. In winter, raw sweets and salads are complemented by a daily hot special (perhaps dal and rice). Takeaway packaging is recyclable but discouraged, with containers available to buy and reuse, and some cushion-pimped wooden pallets to sit on and enjoy.

There's also a communal table in the mini-library, complete with more than 60 Lonely Planet guidebooks! Check Facebook for pop-up dinner parties.

Replete Cafe & Store
Cafe $$

(☎07-377 3011; www.replete.co.nz; 45 Heu Heu St; mains $13-18; ☉8am-5pm Mon-Fri, to 4pm Sat & Sun; 🖻) 'You don't come to Taupo without stopping for coffee here', a customer tells us, 'it's an institution'. He's not wrong. Established in 1993, Replete is split into a cafe and shop selling designer kitchenware, ceramics and souvenirs. The cafe cabinet is one of the best looking in town, while lunch has an Asian flair (Japanese bolognese or Sri Lankan curry, anyone?).

Southern Meat Kitchen
South American $$

(SMK; ☎07-378 3582; www.facebook.com/ smktaupo; 40 Tuwharetoa St; mains $22-34; ☉noon-midnight Wed-Sun, 4-11pm Mon & Tue) Calling all carnivores! SMK slow cooks beef brisket, pulled pork and shredded chicken on an American wood-fire smoker and you can order it by the half-pound (upgrade to a pound for $8). Save room for jalapeño-and-cheddar cornbread, served in a skillet with addictive honey butter. Beer-tasting paddles for $15.

Bistro
Modern NZ $$

(☎07-377 3111; www.thebistro.co.nz; 17 Tamamutu St; mains $26-39; ☉5pm-midnight) Popular with locals – bookings are recommended – the Bistro focuses on doing the basics very, very well. That means harnessing local and seasonal produce for dishes such

Taupo History

Let's start at the start, back in AD 180 when the Taupo eruption became the largest and most violent in recorded history. Debris was deposited as far as 30,000 sq km and all of New Zealand was covered in ash, in some places up to 10m deep. Everything living was destroyed and there were reports from ancient Rome and China of unusual red sunsets. In the process, Lake Taupo formed in the volcanic caldera.

But Māori legend tells of Ngātoro-i-rangi, who created the lake while searching for a place to settle. Climbing to the top of Mt Tauhara, he saw a vast dust bowl. He hurled a totara tree into it and fresh water swelled to form the lake.

Europeans settled here in force during the East Coast Land War (1868–72), when Taupo was a strategic military base. A redoubt was built in 1869 and a garrison of mounted police remained until the defeat of Te Kooti later that year.

In the 20th century the mass ownership of the motorcar saw Taupo grow from a lakeside village of about 750 people to a large resort town, easily accessible from most points on the North Island. Today the population increases considerably at peak holiday times, when New Zealanders and international visitors alike flock to the 'Great Lake'.

Lake Taupo
SLJONES/SHUTTERSTOCK ©

as bacon-wrapped Wharekauhau lamb, washed down with your pick from the small but thoughtful beer-and-wine list.

Storehouse Cafe $$
(☑07-378 8820; www.facebook.com/store housenz; 14 Runanga St; mains $13-18; ☺7am-3.30pm Mon-Fri, 8am-3.30pm Sat, to 3pm Sun; 🛜♿) If you're looking for Taupo's coolest cafe, you've just found it. Setting the scene since 2013, Storehouse is located in an old plumbing store over two levels. The breakfast salad bowl often sells out – guess that means we're having fried-chicken waffles.

Malabar Beyond India Indian $$
(☑07-376 5456, 07-376 5454; www.malabar taupo.com; 2/40 Tuwharetoa St; mains $17-26; ☺11.30am-1pm; 🍴♿) Our pick of Indian restaurants in Taupo, Malabar has a broad menu but is especially good at vegetarian dishes, such as *dal makhani* made with black lentils and *akabari kofta* (cottage-cheese-and-almond dumplings).

Spoon & Paddle Cafe $$
(☑07-378 9664; www.facebook.com/spoonand paddle; 101 Heu Heu St; mains $15-20; ☺8am-4pm; P🛜♿) Filling a 1950s house with colourful decor, this cafe feels like you've popped into a friend's place for brunch with a whole lot of strangers. Breakfast runs all day and from 11.30am you can order tasty international numbers, including pork-belly *bao*, local beef-brisket soft-shell tacos or a lamb-shoulder salad bowl. Great coffee and a playground for the kids.

Brantry Modern NZ $$$
(☑07-378 0484; www.thebrantry.co.nz; 45 Rifle Range Rd; 3-course set menu $55-60; ☺from 5.30pm Tue-Sat, daily Dec-Jan) Operating out of an unobtrusive 1950s house, the Brantry continues its reign as one of the best in the region for well-executed, brilliant-value fine dining centred around a three-course menu. There's an impressive wine list with friendly staff to help with difficult decisions.

 DRINKING & NIGHTLIFE

Lakehouse Craft Beer
(☑07-377 1545; www.lakehousetaupo.co.nz; 10 Roberts St; breakfast $9-20; mains $20-30; ☺8am-late, kitchen closes 9pm) Welcome

to craft-beer central, with a fridge full of interesting bottles and nine taps serving a rotating selection of NZ brews. Order a tasting box of four beers ($15), partner them with a pizza or stone-grilled steak, and sit outside for lake views – and, if the clouds lift, glimpses of the mountains.

Crafty Trout Brewing Brewery
(☎07-989 8570; www.craftytrout.co.nz; 131-135 Tongariro St; mains $18-28, pizzas $14-49; ☺Bier Kafe noon-late Wed-Mon, shop & brewery 10am-4pm Wed-Mon; ☜) Somewhere between an alpine lodge and a fishing lodge, only the five cuckoo clocks at Crafty Trout interrupt the German music. Comfy leather sofas and the sunny veranda are great places to dig into robust meals, including tasty fish and chips and wood-fired pizza, washed down with any of the 10 beers and ciders.

Vine Eatery & Bar Wine Bar
(☎07-378 5704; www.vineeatery.co.nz; 37 Tuwharetoa St; tapas $8-14, mains $17-39; ☺11am-midnight) Wine-glass chandeliers hang from the industrial ceiling at this restaurant-cum-wine bar, where you can sit in cushy booths, at raised stools or by the fire. Share traditional tapas with a glass (there's whisky and craft beer, too) or linger longer with larger mains.

❶ INFORMATION

Taupo i-SITE (☎0800 525 382, 07-376 0027; www.greatlaketaupo.com; 30 Tongariro St; ☺9am-4.30pm May-Oct, 8.30am-5pm Nov-Apr) Handles bookings for accommodation, transport and activities; dispenses cheerful advice; and stocks Department of Conservation (DOC) and town maps.

❶ GETTING THERE & AWAY

Taupo Airport (☎07-378 7771; www.taupo airport.co.nz; Anzac Memorial Dr) is 8km south of town. Expect to pay about $25 for a cab into town.

Air New Zealand (☎09-357 3000, 0800 737 000; www.airnz.co.nz) flies from Auckland to Taupo two to three times daily; **Sounds Air** flies between Wellington and Taupo at least once daily Thursday to Monday.

InterCity (☎07-348 0366; www.intercity coach.co.nz), **Mana Bus** (www.manabus.com) and **Naked Bus** (www.nakedbus.com/nz) services stop outside the Taupo i-SITE.

Ask at the Taupo i-SITE about shuttles to Tongariro National Park.

❶ GETTING AROUND

Local Connector buses are run by **Busit!** (☎0800 4287 5463; www.busit.co.nz), running as far as Huka Falls and Wairakei, twice daily Monday to Friday.

Great Lake Shuttles (☎021 0236 3439; www.greatlakeshuttles.co.nz) offers charter services around the area, and can hook you up with **bike hire**.

Taxi companies include **Blue Bubble Taxis** (☎07-378 5100; www.taupo.bluebubbletaxi. co.nz) and **Top Cabs** (☎07-378 9250).

HAWKE'S BAY

Hawke's Bay at a Glance...

Hawke Bay, the name given to the body of water that stretches from the Mahia Peninsula to Cape Kidnappers, looks like it's been bitten out of the North Island's eastern flank. Add an apostrophe and an 's' and you've got a region that stretches south and inland to encompass the bountiful Hawke's Bay Wine Region. With food, wine and art deco architecture the prevailing obsessions, it's smugly comfortable but thoroughly appealing, and is best viewed through a rosé-tinted wine glass. Napier, Hastings and Havelock North are the happening hubs.

Hawke's Bay in One Day

Check yourself into **Napier** (p126) ASAP with breakfast at **Mister D** (p126) (can't get enough of those chocolate doughnuts), then sign up for an art deco architecture tour at the **Deco Centre** (p122). Having filled your eyes, fill your belly via a tasting menu at **Bistronomy** (p126). Drinks at hidden-away **Monica Loves** (p127) round out the evening.

Hawke's Bay in Two Days

With an extra day in which to play, grab breakfast at Napier's boho **Cafe Ujazi** (p126), then knock on some cellar doors in the Hawke's Bay Wine Region around **Hastings** (p128). **On Yer Bike Winery Tours** (p128) offers self-guided cycles past the vines; myriad other outfits run minibus winery tours. Finish up with a show at **MTG Hawke's Bay** (p126) and drinks at **Emporium** (p127).

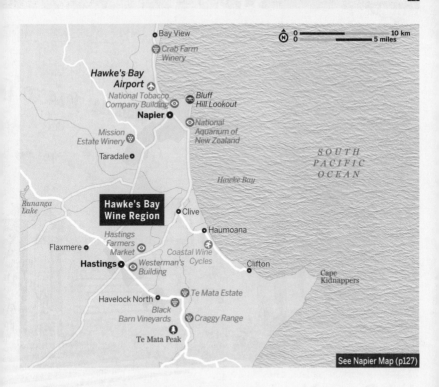

See Napier Map (p127)

Arriving in Hawke's Bay

Hawke's Bay Airport (p128) The airport lies 8km north of Napier and has flights to/from Auckland, Wellington, Christchurch and Blenheim. Air New Zealand, Jetstar and Sounds Air provide things with wings.

Clive Sq Bus Stop (p128) Bus services roll into Napier from Wellington, Taupo, Rotorua and beyond, continuing to Hastings (or passing through en route).

Russell St Bus Stop (p129) In Hastings.

Sleeping

Unless there's a festival happening (eg the **Art Deco Weekend** (p123) in Napier) finding a bed around Hawke's Bay isn't usually a challenge. Expect plenty of good motels, some charismatic hostels and a cache of characterful B&Bs. If you want water views with that, you'll be paying extra.

Art Deco Napier

Napier's claim to fame is undoubtedly its glorious cache of art deco architecture. A close study of these treasures would take days... If you haven't got time for a tour, just hit the streets (particularly Tennyson and Emerson) and remember to look up!

Great For...

☑ Don't Miss

The drop-dead gorgeous National Tobacco Company Building, a little hard to find in Ahuriri.

At 10.46am on 3 February 1931, Napier was levelled by a catastrophic earthquake (7.9 on the Richter scale). Fatalities numbered 258. Napier suddenly found itself 40 sq km larger, as the earthquake heaved sections of what was once a lagoon 2m above sea level (Napier airport was once more 'port', less 'air'). A fevered rebuilding program ensued, resulting in one of the world's most uniformly art deco cities.

Deco Tours

Napier's excellent **Deco Centre** (✆06-835 0022; www.artdeconapier.com; 7 Tennyson St; ⊙9am-5pm;) runs daily one-hour guided art deco walks ($19) departing the Napier i-SITE (p128) at 10am; and daily two-hour tours ($21) leaving the Deco Centre at 2pm. There's also a little shop here, plus

National Tobacco Company Building   Architecture

(☎06-834 1911; www.heritage.org.nz/the-list/details/1170; cnr Bridge & Ossian Sts, Ahuriri; ⊘lobby 9am-5pm Mon-Fri) Around the shore at Ahuriri, the National Tobacco Company Building (1932) is arguably the region's deco masterpiece, combining art deco forms with the natural motifs of art nouveau. Roses, raupo (bulrushes) and grapevines frame the elegantly curved entrance.

Hastings

Like Napier, nearby Hastings was devastated by the 1931 earthquake and also boasts some fine art deco and Spanish Mission buildings, built in the aftermath. Mainstreet highlights include the **Westerman's Building** (cnr Russell St & Heretaunga St E), arguably the bay's best example of the Spanish Mission style. Hastings i-SITE (p129) stocks the *Art Deco Hastings* brochure ($1).

brochures for the self-guided Art Deco Walk ($10), Art Deco Scenic Drive ($3) and Marewa Meander ($3). Other options include a minibus tour ($5, 1¼ hours), vintage car tour ($110, 1¼ hours) and the kids' Art Deco Explorer treasure hunt ($5).

Best Buildings

Daily Telegraph Building   Architecture

(☎06-834 1911; www.heritage.org.nz/the-list/details/1129; 49 Tennyson St; ⊘9am-5pm Mon-Fri) The Daily Telegraph is one of the stars of Napier's art deco show, with superb zigzags, fountain shapes and a ziggurat aesthetic. If the front doors are open, nip inside and ogle the painstakingly restored foyer (it's a real-estate office these days).

HEMIS/ALAMY ©

Hawke's Bay Wine Region

Once upon a time, this district was famous for its orchards. Today, grapevines have top billing, with Hawke's Bay now New Zealand's second-largest wine-producing region (behind Marlborough). Bordeaux-style reds, syrah and chardonnay predominate.

Great For...

☑ **Don't Miss**

The chardonnay at Black Barn Vineyards – like kissing someone pretty on a summer afternoon.

Visit the Napier (p128) or Hastings (p129) i-SITEs for details on minibus and cycling wine-tour operators.

Best Wineries

Black Barn Vineyards Winery

(☎06-877 7985; www.blackbarn.com; Black Barn Rd, Havelock North; ☺cellar door 10am-4pm, restaurant 10am-5pm Sun-Wed, to 9pm Thu-Sat, reduced hours Apr-Oct) This hip, inventive winery has a bistro, gallery, a farmers market in summer and an amphitheatre for regular concerts and movie screenings. Taste the flagship chardonnay.

Crab Farm Winery Winery

(☎06-836 6678; www.crabfarmwinery.co.nz; 511 Main North Rd, Bay View; ☺10am-5pm, plus 6pm-late Fri) Decent, reasonably priced wines, and a great cafe with regular live

Black Barn Vineyards

troubadours and relaxed, rustic vibes. Good for lunch, a glass of rosé or both.

Craggy Range   Winery

(☏06-873 0141; www.craggyrange.com; 253 Waimarama Rd, Havelock North; ⊙10am-6pm, closed Mon & Tue Apr-Oct) Definitely one of Hawke's Bay's flashiest wineries – wonderful wines, excellent restaurant.

Mission Estate Winery   Winery

(☏06-845 9354; www.missionestate.co.nz; 198 Church Rd, Taradale; ⊙9am-5pm Mon-Sat, 10am-4.30pm Sun) New Zealand's oldest winery (1851). Follow the tree-lined driveway up the hill to the restaurant (serving lunch and dinner, mains $28 to $38) and cellar door.

Te Mata Estate   Winery

(☏06-877 4399; www.temata.co.nz; 349 Te Mata Rd, Havelock North; ⊙9am-5pm Mon-Fri, from

10am Sat) 🥬 The legendary Coleraine red at this unpretentious, old-school, family-run winery is worth the trip.

Wining & Dining

Elephant Hill   Modern NZ $$$

(☏06-872 6060; www.elephanthill.co.nz; 86 Clifton Rd, Te Awanga; mains $36-42; ⊙cellar door 11am-5pm Nov-Mar, to 4pm Apr-Oct, restaurant noon-3pm & 6-9pm daily Nov-Mar, Thu-Sat Apr-Oct) 🥬 Huge picture windows provide unencumbered views of Cape Kidnappers and vineyards, and Elephant Hill's award-winning wines partner supremely with seasonal dishes. Exquisite.

Vidal   Modern NZ $$$

(☏06-872 7440; www.vidal.co.nz; 913 St Aubyn St E, Hastings; lunch & dinner mains $30-39, 2-/3-course lunch $28/32; ⊙11.30am-3pm & 6pm-late Mon-Sat, 11.30am-3pm Sun) Vidal's warm, wood-lined dining room is a worthy setting for such elegant food: order the eye fillet steak or the duo of duck, sip some syrah and feel your holiday come to fruition.

Napier

The Napier of today – a charismatic, sunny, composed city with the air of an affluent English seaside resort – is the silver lining of the dark cloud that was the deadly 1931 earthquake. Rebuilt in the popular architectural styles of the time, the city retains a unique concentration of art deco buildings.

◎ SIGHTS

MTG Hawke's Bay   Museum, Theatre
(Museum Theatre Gallery; ☑06-835 7781; www.mtghawkesbay.com; 1 Tennyson St; ☺10am-5pm) FREE Smart-looking MTG is a gleaming-white museum-theatre-gallery space by the water, bringing live performances, film screenings and regularly changing gallery and museum displays together with touring and local exhibitions.

Bluff Hill Lookout   Viewpoint
(Lighthouse Rd) The convoluted route to the top of Bluff Hill (102m) goes up and down like an elevator on speed (best to drive), but rewards with expansive views across the port. Bring a picnic or some fish and chips.

National Aquarium
of New Zealand   Aquarium
(☑06-834 1404; www.nationalaquarium.co.nz; 546 Marine Pde; adult/child/family $20/10.50/57; ☺9am-5pm, feedings 10am & 2pm, last entry 4.30pm) Inside this mod complex with its stingray-inspired roof are piranhas, terrapins, eels, kiwi, tuatara and a whole lotta fish. Snorkellers can swim with sharks ($100), or sign up for a 'Little Penguin Close Encounter' ($70).

☞ TOURS

Absolute de Tours   Bus
(☑06-844 8699; www.absolutedetours.co.nz; tours 90min/half-day from $50/70) Runs quick-fire bus tours of the city, Marewa and Bluff Hill in conjunction with the Deco Centre (p122), as well as half-day tours of Napier and Hastings.

Hawke's Bay Scenic Tours   Tours
(☑06-844 5693, 027 497 9231; www.hbscenic tours.co.nz; tours from $55) A grape-coloured bunch of tour options including the 2½-hour 'Napier Whirlwind' ($55), full-day Hawke's Bay scenic tour ($140), and a 4½-hour wine and brewery jaunt ($100).

✗ EATING

Cafe Ujazi   Cafe $
(☑06-835 1490; www.facebook.com/ujazicafe; 28 Tennyson St; mains $10-22; ☺8am-5pm; ☑) Ujazi folds back its windows and lets the alternative vibes spill out onto the pavement. It's a long-established, consistent performer offering blackboard meals and hearty counter food (vegetarian and vegan a speciality). Try the classic *rewana* special – a big breakfast on traditional Māori bread.

Mister D   Modern NZ $$
(☑06-835 5022; www.misterd.co.nz; 47 Tennyson St; mains $25-36; ☺7.30am-4pm Sun-Wed, to late Thu-Sat) This long, floorboarded room with its green-tiled bar is the pride of the Napier foodie scene. Hip and slick but not unaffordable, with quick-fire service delivering the likes of pulled pork with white polenta or roast-duck risotto. Addictive doughnuts are served with syringes full of chocolate, jam or custard (DIY injecting). Bookings essential.

Milk & Honey   Cafe $$
(☑06-833 6099; www.themilkandhoney.co.nz; 19 Hardinge Rd, Ahuriri; mains & shared plates $15-34; ☺7am-9pm) Milk & Honey combines ocean and boardwalk views with a versatile all-day menu. Hawke's Bay beers and wines feature along with delicate seafood ceviche or a Japanese-influenced chicken salad.

Bistronomy   Modern NZ $$$
(☑06-834 4309; www.bistronomy.co.nz; 40 Hastings St; mains lunch $22-28, dinner 6/9 courses $75/100; ☺noon-late Fri-Sun, from 5pm Wed & Thu; ☑) ✔ Bistronomy's finely judged seasonal tasting menus, which could include sumac-cured kingfish or chicken poached in kawakawa (a NZ forest herb), are highly recommended; they're

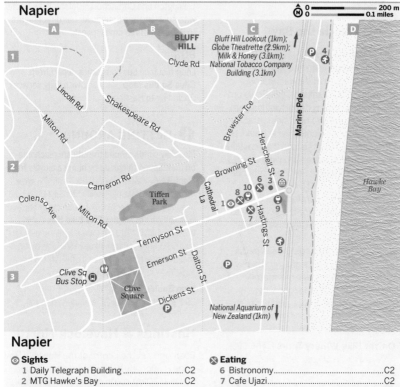

Napier

great-value experiences you'll definitely talk about when you get back home.

◐ DRINKING & NIGHTLIFE

Monica Loves
Bar

(☏06-650 0240; www.monicaloves.co.nz; 39 Tennyson St; ⊙3-11pm Wed-Thu, to midnight Fri & Sat) Big-city laneway style comes to Napier at this bar tucked away off Tennyson St. Look for the big neon sign proclaiming 'Who shot the barman?' and you're in the right place for top cocktails, a beer list with regular surprises on the taps, and a knowingly Hawke's Bay–centric wine list.

Emporium
Bar

(☏06-835 0013; www.emporiumbar.co.nz; Masonic Hotel, cnr Tennyson St & Marine Pde; ⊙7am-late; ☏) Napier's most civilised bar is super atmospheric, with its marble-topped bar, fab art deco details and old-fashioned relics strewn about.

★ ENTERTAINMENT

Globe Theatrette
Cinema

(☏06-833 6011; www.globenapier.co.nz; 15 Hardinge Rd, Ahuriri; tickets adult/child $16/14; ⊙1pm-late Tue-Sun) A vision in purple, this boutique 45-seat cinema screens art-house

Cycle the Bay

The 200km network of Hawke's Bay Trails (www.nzcycletrail.com/hawkes-bay-trails) – part of the national Nga Haerenga, New Zealand Cycle Trails project – offers cycling opportunities from short, city scoots to hilly, single-track shenanigans. Dedicated cycle tracks encircle Napier, Hastings and the coastline, with landscape, water and wine themes. Pick up the *Hawke's Bay Trails* brochure from the Napier i-SITE or online.

Fishbike rents comfortable bikes – including tandems for those willing to risk divorce. Napier City Bike Hire is another option.

Numerous cycle companies pedal fully geared-up tours around the bay, with winery visits near-mandatory. Operators include the following:

Coastal Wine Cycles (06-875 0302; www.winecycles.co.nz; 41 East Rd, Te Awanga; tours per day $40; 👪)

On Yer Bike Winery Tours (📞06-650 4627; www.onyerbikehb.co.nz; full-day tours $55)

Tākaro Trails (📞06-835 9030; www.takarotrails.co.nz; day rides from $40)

flicks in a sumptuous lounge with ready access to upmarket snacks and drinks.

ⓘ INFORMATION

Napier i-SITE (📞06-834 1911; www.napiernz.com; 100 Marine Pde; ⊙9am-5pm, extended hours Dec-Feb; 🛜) Central, helpful and right by the bay.

ⓘ GETTING THERE & AWAY

AIR

Hawke's Bay Airport (www.hawkesbay-airport.co.nz; SH2) is 8km north of the city.

Air New Zealand (📞0800 737 000; www.airnewzealand.co.nz) flies direct to/from Auckland,

Wellington and Christchurch. Jetstar links Napier with Auckland and Sounds Air has direct flights to Blenheim three times a week.

BUS

Long-distance bus companies depart from **Clive Sq bus stop** (Clive Sq), with daily services (including to Hastings).

ⓘ GETTING AROUND

Most key sights around the city are reachable on foot. Speed things up by hiring a bicycle from **Fishbike** (0800 131 600, 06-833 6979; www.fishbike.nz; 22 Marine Pde, Pacific Surf Club; bike hire per half/full day $30/40, tandems per hr $35; ⊙9am-5pm) or **Napier City Bike Hire** (📞021 959 595, 0800 245 344; www.bikehirenapier.co.nz; 117 Marine Pde; half-day kids/city/mountain-bike hire from $20/25/30, full day from $25/35/40; ⊙9am-5pm).

Blue Bubble Taxis (📞06-835 7777, 0800 228 294; www.hawkes-bay.bluebubbletaxi.co.nz)

Hastings & Havelock North

Positioned at the centre of the Hawke's Bay Wine Region, busy Hastings is a commercial hub 20km south of Napier. A few kilometres of vines and orchards still separate it from Havelock North, with its prosperous village atmosphere and the towering backdrop of Te Mata Peak.

◎ SIGHTS

Te Mata Peak   Park
(📞06-873 0080; www.tematapark.co.nz; off Te Mata Rd, Havelock North; ⊙5am-10pm) Rising dramatically from the Heretaunga Plains 16km south of Havelock North, Te Mata Peak (399m) is part of the 1-sq-km **Te Mata Trust Park**. The summit road passes sheep tracks, rickety fences and vertigo-inducing stone escarpments, cowled in a bleak, lunar-meets-Scottish-Highlands atmosphere. On a clear day, views from the **lookout** fall away to Hawke Bay, the Mahia Peninsula and distant Mt Ruapehu.

Hastings Farmers Market   Market

(📞027 697 3737; www.hawkesbayfarmersmarket. co.nz; Showgrounds, Kenilworth Rd; ⏰8.30am-12.30pm Sun) If you're around on Sunday, the Hastings market is mandatory. Bring an empty stomach, some cash and a roomy shopping bag.

SHOPPING

Strawberry Patch   Food

(📞06-877 1350; www.strawberrypatch.co.nz; 76 Havelock Rd, Havelock North; ⏰9am-5.30pm) Pick your own berries in season (late November to April), or visit year-round for fresh produce, picnic supplies, coffee and real fruit ice cream ($4).

✪ EATING

Opera Kitchen   Cafe $$

(📞06-870 6020; www.eatdrinkshareehb.co.nz; 306 Eastbourne St E, Hastings; mains $13-30; ⏰7.30am-4pm Mon-Fri, 9am-3pm Sat & Sun; 🖋) Located in a high-ceilinged heritage building – formerly the HB Electric Power Board – our favourite Hastings cafe serves up sophisticated breakfast and lunch dishes with international accents. Heavenly pastries, great coffee and snappy staff.

Maina   Cafe $$

(📞06-877 1714; www.maina.co.nz; 11 Havelock Rd, Havelock North; mains $12-24; ⏰7am-11pm Mon-Fri, from 8am Sat, 9am-3pm Sun; 🖋) 🍴 Blur the line between breakfast and lunch at the best new cafe in Hawke's Bay. This former post office is infused with stylish retro Kiwiana decor, and highlights include Te Mata mushrooms on organic sourdough or creamy pulled-pork croquettes. Superior homestyle baking includes perfect mid-morning coffee and doughnuts.

Alessandro's   Pizza $$

(📞06-877 8844; www.alessandrospizzeria.co.nz; 24 Havelock Rd, Havelock North; mains $20-27; ⏰4.30-9pm Tue-Sun) Excellent Alessandro's does handmade wood-fired pizzas, thin and flavoursome, just like back in Napoli. Order

the *noci e pere* (pear, Gorgonzola, mozzarella, walnuts and truffle honey).

DRINKING & NIGHTLIFE

Brave Brewing Co   Craft Beer

(📞027 460 8414; www.facebook.com/bravebeer; 408 Warren St; ⏰4-9pm Thu, from noon Fri-Sun) Brave's cool and compact tasting room on the edge of central Hastings showcases its own brews – ask if the Tigermilk IPA is available – and regular guest beers from brewing mates around the country. Partner your brew with a delicious gourmet burger ($15) from the on-site Carr's Kitchen.

Common Room   Bar

(📞027 656 8959; www.commonroombar.com; 227 Heretaunga St E, Hastings; ⏰3pm-late Wed-Sat) There's pretty much nothing wrong with this hip little bar in central Hastings: cheery staff, bar snacks, craft beer, local wines, a creative retro interior, a garden bar, Persian rugs, live music and a tune-scape ranging from jazz to alt-country to indie.

ⓘ INFORMATION

Hastings i-SITE (📞06-873 0080; www.hawkes baynz.com; Westermans Bldg, cnr Russell St & Heretaunga St E; ⏰9am-5pm Mon-Fri, to 3pm Sat, 10am-2pm Sun) The usual array of maps, brochures and bookings.

Havelock North i-SITE (📞06-877 9600; www. havelocknorthnz.com; 1 Te Aute Rd; ⏰10am-5pm Mon-Fri, to 3pm Sat, to 2pm Sun; 📶) Local info in a cute little booth.

ⓘ GETTING THERE & AWAY

Buses stop at the **Russell St Bus Stop**.

ⓘ GETTING AROUND

GoBay (www.hbrc.govt.nz) local buses (with bike racks) run between Hastings, Havelock North and Napier.

Hastings Taxis (📞0800 875 055, 06-878 5055; www.hastingstaxis.co.nz)

WELLINGTON

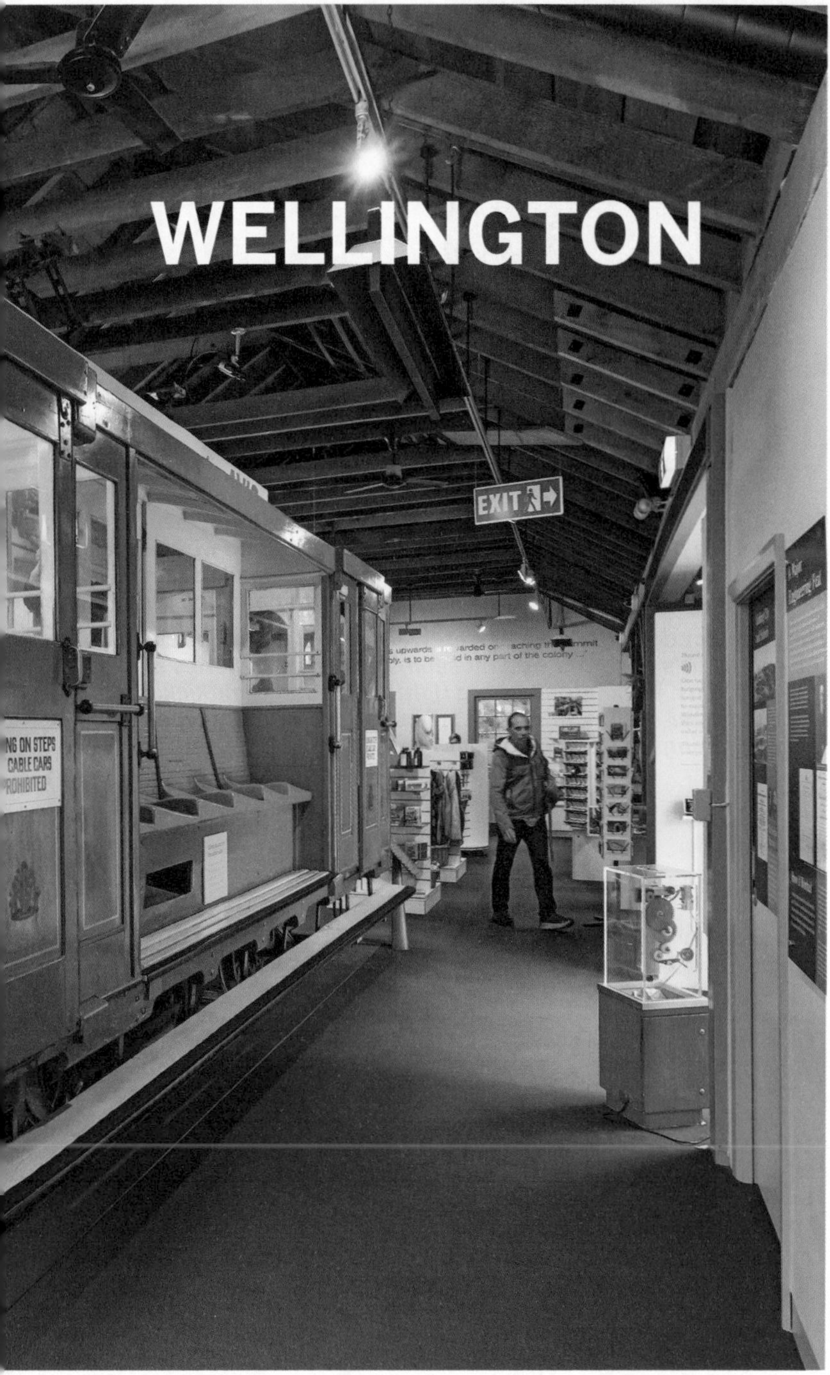

EXIT

ING ON STEPS
CABLE CARS
PROHIBITED

Wellington at a Glance...

On a sunny, windless day, Wellington is up there with the best of them. It's lovely to behold, on a hook-shaped harbour ringed with ranges that are cloaked in winter snow. Victorian timber architecture laces the hillsides above the harbour, which resonate with native birdsong.

The compact downtown area gives 'Welly' a bigger-city buzz and, being the capital, it's endowed with museums, theatres, galleries and arts organisations. Wellingtonians are rightly proud of their kickin' caffeine and craft-beer scenes, and there's no shortage of artsy types doing interesting things in old warehouses across town.

Wellington in Two Days

First up, drive to **Mt Victoria Lookout** (p142) to see the city. Shop and lunch on boho-hipster **Cuba St**, then catch some Kiwi culture at **Te Papa** (p134) or the **Wellington Museum** (p135). Wash off the day at **Golding's Free Dive** (p136).

Reconstitute at **Fidel's** (p148) then visit **Zealandia** (p142) to learn about NZ conservation. Grab dinner at **Logan Brown** (p149) before a movie at the **Embassy Theatre** (p138).

Wellington in Four Days

Break the fast at **Nikau Cafe** (p148), then tour **Parliament** (p143) (is Jacinda in the house?). Catch some live music at **San Fran** (p150), after a French dinner at **Noble Rot** (p147).

The **Wellington Botanic Gardens** (p142) are wander-ful; take the **Wellington Cable Car** (p142) to the top (killer views), then meander downhill. Drinks beckon: hit rooftop **Dirty Little Secret** (p149) and bookish **Library** (p149) for craft beer and cocktails.

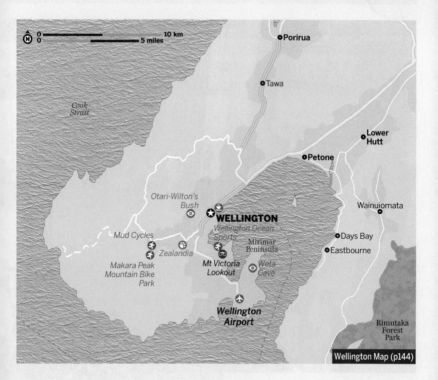

Wellington Map (p144)

Arriving in Wellington

Wellington Airport (p151) Wellington's airport is 6km southeast of the city. Shuttles cost $20 (15 minutes). Airport Flyer buses run 7am to 9pm ($9); a taxi costs about $30.

Ferry To/from Picton on the South Island (3½ hours). Bluebridge Ferries (p151) and Interislander (p151) are the operators.

Buses InterCity (p151) and Mana Bus (p151) depart for North Island destinations.

Trains Depart for Auckland and Palmerston North.

Sleeping

Accommodation in Wellington is more expensive than in regional areas, but there are plenty of options close to the city centre. Free parking spots are a rarity – ask in advance. Wellington's budget accommodation largely takes the form of multistorey hostel megaliths. Motels dot the city fringes. Self-contained apartments are popular, and often offer bargain weekend rates. Book well in advance.

NATHANIEL NOIR/ALAMY ©

Museums & Galleries

Wellington is an arty, learned kinda town – expect quality gallery experiences and some truly fab museums (...particularly useful on those rainy, hurricane-swept Wellington afternoons).

Great For...

☑ Don't Miss

The chance to visit a Māori *marae* (meeting house) at Te Papa.

Te Papa

New Zealand's national museum, **Te Papa** (📞04-381 7000; www.tepapa.govt.nz; 55 Cable St; tours adult/child $20/10; ⊙10am-6pm; 🛒) 🏷**FREE** is hard to miss, taking up a sizeable chunk of the Wellington waterfront. 'Te Papa Tongarewa' loosely translates as 'treasure box' and the riches inside include an amazing collection of Māori artefacts and the museum's own colourful *marae* (meeting house); natural history and environment exhibitions; Pacific and NZ history galleries; themed hands-on 'discovery centres' for children; and Toi Art, a revitalised home for the National Art Collection, which opened in 2018. Big-name temporary exhibitions incur an admission fee, although general admission is free.

Te Papa

NATHANIEL NOIR/ALAMY ©

City Gallery Wellington

Housed in the monumental old library in Civic Sq, Wellington's much-loved **City Gallery** (📞04-913 9032; www.citygallery.org.nz; Civic Sq; ⊙10am-5pm) **FREE** does a cracking job of securing acclaimed contemporary international exhibitions, as well as unearthing up-and-comers and supporting those at the forefront of the NZ scene. Charges may apply for major exhibits.

New Zealand Portrait Gallery

Housed in a heritage red-brick warehouse on the waterfront, this excellent **gallery** (📞04-472 2298; www.nzportraitgallery.org.nz; Shed 11, Customhouse Quay; ⊙10.30am-4.30pm) **FREE** presents a diverse range of NZ portraiture and caricature from its own collection and frequently changing guest exhibitions.

Wellington Museum

For an imaginative, interactive experience of Wellington's social and maritime history, head to this beguiling little **museum** (📞04-472 8904; www.museumswellington.org.nz; 3 Jervois Quay, Queens Wharf; ⊙10am-5pm; 🖐) **FREE**, housed in an 1892 Bond Store on the wharf. Highlights include a moving documentary on the *Wahine*, the interisland ferry that sank in the harbour in 1968 with the loss of 51 lives. Māori legends are dramatically told using tiny holographic actors and special effects.

The 'Attic' has an eclectic set of exhibits including a whiz-bang time machine and a suitably kooky display on Wellington vampire flick *What We Do in the Shadows*.

Craft Beer

Fuelled by a heady mix of musos, web developers and filmmakers, Wellington sustains the best craft-beer scene in the southern hemisphere. It's also a compact scene, easily explored on foot.

Great For...

☑ Don't Miss

Garage Project's Dirty Boots Mosh Pit APA – dank hoppy deliverance.

Bars

Golding's Free Dive   Craft Beer
(📞04-381 3616; www.goldingsfreedive.co.nz; 14 Leeds St; ⊘noon-11pm; 🛜) Hidden down a busy little back alley near Cuba St, gloriously garish Golding's is a bijoux craft-beer bar with far too many merits to mention. We'll single out ex-casino swivel chairs, a ravishing Reuben sandwich and Zappa and Bowie across the airways.

Fortune Favours   Craft Beer
(📞04-595 4092; www.fortunefavours.beer; 7 Leeds St; ⊘11am-11pm) The bold and the beautiful head to the rooftop of this old warehouse to sup on beer brewed in the shiny vats downstairs. Along with seven of its own concoctions it serves guest brews, wine and cocktails.

Garage Project Taproom

Microbreweries

Garage Project Taproom
Craft Beer

(☎04-802 5324; www.garageproject.co.nz; 91 Aro St, Aro Valley; ☺3-10pm Tue-Thu, noon-10pm Fri-Sun) The actual microbrewery occupies a former petrol station just down the road (68 Aro St), where they serve craft beer by the litre, petrol-pump style. If you'd rather consume your brew on premises in less industrial quantities, head to this narrow graffiti-lined bar. Order a tasting flight or chance your arm on the Pernicious Weed or Venusian Pale Ale.

Hashigo Zake
Craft Beer

(☎04-384 7300; www.hashigozake.co.nz; 25 Taranaki St; ☺noon-late; 🛜) This bricky bunker is the HQ for a zealous beer-import business, splicing big-flavoured international brews into a smartly selected NZ range. Hop-heads squeeze into the sweet little side-lounge on live-music nights.

Little Beer Quarter
Craft Beer

(☎04-803 3304; www.littlebeerquarter.co.nz; 6 Edward St; ☺3.30pm-late Sun & Mon, noon-late Tue-Sat) Buried in a back lane, lovely LBQ is warm, inviting and moodily lit in all the right places. Well-curated taps and a broad selection of bottled beer pack a hop-ish punch.

Fork & Brewer
Craft Beer

(☎04-472 0033; www.forkandbrewer.co.nz; 20a Bond St; ☺11.30am-late Mon-Sat) Aiming to improve on the 'kebab at 2am' experience, F&B offers excellent burgers, pizzas, pies, share plates and meaty mains to go along with its crafty brews (of which there are dozens – the Low Blow IPA comes highly recommended). Oh, and dark-beer doughnuts for dessert!

HEMIS/ALAMY ©

Wellywood

In recent years Wellington has stamped its name firmly on the world map as the home of New Zealand's booming film industry and off-piste Hollywood big-screen production, earning itself the nickname 'Wellywood'.

Acclaimed director Sir Peter Jackson still calls Wellington home; the success of his *The Lord of the Rings* films and subsequent productions such as *King Kong, The Adventures of Tintin* and *The Hobbit* have made him a powerful Hollywood player, and have bolstered Wellington's reputation.

Canadian director James Cameron is also in on the action; shooting has commenced for his four *Avatar* sequels, the first of which is due for a 2020 release. Cameron and his family are NZ residents, with landholding in rural Wairarapa. They have that in common with Jackson, who also has a property there.

Great For...

☑ Don't Miss

Winter's **New Zealand International Film Festival** (www.nzff.co.nz; ☺Jul-Aug), a roving two-week indie film fest.

Cinemas

Embassy Theatre   Cinema

(☎04-384 7657; www.embassytheatre.co.nz; 10 Kent Tce; ☺10am-late) Wellywood's cinema

William the Troll at Weta Cave

$28/13, both tours $45/20; ⊗9am-5.30pm) Academy Award–winning special-effects and props company Weta Workshop has been responsible for bringing the likes of *The Lord of the Rings, The Hobbit, King Kong, District 9* and *Thor: Ragnarok* to life. Learn how it does it on entertaining 45-minute guided tours, starting every half-hour; bookings recommended. Weta Cave is 8km east of the city centre: drive, catch a bus (p151) or book transport ($40 return) with your admission.

Wellington Movie Tours Tours

(☑027 419 3077; www.adventuresafari.co.nz; adult/child tours from $45/30) Half- and full-day tours with more props, clips and Middle-earth film locations than you can shake a staff at.

mother ship is an art deco darling, built in the 1920s. Today she screens mainly mainstream films with state-of-the-art sound and vision. Be sure to check out the glamorous Black Sparrow cocktail bar at the rear.

Light House Cinema Cinema

(☑04-385 3337; www.lighthousecinema.co.nz; 29 Wigan St; adult/child $18/13; ⊗10am-late; 🛜) Tucked away near the top end of Cuba St, this small, stylish cinema throws a range of mainstream, art-house and foreign films up onto the screens in three small theatres. High-quality snacks. Tuesday tickets $11.50.

Tours

Weta Cave Workshop

(☑04-909 4035; www.wetaworkshop.com/tours; 1 Weka St, Miramar; single tour adult/child

City Sculpture Tour

Wellington takes street art to sophisticated, sculptural levels. Here's our hit list of the weirdest, most engaging and actually rather moving installations around the city.

Start Post Office Sq
Distance 2.8km
Duration One hour

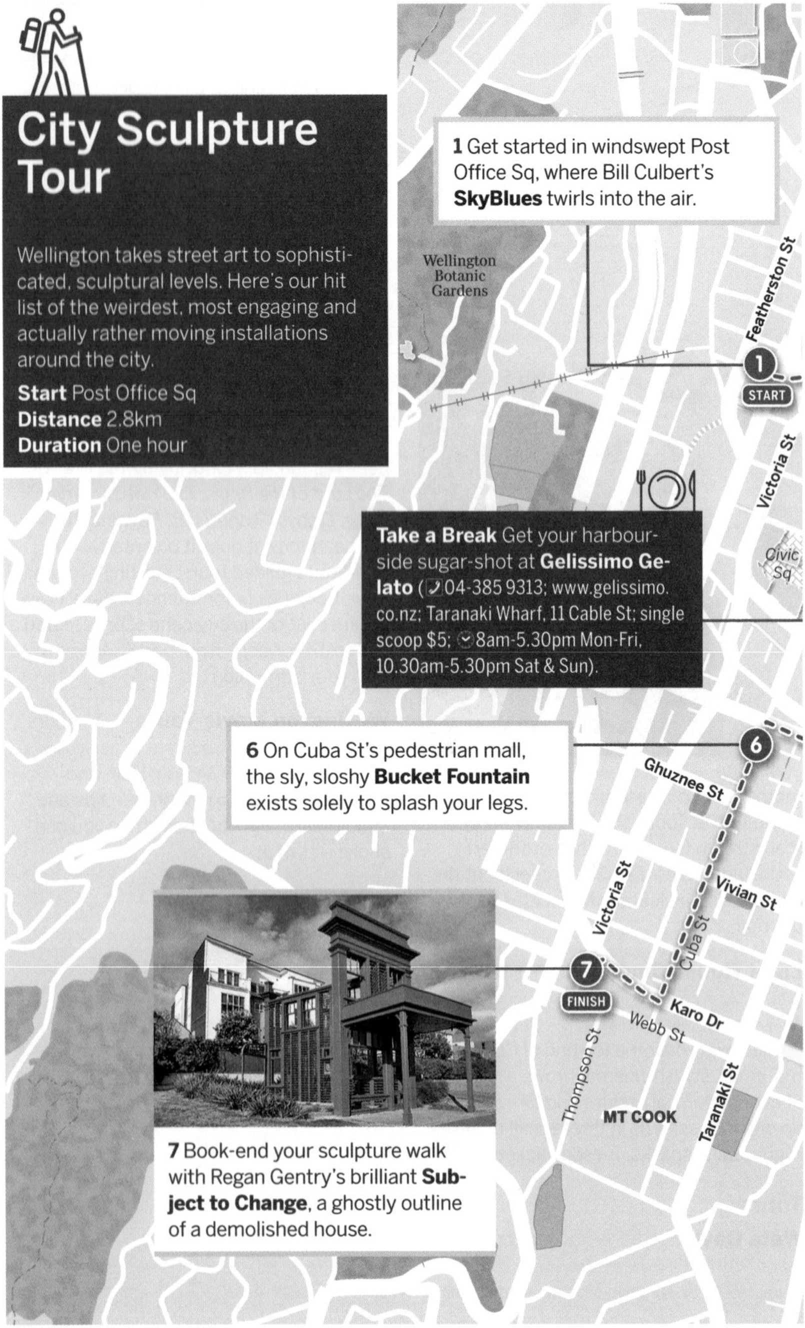

Wellington Botanic Gardens

Featherston St

Victoria St

1 Get started in windswept Post Office Sq, where Bill Culbert's **SkyBlues** twirls into the air.

START

Civic Sq

Take a Break Get your harbour-side sugar-shot at **Gelissimo Gelato** (☎04-385 9313; www.gelissimo.co.nz; Taranaki Wharf, 11 Cable St; single scoop $5; ☺8am-5.30pm Mon-Fri, 10.30am-5.30pm Sat & Sun).

6 On Cuba St's pedestrian mall, the sly, sloshy **Bucket Fountain** exists solely to splash your legs.

6

Ghuznee St

Victoria St

Vivian St

Cuba St

7

FINISH

Karo Dr

Webb St

Thompson St

Taranaki St

MT COOK

7 Book-end your sculpture walk with Regan Gentry's brilliant **Subject to Change**, a ghostly outline of a demolished house.

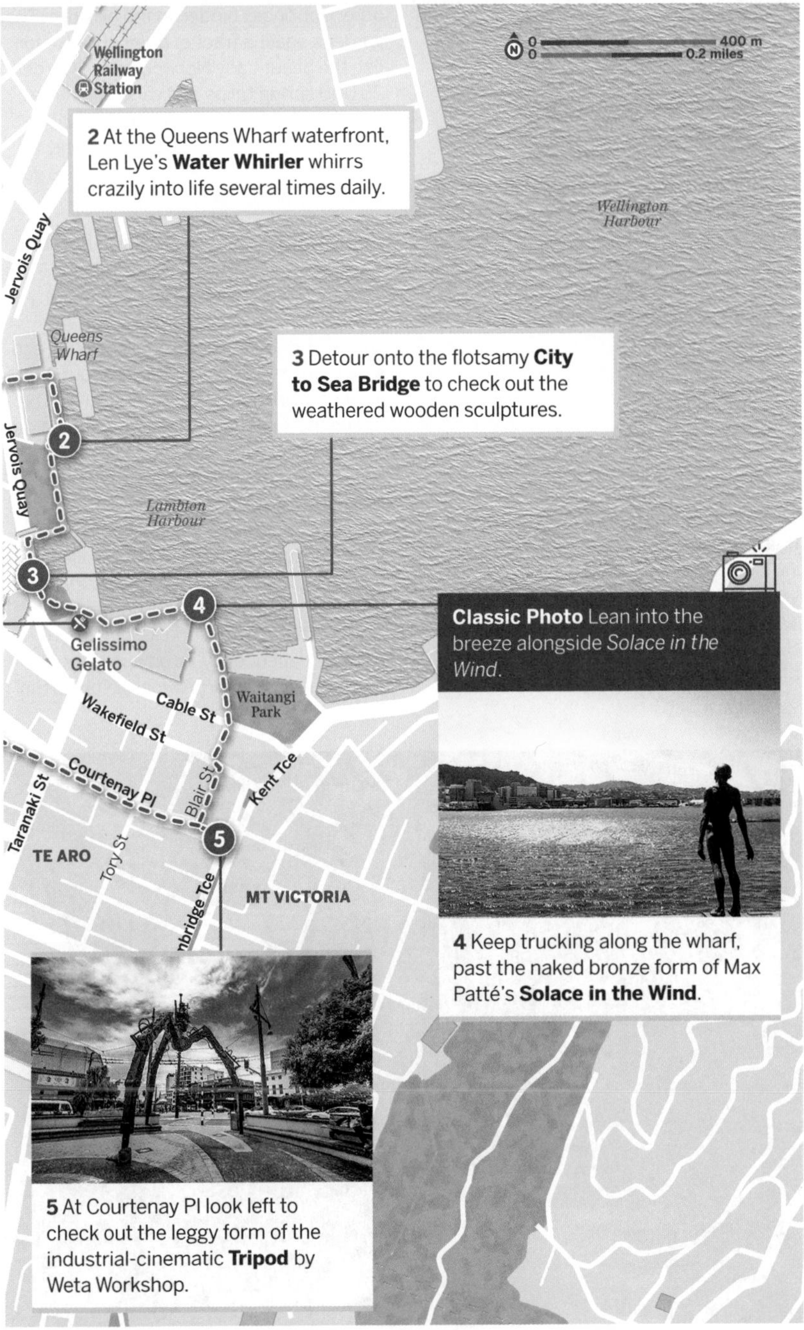

2 At the Queens Wharf waterfront, Len Lye's **Water Whirler** whirrs crazily into life several times daily.

Wellington Harbour

3 Detour onto the flotsamy **City to Sea Bridge** to check out the weathered wooden sculptures.

Wellington Railway Station

Jervois Quay

Queens Wharf

Jervois Quay

Lambton Harbour

Gelissimo Gelato

Cable St

Wakefield St

Courtenay Pl

Taranaki St

Tory St

Blair St

Kent Tce

Waitangi Park

TE ARO

MT VICTORIA

Classic Photo Lean into the breeze alongside *Solace in the Wind*.

4 Keep trucking along the wharf, past the naked bronze form of Max Patté's **Solace in the Wind**.

5 At Courtenay Pl look left to check out the leggy form of the industrial-cinematic **Tripod** by Weta Workshop.

4 MOLLY NZ/SHUTTERSTOCK © 5 YUCHEUNG/SHUTTERSTOCK © 7 CHAMELEONSEYE/SHUTTERSTOCK ©

◉ SIGHTS

Mt Victoria Lookout   Viewpoint

(Lookout Rd) The city's most impressive view point is atop 196m-high Mt Victoria (Matairangi), east of the city centre. You can take the bus 20 most of the way up, but the rite of passage is to sweat it out on the walk (ask a local for directions or just follow your nose). If you've got wheels, take Oriental Pde along the waterfront and then scoot up Carlton Gore Rd. Aside from the views there are some rather interesting info panels.

Wellington Botanic Gardens   Gardens

(☎04-499 4444; www.wellington.govt.nz; 101 Glenmore St, Thorndon; ⊙daylight hours) **FREE** These hilly, 25-hectare botanic gardens can be *almost* effortlessly visited via the **Wellington Cable Car** (☎04-472 2199; www.wellingtoncablecar.co.nz; Cable Car Lane, rear 280 Lambton Quay; adult/child one way $4/2, return $7.50/3.50; ⊙departs every 10min, 7am-10pm Mon-Fri, 8.30am-9pm Sat & Sun; ▥) (nice bit of planning, eh?), although there are several other entrances hidden in the hillsides. The gardens boast a tract of original native forest, the beaut Lady Norwood Rose Garden, 25,000 spring tulips and various international plant collections. Add in fountains, a playground, sculptures, a duck pond, a cafe and city skyline views, and you've got a grand day out indeed.

Zealandia   Wildlife Reserve

(☎04-920 9213; www.visitzealandia.com; 53 Waiapu Rd, Karori; adult/child/family exhibition only $9/5/21, full admission $20/10/46; ⊙9am-5pm; ▥) ✔ This groundbreaking eco-sanctuary is hidden in the hills about 2km west of town: buses 3 and 20 stop nearby, or see the Zealandia website for info on the free shuttle. Living wild within the fenced valley are more than 30 native bird species, including rare little spotted kiwi, takahe, saddleback, hihi and kaka, as well as NZ's little dinosaur, the tuatara. An excellent exhibition relays NZ's natural history and world-renowned conservation story.

More than 30km of tracks can be explored independently, or on regular guided tours. The night tour provides an opportuni-

Wellington Botanic Gardens

BANGKOKFLAME/SHUTTERSTOCK ©

ty to spot nocturnal creatures including kiwi, frogs and glowworms (adult/child $85/40).

New Zealand Parliament   Historic Building

(☑04-817 9503; www.parliament.nz; Molesworth St; ⊙9.30am-4.30pm) **FREE** New Zealand might be a young country but it has one of the oldest continuously functioning parliaments in the world and has chalked up more than its share of firsts, including being the first to give women the vote (in 1893) and the first to include an openly transsexual Member of Parliament (in 1999). You can learn all about NZ's unique version of democracy on a free guided tour.

Space Place   Observatory

(☑04-910 3140; www.museumswellington.org. nz; 40 Salamanca Rd, Kelburn; adult/child/family $13/8/39; ⊙4-11pm Tue & Fri, 10am-11pm Sat, 10am-5.30pm Sun) Located in the Carter Observatory at the top of the Botanic Gardens, this full-dome planetarium offers regular space-themed multimedia shows (eg *We Are Aliens, Dynamic Earth, Matariki Dawn*) and stargazing sessions. Check the website for show times.

Ngā Taonga Sound & Vision   Archives

(☑04-384 7647; www.ngataonga.org.nz; 84 Taranaki St; screenings adult/child $10/8; ⊙library noon-4pm Mon-Fri) **FREE** Ngā Taonga is a vortex of NZ moving images into which you could get sucked for days. Its library holds tens of thousands of titles: feature films, documentaries, short films, home movies, newsreels, TV programs, advertisements... There are regular screenings in the cinema (check the website for the schedule), and a viewing library (free) where you can watch films until you're square-eyed. If the library's closed, there's a media player in the on-site cafe.

Otari-Wilton's Bush   Gardens

(☑04-499 4444; www.wellington.govt.nz; 160 Wilton Rd, Wilton; ⊙daylight hours) **FREE** The only botanic gardens in NZ specialising in native flora, Otari features more than 1200 plant species including an extant section of native

 ### Days Bay & Matiu/ Somes Island

Wellingtonians have been taking day trips across the harbour to Days Bay since the 1880s. At the bay there's a beach, a park and a cafe, and a boat-shed with kayaks and bikes for hire. A 10-minute walk from Days Bay leads to Eastbourne, a beachy township with cafes, a cute pub, a summer swimming pool and a playground.

The sweet little **East by West Ferry** (☑04-499 1282; www.eastbywest.co.nz; Queens Wharf; return adult/child $23/12) plies the 20- to 30-minute route 16 times a day on weekdays and eight times on weekends; some sailings stop in Petone and Seatoun as well.

Three or four of the daily ferries also stop at Matiu/Somes Island in the middle of the harbour, a DOC-managed reserve which is home to weta, tuatara, kakariki and little blue penguins, among other critters. The island is rich in history, having once been a prisoner-of-war camp and quarantine station. Take a picnic lunch, or even stay overnight in the basic campsite (adult/child $13/6.50) or at one of the two DOC cottages (sole-occupancy $200): book online at www.doc.govt.nz or at the **DOC Wellington Visitor Centre** (☑04-384 7770; www.doc.govt.nz; 18 Manners St; ⊙9.30am-5pm Mon-Fri, 10am-3.30pm Sat).

bush containing the city's oldest trees (including an 800-year-old rimu). There's also an information centre, an 18m-high canopy walkway, 11km of walking trails and some beaut picnic areas. It's located about 5km northwest of the centre and well signposted; bus 14 passes the gates.

🏃 ACTIVITIES

Ferg's Kayaks   Kayaking, Climbing

(☑04-499 8898; www.fergskayaks.co.nz; Shed 6, Queens Wharf; ⊙10am-8pm Mon-Fri, 9am-6pm

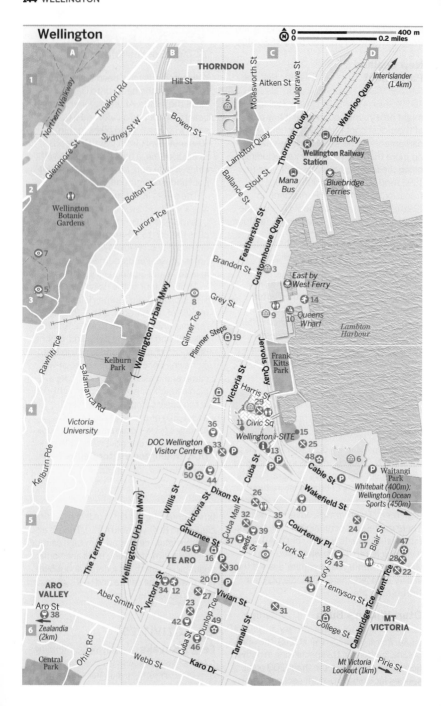

Wellington

N

0   400 m
0   0.2 miles

THORNDON

Hill St

Molesworth St

Aitken St

Mulgrave St

Tinakori Rd

Sydney St W

Bowen St

Lambton Quay

Thorndon Quay

Waterloo Quay

Interislander
(1.4km)

Glenmore St

Bolton St

Ballance St

Stout St

2

Aurora Tce

**Wellington
Botanic
Gardens**

InterCity

**Wellington Railway
Station**

Mana
Bus

*Bluebridge
Ferries*

Featherston St

Customhouse Quay

Brandon St

3

*East by
West Ferry*

14

7

Grey St

8

9

10

*Queens
Wharf*

*Lambton
Harbour*

5

Rawhiti Tce

Wellington Urban Mwy

Glimer Tce

Plimmer Steps

19

Jervois Quay

Frank
Kitts
Park

Salamanca Rd

**Kelburn
Park**

Victoria St

Harris St

21

29

*Victoria
University*

1

36

11   Civic Sq

Wellington i-SITE

15

Kelburn Pde

DOC Wellington
Visitor Centre

33

13

25

48   6

P

*Waitangi
Park*

*Whitebait (400m);
Wellington Ocean
Sports (450m)*

50   44

Cable St

The Terrace

Willis St

Wellington Urban Mwy

Victoria St

Dixon St

Cuba St

26

Wakefield St

40

32

35

Courtenay Pl

24

Ghuznee St

37

Leeds St

39

4

York St

17

Blair St

47

45

16

30

P

Tory St

43

28

22

TE ARO

20

Vivian St

41

Tennyson St

Cambridge Tce

Kent Tce

**MT
VICTORIA**

**ARO
VALLEY**

Aro St

38

*Zealandia
(2km)*

34   12

Abel Smith St

23

27

42   49

Cuba St

Dunlop Tce

Taranaki St

31

18

College St

*Central
Park*

Ohiro Rd

Webb St

46

Karo Dr

*Mt Victoria
Lookout (1km)*

Pirie St

Wellington

Sat & Sun) Stretch your tendons with indoor rock climbing (adult/child $21/17), cruise the waterfront wearing in-line skates (one/two hours $20/25) or go for a paddle in a kayak (one/two hours $25/35) or on a stand-up paddle board (one/two hours $30/40). There's also bike hire (hour/day from $20/80) and guided kayaking trips.

Makara Peak Mountain
Bike Park   Mountain Biking
(www.makarapeak.org; 116 South Karori Rd, Karori; ☉daylight hours) In hilly Karori, 7km west of the city centre, this excellent 230-hectare park is laced with 45km of single-track, ranging from beginner to extreme. The nearby **Mud Cycles** (☎04-476 4961; www.mudcycles.co.nz; 424 Karori Rd, Karori; half-day/full-day/weekend bike hire from $35/60/100; ☉9.30am-6.30pm Mon-Fri, 10am-

5pm Sat & Sun) has mountain bikes for hire. To get here by public transport, catch bus 3.

Wellington
Ocean Sports   Water Sports
(☎04-939 6702; www.oceansports.org.nz; 115 Oriental Pde; harbour sails per person $40; ☉booking office 9am-5pm) Harness Wellington's infamous wind on a one-hour harbour sailing trip, departing most weekends (weather dependent) – no experience required! Ask about stand-up paddle boarding, windsurfing, *waka ama* (outrigger canoeing) and kayaking sessions.

Switched On Bikes   Cycling
(☎022 075 8754; www.switchedonbikes.co.nz; Queens Wharf; city & mountain bike hire 1hr/4hr/day $15/40/60, electric $20/45/75, guided tours from $95; ☉9am-5pm) If you're short on puff

on those notorious Wellington hills, these guys rent out electric bikes for cruising the city or taking on guided tours around the harbour. Look for their shipping-container base near the end of the wharf.

Te Wharewaka o Pōneke　Cultural
(📞04-901 3333; www.wharewakaoponeke.co.nz; Taranaki Wharf, 2 Taranaki St; tours walking $30-40, 2hr waka $100, 3hr waka & walk $125) Get set for (and maybe a little bit wet on) a two-hour paddle tour in a Māori *waka* (canoe) around Wellington's waterfront, with lots of cultural insights along the way. Call for the latest tour times and bookings – minimum numbers apply.

🅖 TOURS

Walk Wellington　Walking
(📞04-473 3145; www.walkwellington.org.nz; departs Wellington i-SITE, 111 Wakefield St; tour $20; ⊙10am daily year-round, plus 5pm Mon, Wed & Fri Dec-Mar) Informative and great-value two-hour walking tours focusing on the city and waterfront, departing from the i-SITE (p150). Book online, by phone or just turn up.

Flat Earth　Driving
(📞04-472 9635; www.flatearth.co.nz; half-/full-day tours from $95/385) An array of themed small-group guided tours: city highlights, Māori treasures, arts, wilderness and Middle-earth filming locations. Martinborough wine tours also available.

Zest Food Tours　Food & Drink
(📞04-801 9198; www.zestfoodtours.co.nz; departs Wellington i-SITE, 111 Wakefield St; tours from $185) Runs 3½- to five-hour small-group foodie tours around the city, plus day tours over the hills into the Wairarapa wine region.

Hop On Hop Off　Bus
(📞0800 246 877; www.hoponhopoff.co.nz; departs 101 Wakefield St; adult/child $45/30; ⊙departs 9.30am, 11am, 12.30pm & 2.30pm) Flexible 1½-hour scenic loop of the city with 11 stops en route. Tickets are valid for 24 hours.

South Coast Shuttles　Driving
(📞04-389 2161; www.southcoastshuttles.co.nz; departs Wellington i-SITE, 111 Wakefield St; 2½hr tours $55; ⊙tours 10am & 1pm) Offers scheduled daily city highlights tours including the south coast, Mt Victoria, Weta Cave and Otari-Wilton's Bush.

🅐 SHOPPING

Unity Books　Books
(📞04-499 4245; www.unitybooks.co.nz; 57 Willis St; ⊙9am-6pm Mon-Sat, 11am-5pm Sun) Sets the standard for every bookshop in the land, with dedicated NZ tables piled high.

Slow Boat Records　Music
(📞04-385 1330; www.slowboatrecords.co.nz; 183 Cuba St; ⊙9.30am-5.30pm Sat-Thu, to 7.30pm Fri) Country, folk, pop, indie, metal, blues, soul, rock, Hawaiian nose-flute music – it's all here at Slow Boat, Wellington's long-running music shop and Cuba St mainstay.

Kura　Art
(📞04-802 4934; www.kuragallery.co.nz; 19 Allen St; ⊙10am-6pm Mon-Fri, 11am-4pm Sat & Sun) Contemporary Māori and NZ art: painting, ceramics, jewellery and sculpture. A gorgeous galley – come for a look even if you're not buying.

Moore Wilson's　Food & Drinks
(📞04-384 9906; www.moorewilsons.co.nz; 93 Tory St; ⊙7.30am-7pm) A call-out to self-caterers: this positively swoon-inducing grocer is one of NZ's most committed supporters of independently produced and artisanal produce. If you want to chew on the best of Wellington and NZ, here's your chance. Head upstairs for dry goods, wine, beer and kitchenware.

Hunters & Collectors　Clothing
(📞04-384 8948; www.facebook.com/huntersandcollectorswellington; 134 Cuba St; ⊙10.30am-6pm) Beyond the best-dressed window in NZ you'll find off-the-rack and vintage clothing (punk, skate, Western and mod), plus shoes and accessories.

Old Bank
Shopping Centre

(☑04-922 0600; www.oldbank.co.nz; 233-237 Lambton Quay; ⊗9am-6pm Mon-Fri, 11am-3pm Sat & Sun) This dear old building on a wedge-shaped city site is home to an arcade of indulgent, high-end shops, predominantly jewellers and boutiques. Check out the fab tiled floors and Corinthian columns.

⊗ EATING

Little Penang
Malaysian $

(☑04-382 9818; www.facebook.com/little penang; 40 Dixon St; mains $12-17; ⊗11am-3pm & 5-9pm Mon-Fri, 11am-9pm Sat; ☑) Among a troupe of great Malaysian diners, Little Penang steals the show with its fresh-flavoured, fiery street food. Order a *nasi le-mak* with the good eggy, nutty, saucy stuff; or go for the bargain $9 roti bread with curry. And don't bypass the curry puffs. The lunchtime rush can border on the absurd.

Noble Rot
French $$

(☑04-385 6671; www.noblerot.co.nz; 6 Swan Lane; mains $29-34; ⊗4pm-late) Noble Rot thinks of itself as a wine bar, but this cosy

nook serves some of Wellington's best food too. A French influence pervades the menu (charcuterie, duck parfait, smoked-cheese soufflé, slow-cooked lamb), alongside a few distinctly Kiwi touches such as spaghetti with *puha* (a native green vegetable). Need-less to say, the wine list is exceptional.

Loretta
Cafe $$

(☑04-384 2213; www.loretta.net.nz; 181 Cuba St; mains $13-28; ⊗9am-10pm Tue-Sun; ☑) From breakfast (waffles, crumpets, cereal) through lunch (sandwiches, fritters, soup) and into dinner (pizzas, roast chicken, schnitzel), Loretta has won leagues of fans with her classy, well-proportioned offerings served in bright, airy surrounds. We recom-mend splitting a pizza and grain-filled salad between two. Bookings for lunch only.

Shepherd
Contemporary $$

(☑04-385 7274; www.shepherdrestaurant.co.nz; 1/5 Eva St; mains $26-30; ⊗5.30pm-late Wed-Sun) This good Shepherd leads the way with on-trend contemporary cuisine, guiding its eager flock through fusion flavours, unusu-al produce and pickled accompaniments. A

Old Bank

Library

long bar on one side faces off with an open kitchen on the other, with an assortment of brightly painted stools and high tables in between. The vibe is young and edgy, and the food's thrilling.

Fidel's   Cafe $$

(☏04-801 6868; www.fidelscafe.com; 234 Cuba St; mains brunch $9-22, dinner $13-26; ☺8am-10pm; 🎵) A Cuba St institution for caffeine-craving alternative types, Fidel's cranks out eggs any which way, pizza and super salads from its itsy kitchen, along with Welly's best milk-shakes. Revolutionary memorabilia adorns the walls of the low-lit interior, and there's a small outdoor area and a street-facing booth for takeaway coffees. The ever-busy crew copes with the chaos admirably.

Nikau Cafe   Cafe $$

(☏04-801 4168; www.nikaucafe.co.nz; City Gallery, Civic Sq; mains $15-27; ☺7am-4pm Mon-Sat) 🌿 An airy affair at the sophisticated end of Wellington's cafe spectrum, Nikau consistently dishes up simple but sublime stuff (pan-fried halloumi, legendary kedgeree). Refreshing aperitifs, divine sweets, charming staff and a

sunny courtyard complete the package. The organic, seasonal menu changes daily.

Capitol   Italian $$

(☏04-384 2855; www.capitolrestaurant.co.nz; 10 Kent Tce, Mt Victoria; mains brunch $10-27, lunch $18-27, dinner $28-38; ☺noon-3pm & 5.30-9.30pm Mon-Fri, 9.30am-3pm & 5.30-9.30pm Sat & Sun) This consistent culinary star serves simple, seasonal fare using premium local ingredients, with a nod to classic Italian cuisine (try the homemade tagliolini or the Parmesan-crusted lamb's liver). The dining room is a bit cramped and noisy, but elegant nonetheless.

Field & Green   British $$

(☏04-384 4992; www.fieldandgreen.co.nz; 262 Wakefield St; mains $14-33; ☺8am-10pm Wed-Sat, to 3pm Sun) 'European soul food' is their slogan, but it's the best of British that dominates here, including red Leicester scones, Welsh rarebit, kedgeree, fish finger sarnies, bacon butties with HP sauce and pan-fried pork chops. It's actually way more sophisticated than it sounds, with a Scandi-chic sensibility to the decor and accomplished London-born chef Laura Greenfield at the helm.

WBC
Fusion $$

(📞04-499 9379; www.wbcrestaurant.co.nz; Level 1, 107 Victoria St; small plates $14-18, large $25-28; ⏰10.30am-late Tue-Sat) At the Wholesale Boot Company (wonder why they use the acronym?), flavours from Thailand, China and Japan punctuate a menu filled with the best of NZ produce, including freshly shucked oysters and clams (served raw, steamed or tempura-battered), and game meats (tahr tacos, kung pow venison). Everything's packed with flavour and de-signed to be shared.

Prefab
Cafe $$

(📞04-385 2263; www.pre-fab.co.nz; 14 Jessie St; mains $11-26; ⏰7am-4pm Mon-Sat; 📶🚻) A big, industrial-minimalist space houses the city's slickest espresso bar and roastery, owned by long-time Wellington caffeine fiends. Beautiful house-baked bread features on a menu of flavourful, well-executed offerings. Dogs doze on the sunny terrace while the staff efficiently handle the bustle inside.

Mt Vic Chippery
Fish & Chips $$

(📞04-382 8713; www.thechippery.co.nz; 5 Major-ibanks St, Mt Victoria; meals $12-20; ⏰noon-8.30pm; 🚻) At this backwater fish shack it's fish and chips by numbers: 1. Choose your fish (from at least three varieties). 2. Choose your coating (beer batter, panko crumb, tempura...). 3. Choose your chips (five varieties!). 4. Add aioli, coleslaw, salad or sauce, and a quality soft drink. 5. Chow down inside or takeaway. There are burgers and battered sausages too.

Logan Brown
Contemporary $$$

(📞04-801 5114; www.loganbrown.co.nz; 192 Cuba St; mains $39-45; ⏰noon-2pm Wed-Sat & 5pm-late Tue-Sun; 📶) 🍴 Deservedly ranked amongst Wellington's best restaurants, Logan Brown oozes class without being overly formal. Its 1920s banking-chamber dining room is a neoclassical stunner – a fitting complement to the produce-driven modern NZ cuisine. The three-course bistro menu ($45) won't hurt your wallet too badly (but the epic wine list might force a blowout). There's also a great-value $25 main-plus-wine lunch deal.

Whitebait
Seafood $$$

(📞04-385 8555; www.white-bait.nz; 1 Clyde Quay Wharf; mains $38; ⏰5.30pm-late year-round, plus noon-3pm Wed-Fri Nov-Mar) Neutral colours and gauzy screens set an upmarket tone for this top-rated seafood restaurant. All of the fish are sustainably sourced and deftly prepared, with a scattering of quality non-fishy options rounding out the contemporary menu. Early diners (seatings before 6.30pm) can take advantage of a good-value set 'bistro' menu ($55 for an oyster, entree, main and petit four).

🍸 DRINKING & NIGHTLIFE

The inner city is riddled with bars, with high concentrations around raucous Courte-nay Pl, bohemian Cuba St and along the waterfront.

Library
Bar

(📞04-382 8593; www.thelibrary.co.nz; Level 1, 53 Courtenay Pl; ⏰5pm-late) You'll find yourself in the right kind of bind at moody, bookish Library, with its velveteen booths, board games and swish cocktails. An excellent all-round drink selection is complemented by a highly shareable menu of sweet and sa-voury treats. There's live music on occasion.

Dirty Little Secret
Rooftop Bar

(📞021 0824 0298; www.dirtylittlesecret.co.nz; Level 8, 7-8 Dixon St; ⏰4pm-late Mon-Thu, noon-late Fri-Sun; 📶) While it's not strictly a secret (it's packed to the gills on balmy eve-nings) this hip bar atop the historic Hope Gibbons Ltd building plays hard to get, with a nondescript entrance on Taranaki St next to Jack Hackett's Irish Pub. Expect craft beer, slugged together cocktails, loud indie music and plastic awnings straining to keep the elements at bay.

Hawthorn Lounge
Cocktail Bar

(📞04-890 3724; www.hawthornlounge.co.nz; Level 1, 82 Tory St; ⏰5pm-3am) This uppercut cocktail bar has a 1920s speakeasy feel, suited-up in waistcoats and wide-brimmed fedoras. Sip a whisky sour and play poker, or watch the behind-the-bar theatrics from the Hawthorn's mixologists, twisting and turning classics into modern-day masterpieces. Open 'til the wee small hours.

Rogue & Vagabond
Craft Beer

(☑04-381 2321; www.rogueandvagabond. co.nz; 18 Garrett St; ☺11am-late) Fronting on to a precious pocket park, the Rogue is a lovably scruffy, colourful, kaleidoscopic craft-beer bar with heaps going on – via 18 taps including two hand-pulls. Voluminous, chewy-crust pizza, burgers, po' boys, alcoholic milkshakes and regular, rockin' gigs add further appeal. Swill around on the patio or slouch on the lawn.

Counterculture
Bar

(☑04-891 2345; www.counterculture.co.nz; 211 Victoria St; unlimited games $5; ☺noon-10pm Mon-Fri, 10am-10pm Sat & Sun; 📶📶) Who doesn't secretly love a board game? Assume an ironic stance if you must, but here's the chance to embrace your inner games nerd in public. There are almost 400 games to choose from, staff to advise on rules, and craft beers and cocktails to take the edge off your ugly competitive streak.

Motel
Cocktail Bar

(☑04-384 9084; www.motelbar.co.nz; Forresters Lane; ☺5pm-late Mon-Sat) The back lane location, retro neon sign and unpromising staircase generates a suitably seedy NYC-in-the-'70s first impression but inside is a louche, low-lit tiki bar, where the bar staff shake up fruity cocktails before a backdrop of giant clams, Polynesian-style statues and pineapple lights. Campy, fun and a great place for a sneaky rendezvous.

Laundry
Bar

(☑04-384 4280; www.laundry.net.nz; 240 Cuba St; ☺4pm-2am) Tumble into this lurid-green, junk-shop, juke joint any time of the day or night for a tipple and a plate of jerk chicken. Regular live music and DJs offset Southern-style bar food and carnivalesque decor. There's also a trailer-trash backyard complete with a caravan.

Southern Cross
Pub

(☑04-384 9085; www.thecross.co.nz; 39 Abel Smith St; ☺8am-late; 📶) Welcoming to all – from frenetic five-year-olds to knitting nanas – the democratic Cross rambles through a series of colourful rooms, combining a lively bar, a dance floor, a pool table and the best garden bar in town. There's good beer on tap, food for all budgets and regular events (gigs, quiz nights, karaoke, coffee groups).

✪ ENTERTAINMENT

San Fran
Live Music

(☑04-801 6797; www.sanfran.co.nz; 171 Cuba St; ☺3pm-late Tue-Sat) This much-loved, mid-size music venue is moving to a new beat; it's boarded the craft-beer bandwagon and rocks out smoky, meaty food along the way. Gigs still rule, dancing is de rigueur, and the balcony still gets good afternoon sun.

Circa Theatre
Theatre

(☑04-801 7992; www.circa.co.nz; 1 Taranaki St) This attractive waterfront theatre has two auditoriums in which it shows everything from edgy new works to Christmas panto.

Meow
Live Music

(☑04-385 8883; www.welovemeow.co.nz; 9 Edward St; ☺4pm-late Tue-Fri, 6pm-late Sat) Truly the cat's pyjamas, Meow goes out on a limb to host a diverse range of gigs and performances: country, ragtime, DJs, acoustic rock, jazz, poetry... At the same time the kitchen plates up good-quality, inexpensive food at any tick of the clock. Mishmashed retro decor; cool craft beers.

BATS
Theatre

(☑04-802 4175; www.bats.co.nz; 1 Kent Tce) Wildly alternative but accessible BATS presents cutting-edge and experimental NZ theatre – varied, cheap and intimate – in its revamped theatre.

❶ INFORMATION

Wellington i-SITE (☑04-802 4860; www.welling tonnz.com; 111 Wakefield St; ☺8.30am-5pm;) After an earthquake chased it out of its regular digs, the i-SITE has taken over the Michael Fowler

Centre's old booking office. It looks like it'll be here for the foreseeable future, but check its website for the latest. Staff book almost everything here, and cheerfully distribute Wellington's *Official Visitor Guide*, along with other maps and pamphlets.

❶ GETTING THERE & AWAY

AIR

Wellington Airport (WLG; ☑04-385 5100; www.wellingtonairport.co.nz; Stewart Duff Dr, Rongotai) is an international gateway to NZ.

Domestic services:

Air New Zealand (☑0800 737 000; www.airnewzealand.co.nz) Flies to/from Auckland, Rotorua, Napier, Blenheim, Christchurch, Queenstown, Dunedin and many other hubs.

Jetstar (www.jetstar.com) Auckland, Christchurch and Dunedin.

Sounds Air (☑0800 505 005; www.soundsair.com) Taupo, Blenheim and Picton.

BOAT

To cross Cook Strait to Picton there are two ferry options:

Bluebridge Ferries (☑04-471 6188; www.bluebridge.co.nz; 50 Waterloo Quay; adult/child/car/campervan/motorbike from $53/27/120/155/51; 🛜) ✐ Up to four sailings between Wellington and Picton daily (3½ hours).

Interislander (☑04-498 3302; www.interislander.co.nz; Aotea Quay; adult/child/car/campervan/motorbike from $56/28/149/181/84) Up to five sailings between Wellington and Picton daily; crossings take 3¼ to 3½ hours. A free shuttle bus heads from platform 9 at Wellington Railway Station to Aotea Quay, 50 minutes before every daytime sailing, and returns 20 minutes after every arrival.

BUS

Wellington is a major terminus for North Island bus services. **InterCity** (☑04-385 0520; www.intercity.co.nz) and **Mana Bus** (☑09-367 9140; www.manabus.com) are the main players.

TRAIN

The **Northern Explorer** (www.greatjourneysofnz.co.nz) train heads to/from Auckland (from $139, 11 hours).

History on the Harbour

Māori tradition has it that the explorer Kupe was first to discover Wellington Harbour. Wellington's original Māori name was Te Whanganui-a-Tara (great harbour of Tara), named after the son of a chief named Whatonga who had settled on the Hawke's Bay coast. Whatonga's followers moved to the Wellington area and founded the Ngāi Tara tribe.

On 22 January 1840 the first European settlers arrived in the New Zealand Company's ship *Aurora*, expecting to take possession of land that the local Māori denied selling. The Treaty of Waitangi was signed a few weeks later and in the years that followed the Land Claims Commission was established to sort out the mess.

By 1850 Wellington was a thriving settlement of around 5500 people, despite a shortage of flat land. Originally the waterfront was along Lambton Quay, but reclamation of parts of the harbour began in 1852. In 1855 a significant earthquake raised many parts of Wellington.

In 1865 the seat of government was moved from Auckland to Wellington, although it took until the turn of the century for the city to really flourish. In the early 1900s the port prospered, with export boards and banks springing up in its surrounds.

❶ GETTING AROUND

Downtown Wellington isn't too hilly and can easily be explored on foot or by bike.

Metlink (☑0800 801 700; www.metlink.org.nz) is the one-stop shop for Wellington's regional bus, train and harbour ferry networks; there's a handy journey planner on its website.

On Yer Bike (☑04-384 8480; www.avantiplus.co.nz/wellington; 181 Vivian St; city/mountain/electric bike per day $30/40/60; ⏰8.30am-5.30pm Mon-Sat) Quality bike hire in the city centre.

Wellington Combined Taxis (☑04-384 4444; www.taxis.co.nz)

MARLBOROUGH

Marlborough at a Glance...

Sunny Marlborough is a region of two main enticements: the aston-ishingly gorgeous Marlborough Sounds, where you can hike, bike and kayak to your heart's content; and the world-trumping Marlborough Wine Region, home to grapes that, with a bit of New Zealand know-how, become the cool-climate wines that grace the world's best restaurants.

Local produce, including hops, wild game, seafood and summer fruits, is also a highlight, best enjoyed in hip local cafes and classy vine-side eateries. The amazing Abel Tasman National Park (p170) isn't too far away, either.

Marlborough in Two Days

Picturesque little **Picton** (p164) is much more than just a drive-thru ferry hub – spend a day touring the Marlborough Sounds or tackling lovely local walks.

On day two hit the **Marlborough Wine Region** (p158). Standout vine-yards include **Saint Clair Estate** (p160) and **Framingham** (p160), while in little Renwick near Blenheim, **Arbour** (p161) delivers the best of Marlborough pro-duce in seamlessly elegant surrounds.

Marlborough in Four Days

For days three and four rev up the en-ergy levels by exploring the photogenic Marlborough Sounds along the **Queen Charlotte Track** (p156). This convolut-ed 70km waterside trail is one of NZ's 'Great Rides', but you can hike it or (with a little help from water taxis) kayak sections of it too.

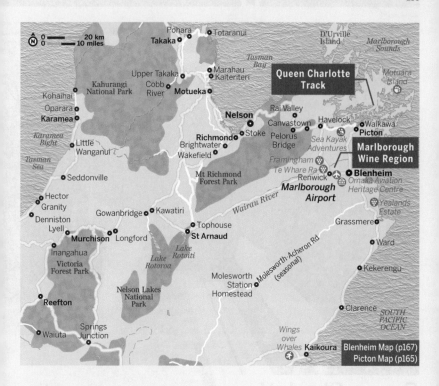

N
0 —— 20 km
0 —— 10 miles

Pohara
Totaranui
Takaka

D'Urville
Island
Marlborough
Sounds

Tasman
Bay

Upper Takaka
Marahau
Kaiteriteri

Motuara
Island

Kahurangi
National Park
Cobb
River
Motueka

**Queen Charlotte
Track**

Kohaihai
Oparara
Karamea

Nelson

Rai Valley
Canvastown
Havelock
Waikawa
Picton

Karamea
Bight
Little
Wanganui

Richmond
Brightwater
Wakefield

Stoke
Pelorus
Bridge

Sea Kayak
Adventures

**Marlborough
Wine Region**

Tasman
Sea

Seddonville

Mt Richmond
Forest Park

Framingham
Te Whare Ra

Blenheim
Omaka Aviation
Heritage Centre

Hector
Granity
Denniston
Lyell

Gowanbridge
Kawatiri

Wairau River

Renwick
*Marlborough
Airport*

Yealands
Estate

Tophouse
St Arnaud

Grassmere

Murchison
Longford

Lake
Rotoiti

Ward

Inangahua
Victoria
Forest Park

Lake
Rotoroa

Molesworth-Acheron Rd
(seasonal)

Kekerengu

Reefton

Nelson Lakes
National
Park

Molesworth
Station
Homestead

Clarence
SOUTH
PACIFIC
OCEAN

Waiuta
Springs
Junction

Wings
over
Whales **Kaikoura**

Blenheim Map (p167)
Picton Map (p165)

Arriving in Marlborough

Picton Ferry Terminal Terminus for vehicle ferries from Wellington. Buses and shuttles depart from here or the nearby i-SITE for Christchurch, Kaikoura, Nelson and beyond.

Picton Train Station The *Coastal Pacific* train to Christchurch was closed following an earthquake, but was planned to be back up and running in late 2018.

Blenheim Buses from Queenstown, Christchurch, Picton and Kaikoura.

Marlborough Airport (p169) The airport is 6km west of Blenheim, with flights to/from Wellington, Auckland, Napier and Kaikoura.

Sleeping

As a popular holiday destination for domestic and international travellers alike (these are NZ's sunniest latitudes!), Marlborough delivers a plethora of accommodation options across all budgets. The broadest selection can be found in and around Blenheim in the Marlborough Wine Region, plus pretty little Picton and Kaikoura.

Queen Charlotte Track

One of New Zealand's classic walks — and now one of its Great Rides, too — the meandering, 70km Queen Charlotte Track offers gorgeous coastal scenery through the hushed, tranquil Marlborough Sounds.

Great For...

☑ Don't Miss

Cooling off with a swim in a mirror-flat, isolated cove along the track.

The track runs from historic Ship Cove to Anakiwa, passing through a mixture of privately owned land and DOC reserves. Access depends on the cooperation of local landowners; respect their property by utilising designated campsites and toilets, and carrying out your rubbish. Your purchase of the **Track Pass** ($10 to $18), available from the Picton i-SITE (p166) and track-related businesses, provides the co-op with the means to maintain and enhance the experience for all. The i-SITE also handles bookings for transport and accommodation. See also the Queen Charlotte Track website (www.qc track.co.nz) and the Queen Charlotte Track Land Cooperative website (www.qctlc.com).

Hiking & Biking

Queen Charlotte is a well-defined track, suitable for people of average fitness.

✕ Take a Break

The in-house restaurant at the stylish **Bay of Many Coves Resort** (📞0800 579 9771, 03-579 9771; www.bayofmanycoves.co.nz; Bay of Many Coves; 1-/2-/3-bedroom apt $860/1090/1435; 🛜🏊) is the best QCT eating option.

★ Top Tip

Unless you're camping, book your accommodation *waaay* in advance, especially in summer.

Numerous boat and tour operators service the track, allowing you to tramp the whole three- to five-day journey, or to start and finish where you like, on foot or by kayak or bike. We're talking mountain biking here, and a whole lot of fun for fit, competent off-roaders. Part of the track is off-limits to cyclists from 1 December to the end of February, but there is still good riding to be had during this time.

Ship Cove is the usual (and recommended) starting point – mainly because it's easier to arrange a boat from Picton to Ship Cove than vice versa – but the track can be started from Anakiwa. There's a public phone at Anakiwa but not at Ship Cove.

Sleeping

There are lots of great day-trip options, allowing you to base yourself in Picton.

There's also plenty of accommodation spaced along the way; boat operators will transport your luggage along the track.

There are six DOC campsites, all with toilets and a water supply but no cooking facilities, and a variety of resorts, lodges, backpackers and guesthouses.

Getting There & Away

Picton water taxis can drop you off and pick you up at numerous locations along the track.

Winery in Blenheim (p166)

Marlborough Wine Region

Languidly exploring the wineries of the Marlborough Wine Region is a quintessential NZ experience. Dining among the vines on a sunny southern hemisphere afternoon is also an absolute highlight.

Great For...

ⓘ Need to Know

Pick up a copy of the Marlborough Wine Trail map from Blenheim i-SITE (p169), also available online at www.wine-marlborough.co.nz.

★ **Top Tip**

If you don't have time to visit the wineries, Wino's (p167) in Blenheim stocks some mighty fine local bottles.

Marlborough is NZ's vinous colossus, producing around three-quarters of the country's wine. At last count, there were 244 sq km of vines planted – that's more than 28,000 rugby pitches! Sunny days and cool nights create the perfect conditions for cool-climate grapes: world-famous sauvignon blanc, top-notch pinot noir, and notable chardonnay, riesling, gewürztraminer, pinot gris and bubbly. Drifting between tasting rooms and dining among the vines is a quintessential South Island experience.

Wine Tastings

Around 35 wineries are open to the public. Our picks of the bunch provide a range of high-quality cellar-door experiences, with most being open from around 10.30am till 4.30pm (some scale back operations in winter). Wineries may charge a small fee for tasting, normally refunded if you purchase a bottle.

Framingham (☏03-572 8884; www.framingham.co.nz; 19 Conders Bend Rd, Renwick; ☉10.30am-4.30pm) 🍃

Saint Clair Estate (☏03-570 5280; www.saintclair.co.nz; 13 Selmes Rd, Rapaura; ☉9am-5pm Nov-Apr, 11am-4pm May-Oct)

Yealands Estate (☏03-575 7618; www.yealandsestate.co.nz; cnr Seaview & Reserve Rds, Seddon; ☉10am-4.30pm) 🍃

Te Whare Ra (☏03-572 8581; www.twrwines.co.nz; 56 Anglesea St, Renwick; ☉11am-4pm Mon-Fri Nov–mid-Mar) 🍃

Bladen (☏03-572 9417; www.bladen.co.nz; 83 Conders Bend Rd; ☉11am-4.30pm late Oct-Apr)

Brancott Estate Heritage Centre (☏03-520 6975; www.brancottestate.com; 180 Brancott Rd; ☉10am-4.30pm)

Interior of Cloudy Bay

Clos Henri Vineyard (☏03-572 7293; www. clos-henri.com; 639 State Hwy 63, RD1; ☺10am-4pm Mon-Fri Oct-Apr)

Cloudy Bay (☏03-520 9147; www.cloudybay. co.nz; 230 Jacksons Rd; ☺10am-4pm) ✦

Forrest (☏03-572 9084; www.forrest.co.nz; 19 Blicks Rd; ☺10am-4.30pm)

Huia (☏03-572 8326; www.huiavineyards.com; 22 Boyces Rd; ☺10am-5pm Nov-Mar) ✦

Spy Valley Wines (☏03-572 6207; www. spyvalleywine.co.nz; 37 Lake Timara Rd, Waihopai Valley; ☺10.30am-4.30pm mid-Oct–mid-May, 10.30am-4.30pm Mon-Fri mid-May–mid-Oct) ✦

Vines Village (☏03-579 5424; www.thevines village.co.nz; 193 Rapaura Rd; ☺10am-5pm)

☑ Don't Miss

For some extra pizzazz, don't miss February's Marlborough Wine & Food Festival (p22).

Wairau River (☏03-572 9800; www.wairau riverwines.com; 11 Rapaura Rd; ☺10am-5pm) ✦

Auntsfield Estate (☏03-578 0622; www. auntsfield.co.nz; 270 Paynters Rd; ☺by appoint-ment 11am-4.30pm Mon-Fri late Oct-Easter)

Wining & Dining

With wine there must be food, and here are our recommendations for dining among the vines. Opening hours are for summer, when bookings are recommended.

Arbour (☏03-572 7989; www.arbour.co.nz; 36 Godfrey Rd, Renwick; mains $37-39; ☺5-11pm Tue-Sat Aug-Jun; ☑) ✦

Wairau River Restaurant (☏03-572 9800; www.wairauriverwines.com; cnr Rapaura Rd & SH6, Renwick; mains $21-27; ☺noon-3pm) ✦

Rock Ferry (☏03-579 6431; www.rockferry. co.nz; 130 Hammerichs Rd; mains $25-29; ☺11.30am-3pm) ✦

Wither Hills (☏03-520 8284; www.witherhills. co.nz; 211 New Renwick Rd; mains $27-30, platters $22-24; ☺11am-4pm)

Wine Tours

Wine tours are generally conducted in a minibus (or on a bike!), last between four and seven hours, take in four to seven wineries and range in price from $65 to $95 (with a few grand tours up to around $200 for the day, including a winery lunch). Recommended operators:

Bike2Wine (☏0800 653 262, 03-572 8458; www.bike2wine.co.nz; 9 Wilson St, Renwick; standard/tandem per day $30/60, pick-ups from $10; ☺10am-5.30pm)

Bubbly Grape Wine Tours (☏027 672 2195, 0800 228 2253; www.bubblygrape.co.nz; tours $100-195)

Highlight Wine Tours (☏027 434 6451, 03-577 9046; www.highlightwinetours.co.nz; tours $115-130)

✕ Take a Break

For a fortifying brunch before a wine-soaked afternoon, try Rock Ferry (p167) in Blenheim.

SHARON JONES/ALAMY ©

Wildlife Watching in Kaikoura

Around 129km southeast of Blenheim (or 180km north of Christchurch) is pretty Kaikoura – one of the best places on the planet to spy whales, dolphins, NZ fur seals, penguins, shearwaters, petrels and several species of albatross.

Great For...

☑ Don't Miss

Snorkelling with curious NZ fur seal pups as they swoop and dive around you.

Marine animals are abundant here due to ocean-current and continental-shelf conditions: the seabed gradually slopes away from the land before plunging to more than 800m where the southerly current hits the continental shelf. This creates an upwelling of nutrients from the ocean floor into the feeding zone.

Whale-watching happens by boat, plane or helicopter. Aerial options are shorter and pricier, but allow you to see the whole whale, as opposed to just a tail, flipper or spout.

Whale Watch Kaikoura

Wildlife Watching

(☎0800 655 121, 03-319 6767; www.whalewatch.co.nz; Railway Station; 3½hr tours adult/child $150/60) ⚑ With knowledgeable guides and fascinating on-board animation, Kaikoura's

biggest operator heads out on boat trips in search of the big fellas (success rate 95%).

Albatross Encounter   Birdwatching

(☎03-319 6777, 0800 733 365; www.encounter kaikoura.co.nz; 96 Esplanade; adult/child $125/60; ⊙tours 9am & 1pm year-round, plus 6am Nov-Apr) ✐ A close encounter with various albatross species, plus shearwaters, shags, mollymawks and petrels.

Dolphin Encounter   Ecotour

(☎03-319 6777, 0800 733 365; www.encounter kaikoura.co.nz; 96 Esplanade; swim adult/child $175/160, observation $95/50; ⊙tours 8.30am & 12.30pm year-round, plus 5.30am Nov-Apr) ✐ Claiming NZ's highest success rate (90%) for both locating and swimming with dolphins, this operator runs feel-good three-hour tours.

Seal Swim Kaikoura   Ecotour

(☎03-319 6182, 0800 732 579; www.sealswim kaikoura.co.nz; 58 West End; adult/child $110/70, viewing $55/35; ⊙Oct-May) ✐ Take a (warmly wet-suited) swim with Kaikoura's playful seals on two-hour guided snorkelling tours (by boat).

Wings over Whales   Scenic Flights

(☎03-319 6580, 0800 226 629; www.whales. co.nz; 30min flights adult/child $180/75) Light-plane flights departing from Kaikoura Airport, 8km south of town on SH1. Spotting success rate: 95%.

South Pacific Whale Watch   Whale Watching

(☎0800 360 886; www.southpacificwhales. co.nz; 72 West End; per person $350-650) Offers a wide range of whale-watching and flight-seeing trips by helicopter.

Picton

Boaty Picton clusters around a deep gulch at the head of Queen Charlotte Sound. It's the main traveller port for the South Island, and the best base for tackling the Marlborough Sounds and Queen Charlotte Track.

◎ SIGHTS

Edwin Fox
Maritime Museum   Museum
(☏03-573 6868; www.edwinfoxsociety.co.nz; Dunbar Wharf; adult/child $15/5; ☺9am-5pm) Purportedly the world's ninth-oldest surviving wooden ship, the *Edwin Fox* was built near Calcutta and launched in 1853. This museum has maritime exhibits, including this venerable old dear.

✪ ACTIVITIES

A free i-SITE map details local walks, including an easy 1km track to **Bob's Bay**. The **Snout Track** (three hours return) continues along the ridge offering superb water views. Climbing a hill behind the town, the **Tirohanga Track** is a two-hour leg-stretching loop offering the best view in the house.

⊙ TOURS

Wilderness Guides   Tours
(☏0800 266 266, 03-573 5432; www.wilderness guidesnz.com; Town Wharf; 1-day guided trips from $130, kayak/bike hire per day $60) Host of the popular and flexible one- to three-day 'multisport' trips (kayak/walk/cycle) plus many other guided and independent biking, tramping and kayaking tours. Mountain bikes and kayaks for hire, too.

Cougar Line   Tours
(☏03-573 7925, 0800 504 090; www.cougarline. co.nz; Town Wharf; track round trips $105, cruises from $85) Queen Charlotte Track transport, plus various half- and full-day cruise/walk trips, including the rather special (and flexible) eco-cruise to Motuara Island (p169) and a day walk from Resolution Bay to Furneaux Lodge.

Sea Kayak
Adventures   Kayaking, Biking
(☏03-574 2765, 0800 262 5492; www.nzseakay aking.com; cnr Queen Charlotte Dr & Anakiwa Rd; half-/1-day guided paddles $90/125) Guided and 'guided then go' kayaking with bike/hike options around Queen Charlotte, Kenepuru and Pelorus Sounds. Also offers kayak and mountain-bike rental (half/full day $40/60).

Beachcomber Cruises   Tours
(☏03-573 6175, 0800 624 526; www.beach combercruises.co.nz; Town Wharf; mail runs $101, cruises from $85, track round trips $103) Two- to eight-hour cruise adventures, including the classic 'Magic Mail Run', plus walking, biking and resort lunch options and round-trip track transport.

Marlborough Sounds
Adventure Company   Tours
(☏03-573 6078, 0800 283 283; www.marlbo roughsounds.co.nz; Town Wharf; half-/5-day guided packages $95/2420, kayak hire per half day from $40) Bike-walk-kayak trips, with options to suit every inclination and interest. Bikes, kayaks and camping equipment are also available for rent. The popular Kayak & Hike option combines one day of kayaking, one day of walking and an overnight stay in the Sounds.

Escape to Marlborough   Tours
(☏0800 6937 2273; www.escapetomarlborough. co.nz; adult/child $69.50/15.50; ☺8am-6pm) Hop-on, hop-off bus services running at hourly intervals and linking Picton and Blenheim, stopping at 18 key attractions, vineyards and breweries. There are two routes, both taking eight hours in full, and it's possible to change onto the other service en route.

✪ EATING

Picton Village Bakkerij   Bakery $
(☏03-573 7082; www.facebook.com/Picton VillageBakery; cnr Auckland & Dublin Sts; bakery items $2-8; ☺6am-4pm Mon-Fri, to 3.30pm Sat; ☑) Dutch owners bake trays of European goodies here, including interesting breads,

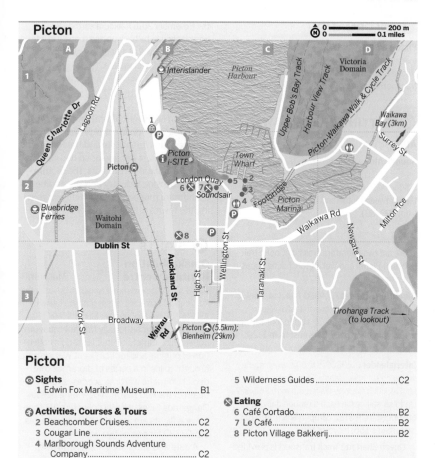

Picton

Sights
1 Edwin Fox Maritime Museum...................B1

Activities, Courses & Tours
2 Beachcomber Cruises...............................C2
3 Cougar Line C2
4 Marlborough Sounds Adventure
    Company..C2

5 Wilderness Guides C2

Eating
6 Café Cortado...B2
7 Le Café..B2
8 Picton Village Bakkerij.............................B2

filled rolls, cakes and custardy, tarty treats. The savoury pies are very good – ask if the chicken, chilli and cream cheese one is available (trust us, it's a winning combo).

Le Café
Cafe $$

(☑03-573 5588; www.lecafepicton.co.nz; London Quay; breakfast & lunch $14-25, dinner $24-30; ⊙7.30am-8pm Sun-Thu, to late Fri & Sat; ☑) A spot perennially popular for its quayside location, dependable food and Havana coffee. A good antipasto platter, generous pasta dishes, local mussels, and lamb and fish dishes feature à la carte. The laid-back

atmosphere, craft beer and occasional live gigs make this a good evening hang-out.

Café Cortado
Cafe $$

(☑03-573 5630; www.cafecortado.co.nz; cnr High St & London Quay; mains $17-35; ⊙8am-late Nov-Apr, 8am-late Wed-Sun May-Oct) Pleasant corner cafe and bar with views of the harbour through the foreshore's pohutukawa and palms. There's a surprisingly eclectic selection of local Marlborough wines and a few craft beers on tap. Kick off with the breakfast burrito and come back for a dinner of beer-battered blue cod.

ℹ️ INFORMATION

Picton i-SITE (📱03-520 3113; www.marlbor oughnz.com; foreshore; ⏰8am-5pm) **Maps, Queen Charlotte Track information, lockers and transport bookings. Dedicated DOC counter.**

ℹ️ GETTING THERE & AWAY

AIR

Sounds Air (📱0800 505 005, 03-520 3080; www.soundsair.co.nz; 10 London Quay; ⏰7.30am-5.30pm Mon-Thu & Sat, to 7pm Fri, 9am-7pm Sun) flies between Picton and Wellington (adult/child from $99/89).

BOAT

There are two operators crossing Cook Strait between Picton and Wellington, taking about three hours.

Bluebridge Ferries (📱0800 844 844, 04-471 6188; www.bluebridge.co.nz; adult/child to Wellington from $53/27; 📶) **Up to four sailings in each direction daily. Cars cost from $120; campervans from $155.**

Interislander (📱0800 802 802; www.interis lander.co.nz; Interislander Ferry Terminal, Auckland St; adult/child to Wellington from $52/32) Up to six sailings in each direction daily. Cars are priced from $121; campervans from $153; motorbikes $56; bicycles $15.

Queen Charlotte Track transport is provided by Picton's water taxis.

BUS

Buses for Christchurch, Blenheim, Kaikoura, Dunedin, Queenstown and beyond leave from from the Interislander ferry terminal or the i-SITE.

Escape to Marlborough (p164) runs hourly services linking Picton to Blenheim ($12.50) and Blenheim airport ($17.50).

TRAIN

KiwiRail Scenic (📱0800 872 467; www. greatjourneysofnz.co.nz) runs the *Coastal Pacific* between Picton and Christchurch via Blenheim and Kaikoura connecting with the Interislander ferry. Note this service was suspended following

the November 2016 Kaikoura earthquake, but was planned to be back up and running in late 2018. Check KiwiRail's website (www.kiwirail. co.nz) for the latest update.

Blenheim

Blenheim is an agricultural town 29km south of Picton on the pretty Wairau Plains between the Wither Hills and the Richmond Ranges. The last decade or so has seen town beautification projects, the maturation of the wine industry and the addition of a landmark museum, significantly increasing the town's appeal to visitors.

◎ SIGHTS

Omaka Aviation Heritage Centre   Museum

(📱03-579 1305; www.omaka.org.nz; 79 Aerodrome Rd, Omaka; adult/child/family both exhibitions $30/16/99; ⏰9am-5pm Dec-Mar, 10am-5pm Apr-Nov) This exceptionally brilliant museum houses film-director Peter Jackson's collection of original and replica Great War aircraft, brought to life in a series of dioramas that depict dramatic wartime scenes, such as the death of the Red Baron. A new wing houses Dangerous Skies, a WWII collection. Vintage biplane flights are available (10/20 minutes, $250/380 for one or two people).

A cafe and shop are on-site, and next door is **Omaka Classic Cars** (📱03-577 9419; www.omakaclassiccars.co.nz; Aerodrome Rd, Omaka; adult/child $15/free; ⏰10am-4pm), which houses more than 100 vehicles dating from the '50s to the '80s.

⚙️ ACTIVITIES

Driftwood Eco-Tours   Kayaking, Ecotour

(📱03-577 7651; www.driftwoodecotours.co.nz; 749 Dillons Point Rd; kayak & 4WD tours $200) Go on a kayak or 4WD tour for fascinating natural history on and around the ecologically and historically significant Wairau Lagoon, 10 minutes' drive from Blenheim. Rare birds and the muppetty royal spoonbill may well be spotted.

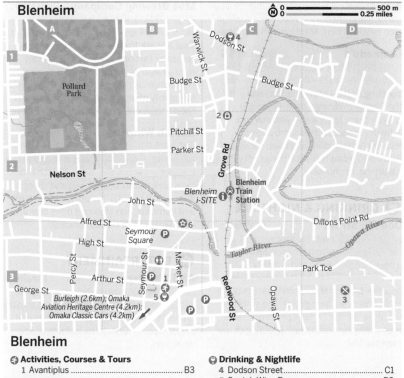

Blenheim

Activities, Courses & Tours
1 Avantiplus B3

Shopping
2 Wino's C2

Eating
3 Gramado's D3

Drinking & Nightlife
4 Dodson Street C1
5 Scotch Wine Bar B3

Entertainment
6 ASB Theatre B3

🛍 SHOPPING

Wino's   Wine

(☎03-578 4196; www.winos.co.nz; 49 Grove Rd;
⏰10am-7pm Sun-Thu, to 8pm Fri & Sat) If your
time is limited, pop into Wino's, a sterling
one-stop shop for some of Marlborough's
finer and less common drops.

🍴 EATING

Burleigh   Deli $

(☎03-579 2531; www.facebook.com/the
burleighnz; 72 New Renwick Rd; pies $6;
⏰7.30am-3pm Mon-Fri, 9am-1pm Sat) The
humble pie rises to stratospheric heights
at this fabulous deli; try the sweet pork
belly or savoury steak and blue cheese, or
perhaps both. Fresh-filled baguettes, local
sausage, French cheeses and great coffee
also make tempting appearances. Avoid the
lunchtime rush.

Rock Ferry   Cafe $$

(☎03-579 6431; www.rockferry.co.nz; 130
Hammerichs Rd; mains $25-29; ⏰11.30am-3pm)
🌿 Pleasant environment inside and out,
with a slightly groovy edge. The compact
summery menu – think miso-marinated
salmon with an Asian slaw or the organic

open steak sandwich topped with a creamy spinach and anchovy spread – is accompanied by wines from Marlborough and Otago.

Gramado's   Brazilian $$

(☏03-579 1192; www.gramadosrestaurant.com; 74 Main St; mains $28-40; ⊙4pm-late Tue-Sat) Injecting a little Latin American flair into the Blenheim dining scene, Gramado's is a fun place to tuck into unashamedly hearty meals such as lamb *assado*, *feijoada* (smoky pork and bean stew) and Brazilian-spiced fish. Kick things off with a caipirinha, of course.

🍷 DRINKING & NIGHTLIFE

Dodson Street   Craft Beer

(☏03-577 8348; www.dodsonstreet.co.nz; 1 Dodson St; ⊙11am-11pm) Pub and garden with a beer-hall ambience and suitably Teutonic menu (mains $17 to $27) featuring pork knuckle, bratwurst and schnitzel (its pizza and burgers are also good). The stars of the show are the 24 taps pouring quality, ever-changing craft beers. A tasting of five brews is $10.

Moa Brewing Company   Craft Beer

(☏03-572 5146; www.moabeer.com; 258 Jacksons Rd, Rapaura; tastings $8; ⊙11am-5pm) Take a break from wine tasting at Moa's laid-back tasting room amid Rapaura's rural vineyards. You won't find any giant flightless moa roaming around, but there's still plenty of other bird life in the gardens. Food trucks often rock up Friday to Sunday.

Scotch Wine Bar   Wine Bar

(☏03-579 1176; www.scotchbar.co.nz; 24-26 Maxwell Rd; ⊙4pm-late) A versatile and sociable spot in central Blenheim, Scotch offers local wines, craft beer on tap and shared plates ($18 to $30), including spiced lamb and hummus, and steamed buns crammed with Japanese-style fried chicken.

🎭 ENTERTAINMENT

ASB Theatre   Theatre

(☏03-520 8558; www.asbtheatre.com; 42a Alfred St) Opened in 2016, this modern theatre presents a wide program of concerts and performances. Check the website to see what's on.

Death of the Red Baron at Omaka Aviation Heritage Centre (p166)

PARK DALE/ALAMY ©

INFORMATION

Blenheim i-SITE (☎03-577 8080; www.marl boroughnz.com; Railway Station, 8 Sinclair St; ⊙9am-5pm Mon-Fri, to 3pm Sat, 10am-3pm Sun) Wine-trail maps and bookings for everything under the sun.

GETTING THERE & AWAY

AIR

Marlborough Airport (www.marlboroughairport. co.nz; Tancred Cres, Woodbourne) is 6km west of town.

Air New Zealand (☎0800 747 000; www.air newzealand.co.nz) flies to/from Wellington and Auckland. Sounds Air (p166) flies to Wellington, Napier and Kaikoura.

BUS

InterCity (☎03-365 1113; www.intercity.co.nz) and **Naked Bus** (☎0900 625 33; https://naked bus.com) services for places across the South Island depart Blenheim i-SITE.

TRAIN

KiwiRail Scenic (p166) runs the *Coastal Pacific*, stopping at Blenheim on its Picton–Christchurch run. Closed for earthquake repairs after 2016; check the website for updates.

 Motuara Island

Bird nerd? This DOC-managed, predator-free **island** (www.doc.govt.nz; Queen Charlotte Sound) 🏃 reserve is chock-full of rare NZ birds including Okarito kiwi (rowi), native pigeons (kereru), saddleback (tieke) and king shags. You can get here by water taxi and with tour operators working out of Picton.

Saddleback (tieke)
CMH IMAGES/ALAMY ©

GETTING AROUND

Avantiplus (☎03-578 0433; www.bikemarlbor ough.co.nz; 61 Queen St; hire per half/full day from $25/40; ⊙8am-5.30pm Mon-Fri, 10am-2pm Sat) and Bike2Wine (p161) rent bikes.

Marlborough Taxis (☎03-577 5511) Four-wheeled winery rescue.

Abel Tasman National Park

Sea kayaking, boating and tramping are the best ways to experience the beautiful beaches and forested coves of this national park on the South Island's northwestern tip.

Great For...

ℹ Need to Know

See www.doc.govt.nz/abeltasmantrack for detailed Abel Tasman Coast Track planning information.

★ **Top Tip**

Tour companies usually offer free Motueka pick-up/drop-off, with Nelson pick-up available at extra cost.

Abel Tasman Coast Track

This is arguably NZ's most beautiful Great Walk – 60km of sparkling seas, golden sand, quintessential coastal forest and hidden surprises such as Cleopatra's Pool. Such pulling power attracts around 30,000 overnight trampers and kayakers per year. Across easy terrain, it's almost impossible to get lost here and you can hike the track in sneakers.

The Route

You will, however, probably get your feet wet, as this track features long stretches of beach and crazy tides. In fact, the tidal differences in the park are among the greatest in the country, up to a staggering 6m. At Torrent and Bark Bays, it's much easier and more fun to cross the soggy sands, rather than take the high-tide track. At Awaroa Bay you have no choice but to plan on crossing close to low tide. Tide tables are posted along the track and on the DOC website; regional i-SITEs also have them.

The entire tramp takes three to five days, although with water taxi transport you can tackle it in myriad ways, particularly if you combine it with a kayak leg. A rewarding short option (beaches, seals, coastal scenery) is to loop through the northern end of the park, hiking the Coast Track from Totaranui, passing Anapai Bay and Mutton Cove, overnighting at Whariwharangi Hut, then returning to Totaranui via the Gibbs Hill Track.

Bookings

The track operates on DOC's Great Walks Pass. Book online (www.doc.govt.nz), contact the **Nelson Marlborough Book-**

ings Helpdesk (☑03-546 8210), or book in person at the Nelson, Motueka or Takaka i-SITES or DOC offices, where staff can offer suggestions to tailor the track to your needs and organise transport at each end. Book well in advance, especially between December and March.

Accommodation

Along the Abel Tasman Coast Track are four Great Walk huts ($38) with bunks, heating, flush toilets and limited lighting, but no cooking facilities. There are also 19 designated Great Walk campsites ($14). An interesting alternative is **Aquapackers** (☑0800 430 744; www.aquapackers.co.nz;

Anchorage; dm/d $85/245; ⊘closed May-Sep), a catamaran moored permanently in Anchorage Bay.

Paddling the Abel Tasman

The Abel Tasman Coast Track has long been tramping territory, but its coastal beauty makes it an equally seductive spot for sea kayaking, which can easily be combined with walking and camping. Options include either guided tours or freedom trips. Recommended operators (shop around):

Kahu Kayaks (☑0800 300 101, 03-527 8300; www.kahukayaks.co.nz; 11 Marahau Valley Rd; self-guided/guided tours from $75/215)

R&R Kayaks (☑0508 223 224; www.rrkayaks. co.nz; 279 Sandy Bay-Marahau Rd; tours from $135)

Tasman Bay Sea Kayaking (☑0800 827 525; www.tasmanbayseakayaking.co.nz; Harvey Rd, Marahau; tours from $110)

Wilsons Abel Tasman (☑03-528 2027, 0800 223 582; www.abeltasman.co.nz; 409 High St, Motueka; walk/kayak from $62/90)

Getting There & Around

The closest big town to Abel Tasman is Motueka. Marahau is the southern gateway; Totaranui is the usual finishing point. **Abel Tasman Coachlines** (☑03-548 0285; www.abeltasmantravel.co.nz) and/or **Golden Bay Coachlines** (☑03-525 8352; www.gb coachlines.co.nz) service these towns.

Water taxis can shunt you to/from any point on the track. Operators include **Abel Tasman Aqua Taxi** (☑03-527 8083, 0800 278 282; www.aquataxi.co.nz; Marahau-Sandy Bay Rd, Marahau) and **Marahau Water Taxis** (☑03-527 8176, 0800 808 018; www.marahauwater taxis.co.nz; Abel Tasman Centre, Franklin St, Marahau).

☑ Don't Miss

A swim at one golden-sand bay along the Coast Track, regardless of season.

JIRI FOLTYN/SHUTTERSTOCK ©

✕ Take a Break

Food is available at Marahau and Kaiteriteri; within the park it's self-catering all the way.

CHRISTCHURCH

Christchurch at a Glance...

Nowhere in New Zealand is changing and developing as fast as post-quake Christchurch. The scaffolding is coming down, the hospitality scene is flourishing and the central city is once again drawing visitors to its pedestrian-friendly streets. Cranes and road cones will be part of the Christchurch landscape for a while yet, but don't be deterred; exciting new buildings are opening at an astonishing pace. Curious travellers will revel in this chaotic, crazy and colourful mix, full of surprises and inspiring in ways you can't even imagine.

Christchurch in Two Days

After breakfast at **Supreme Supreme** (p187), visit **Quake City** (p179) and wander through **Cathedral Square** (p183), at the heart of rebuilding efforts. Visit **Christchurch Art Gallery** (p182) then explore the Victoria St restaurant strip.

Start day two at **Addington Coffee Co-op** (p187) and then head up Mt Cavendish on the **gondola** (p182) for views and a walk at the top. **Smash Palace** (p188) awaits for beers and burgers.

Christchurch in Four Days

Gather picnic supplies at **Canterbury Cheesemongers** (p187) and head to the lovely **Botanic Gardens** (p182). After lunch, visit the excellent **Canterbury Museum** (p182), before dinner at **Twenty Seven Steps** (p187).

On day four, soak up the nautical vibes in soulful **Lyttelton** (p180), Christchurch's port town, before finishing with dinner and drinks at **Pomeroy's Old Brewery Inn** (p188).

Christchurch Map (p184)

Arriving in Christchurch

Christchurch Airport Located 10km from the city centre. A taxi into town costs $45 to $65. Public buses (www.metroinfo.co.nz) also run to the airport ($8.50, 7am to 11pm). Shuttle services cost around $25 per person.

Bus Interchange (p189) Local and some long-distance services depart from the inner-city Bus Interchange on the corner of Lichfield and Colombo Sts.

Sleeping

Sleepy? Christchurch has a wide variety of accommodation available, from luxury hotels to a plethora of backpacker beds. As the city's rebuild progresses, more and more beds are becoming available in the city centre and its inner fringes. Merivale, Riccarton and around Colombo St offer good motels, while the heritage suburb of Fendalton has boutique B&Bs.

HEMIS/ALAMY ©

Post-Quake Christchurch

Resilience and creativity have defined the people of Christchurch since the lethal 6.3-magnitude 2011 earthquake, and while the planned rebuild slowly progresses, quirky initiatives are also inspiring NZ's second biggest city.

Great For...

☑ Don't Miss

Hearing harrowing earthquake survival stories at Quake City.

Following the Christchurch earthquake of 22 February 2011, diverse creativity and DIY entrepreneurship have emerged as the city works through the painstaking process of a 20-year rebuild that's been estimated to cost up to $50 billion. Around 80% of the buildings within the city centre's famed four avenues have been or are due to be demolished. Amid the doomed, the saved and the shiny new builds are countless construction sites and empty plots still strewn with rubble...but a compact new low-rise city centre with parks and cycleways along the Avon River is slowly taking shape. Meanwhile, locals are getting on with making the city a more interesting and rewarding place to live.

Quake City

A must-visit for anyone interested in understanding the impact of the Canterbury

Transitional Cathedral interior

❶ Need to Know

See www.rebuildchristchurch.co.nz for an independent point of view on the progress of the city's rebuild.

✖ Take a Break

Much more than just a food hall, Little High Eatery (p187) is a stylish pan-planet eating option.

★ Top Tip

See www.neatplaces.co.nz to find out about newly opened shops, bars and restaurants in ever-changing Christchurch.

city's temporary Anglican cathedral and as a concert venue. Designed by Japanese 'disaster architect' Shigeru Ban, the entire building was constructed in 11 months.

Gap Filler

Starting from the ground up after the earthquakes, the Gap Filler folks fill the city's empty spaces with creativity and colour. Projects range from temporary art installations, performance spaces and gardens, to a minigolf course scattered through empty building sites, to the world's first giant outdoor arcade game. Gaps open up and get filled, so check out the Gap Map on the website (www.gapfiller.org.nz), or simply wander the streets and see what you can find.

earthquakes, compact museum **Quake City** (☎03-366 5000; www.quakecity.co.nz; 299 Durham St N; adult $20, child accompanied/unaccompanied free/$8; ⏰10am-5pm) tells stories through photography, video footage and various artefacts, including the remnants of ChristChurch Cathedral's celebrated rose window and other similarly moving debris. There are exhibits aimed at engaging both adults and children. Most affecting of all is the film featuring survivors recounting their own experiences.

Transitional Cathedral

Universally known as the **Cardboard Cathedral** (www.cardboardcathedral.org.nz; 234 Hereford St; entry by donation; ⏰9am-5pm Apr-Oct, to 7pm Nov-Mar) due to the 98 cardboard tubes used in its construction, this interesting structure serves as both the

GREG BALFOUR EVANS/ALAMY ©

Lyttelton

Christchurch's port, little Lyttelton is a raffish, artsy harbour town – like Fremantle in Western Australia or Valparaiso in Chile – where the world washes in on the tide and washes out again, leaving the locals buzzing with global zeitgeist. It's a funky enclave with sea-salty soul to burn.

Great For...

☑ **Don't Miss**

A visit on Saturday morning when the farmers market is buzzing.

Christchurch's first European settlers landed at Lyttelton in 1850 to embark on their historic trek over the hills. These days a 2km road tunnel makes the journey considerably quicker.

Lyttelton was badly damaged during the 2010 and 2011 earthquakes, and sadly, many of the town's heritage buildings along London St were subsequently demolished. Today, however, Lyttelton has re-emerged as one of Christchurch's most interesting communities. The town's arty, independent and bohemian vibe is stronger than ever, and it is once again a hub for great bars, cafes and shops. It's well worth catching the bus from Christchurch and getting immersed in the local scene.

Lyttelton Farmers Market

ⓘ Need to Know

Contact the **Lyttelton Visitor Information Centre** (☎03-328 9093; www.lyttelton harbour.info; 20 Oxford St; ⊙10am-4pm) for the local low-down.

✕ Take a Break

Rootsy Roots is king of the Lyttelton dining scene. Book ahead.

★ Top Tip

Nowhere expresses Lyttelton's bohemian soul better than Wunderbar – mandatory drinking.

food in its cavernous, exposed-brick warehouse space.

Eating & Drinking

Lyttelton Farmers Market
Market $

(www.lyttelton.net.nz; London St; ⊙10am-1pm Sat) Every Saturday morning food stalls take the place of cars on Lyttelton's main street. Stock up alongside locals on fresh bread, baked goods, flowers, cheeses, local produce and good coffee.

Lyttelton Coffee Company
Cafe $$

(☎03-328 8096; www.lytteltoncoffee.co.nz; 29 London St; mains $12-20; ⊙7am-4pm Mon-Fri, 8am-4pm Sat & Sun; ⚲🚼) Local institution Lyttelton Coffee Company has risen from the rubble and continues its role as a stalwart of the London St foodie scene, serving consistently great coffee and wholesome

Roots
Modern NZ $$$

(☎03-328 7658; www.rootsrestaurant.co.nz; 8 London St; 5-/8-/12-course degustation $90/125/185, incl wine $140/205/305; ⊙6-11pm Tue-Sat, plus noon-2pm Fri & Sat) ⚲ Let chef-owner Giulio Sturla take you on a magical tasting tour with his renowned degustation menus, which champion all things local and seasonal. Dishes can also be accompanied by carefully paired wines, should you choose to splurge. Reserve ahead.

Wunderbar
Bar

(☎03-328 8818; www.wunderbar.co.nz; 19 London St; ⊙5pm-late Mon-Fri, 1pm-3am Sat & Sun) Wunderbar is a top spot to get down, with regular live music covering all spectra, and clientele to match. The kooky decor and decapitated dolls' heads alone are worth the trip. Enter via the stairs in the rear car park.

◉ SIGHTS

Christchurch Art Gallery   Gallery
(Te Puna o Waiwhetu; ☏03-941 7300; www.
christchurchartgallery.org.nz; cnr Montreal St &
Worcester Blvd; ⊙10am-5pm Thu-Tue, to 9pm
Wed; P) **FREE** Damaged in the earthquakes,
Christchurch's fantastic art gallery has
reopened brighter and bolder, presenting
a stimulating mix of local and international
exhibitions. Collection items range from the
traditional to the startlingly contemporary.
Free guided tours (one hour) happen at
11am and 2pm daily.

Botanic Gardens   Gardens
(www.ccc.govt.nz; Rolleston Ave; ⊙7am-9pm
Nov-Feb, to 8.30pm Oct & Mar, to 6.30pm Apr-
Sep) **FREE** Gorgeous at any time of the year,
these gardens are particularly impressive
in spring when the rhododendrons, azaleas
and daffodil woodland are in riotous bloom.
The **Botanic Gardens Visitor Centre**
(☏03-941 7590; ⊙9am-4pm) also contains a
lovely **cafe** and gift shop.

Guided walks ($10, 1½ hours) depart at
1.30pm (October to May).

Canterbury Museum   Museum
(☏03-366 5000; www.canterburymuseum.com;
Rolleston Ave; ⊙9am-5.30pm Oct-Mar, to 5pm
Apr-Sep; ⓜ) **FREE** Yes, there's a mummy and
dinosaur bones, but the highlights of this
museum are more local and more recent.
The Māori galleries contain some beautiful
pounamu (greenstone) pieces, while
Christchurch Street is an atmospheric walk
through the colonial past. Free guided tours
(one hour) depart from the foyer at 3.30pm
on Tuesdays and Thursdays.

Canterbury Earthquake
National Memorial   Memorial
(Oi Manawa; www.canterburyearthquakememo
rial.co.nz; Oxford Tce) Unveiled in 2017, this
moving monument comprises a 100m-long
memorial wall, curved along the south bank
of the Avon and engraved with the names
of the 185 people who died as a result of
the 2011 earthquake.

Christchurch Gondola   Cable Car
(www.welcomeaboard.co.nz/gondola; 10 Bridle
Path Rd; return adult/child $28/12; ⊙10am-5pm;
P) Take a ride to the top of Mt Cavendish

Botanic Gardens

HO SU A BV/SHUTTERSTOCK ©

(500m) on this 862m cable car for wonderful views over the city, Lyttelton, the Banks Peninsula and the Canterbury Plains.

Cathedral Square   Square

Christchurch's city square stands at the heart of the rebuilding efforts, with the remains of ChristChurch Cathedral emblematic of what has been lost. The February 2011 earthquake brought down the 63m-high spire, while subsequent earthquakes in June 2011 and December 2011 destroyed the prized stained-glass rose window. Other heritage buildings around the square were also badly damaged, but one modern landmark left unscathed is the 18m-high metal sculpture *Chalice,* designed by Neil Dawson. It was erected in 2001 to commemorate the new millennium.

The much-loved Gothic cathedral has been at the centre of a battle between those who seek to preserve what remains of Christchurch's heritage, the fiscal pragmatists, and those ideologically inclined to things new. In 2012 the Anglican Diocese announced that the cathedral was to be demolished, but work was stayed when heritage advocates launched court proceedings. Eventually, in September 2017, the church leadership voted to preserve the building after the government and Christchurch City Council banded together to offer significant financial support. It's thought that the rebuild could take up to 10 years, with an estimated cost of $104 million.

Hagley Park   Park

(Riccarton Ave) Wrapped around the Botanic Gardens, Hagley Park is Christchurch's biggest green space, stretching for 165 hectares. Riccarton Ave splits it in two, while the Avon River snakes through the northern half. It's a great place to stroll, whether on a foggy autumn morning, or a warm spring day when the cherry trees lining Harper Ave are in flower. Joggers make the most of the tree-lined avenues year-round.

Arts Centre   Historic Building

(www.artscentre.org.nz; 2 Worcester Blvd; ☾10am-5pm) **FREE** Dating from 1877, this

 The Christchurch Earthquakes

Christchurch's seismic nightmare began at 4.35am on 4 September 2010. Centred 40km west of the city, a 40-second, 7.1-magnitude earthquake caused widespread damage to older buildings in the central city. There were no fatalities, and many Christchurch residents felt that the city had dodged a bullet.

Fast forward to 12.51pm on 22 February 2011, when central Christchurch was busy with shoppers and workers enjoying their lunch break. This time the 6.3-magnitude quake was much closer, centred just 10km southeast of the city and only 5km deep. The tremor was significantly greater, and many locals report being flung violently and almost vertically into the air.

When the dust settled after 24 traumatic seconds, NZ's second-largest city had changed forever. The towering spire of the iconic ChristChurch Cathedral lay in ruins; walls and verandas had cascaded down on shopping strips; and two multistorey buildings had pancaked. Elsewhere, the historic port town of Lyttelton was badly damaged; roads and bridges were crumpled; and residential suburbs in the east were inundated by oozy silt.

The earthquakes resulted in 185 deaths across 20 nationalities.

Ruined ChristChurch Cathedral
ELENA YAKUSHEVA/SHUTTERSTOCK ©

enclave of Gothic Revival buildings was originally Canterbury College, the forerunner of Canterbury University. The buildings are

Christchurch

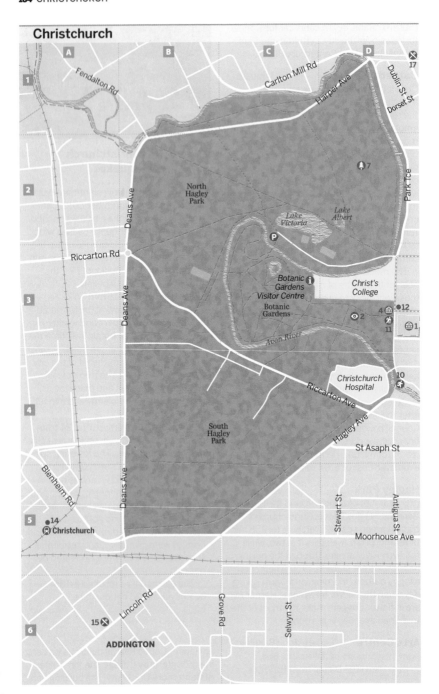

Christchurch

slowly reopening to the public after extensive restoration work due to quake damage, with the entire site due to reopen by 2019. Inside you'll find an array of shops, cafes and museums and galleries, as well as the i-SITE (p189). Exhibition spaces play host to regular concerts, markets and events.

International Antarctic Centre   Museum

(☎0508 736 4846, 03-357 0519; www.iceberg. co.nz; Christchurch Airport, 38 Orchard Rd; adult/child $39/19; ⊗9am-5.30pm; P) As one of only five 'gateway cities' to Antarctica, Christchurch has played a special role in Antarctic exploration since expeditionary ships to the icy continent began departing from Lyttelton in the early 1900s. This huge complex, built for the administration of the NZ, US and Italian Antarctic programs, gives visitors the opportunity to learn about Antarctica in a fun, interactive environment.

Attractions include the Antarctic Storm chamber (where you can get a taste of -18°C wind chill), face-to-face encounters with resident little blue penguins, and a meet-and-greet with rescue huskies (Friday to Sunday only). The 'Xtreme Pass' (adult/child $59/29) includes the '4D theatre' (a 3D film with moving seats and a water spray) and a joyride on a Hägglund all-terrain amphibious Antarctic vehicle. An optional extra is the Penguin Backstage Tour (adult/child $25/15), which allows visitors behind the scenes of the Penguin Encounter.

A free shuttle to the centre departs from outside Canterbury Museum (p182) at 9am, 11am, 1pm and 3pm, returning at 10am, noon, 2pm and 4pm.

◎ ACTIVITIES

Tram   Tram

(☎03-366 7830; www.welcomeaboard.co.nz; adult/child $25/free; ⊗9am-6pm Sep-Mar, 10am-5pm Apr-Aug) Excellent driver commentary makes this so much more than just a tram ride. The beautifully restored old dears trundle around a 17-stop loop, departing every 15 minutes, taking in a host of city highlights. A circuit takes an hour; hop on and off all day.

Punting on the Avon   Boating

(www.punting.co.nz; 2 Cambridge Tce; adult/child $28/12; ⊗9am-6pm Oct-Mar, 10am-4pm

Apr-Sep) 🚣 If rowing your own boat down the Avon sounds a bit too much like hard work, why not relax in a flat-bottomed punt while a strapping lad in Edwardian clobber glides you peaceably through the Botanic Gardens. Tours depart year-round from the **Antigua Boat Sheds** (📞03-366 5885; www. boatsheds.co.nz; 2 Cambridge Tce; ⊙9am-5pm).

🏛 TOURS

Guided City Walks
Walking

(📞0800 423 783; www.walkchristchurch.nz; Rolleston Ave; adult/child $20/free; ⊙10.30am & 1pm) Departing from the red kiosk outside Canterbury Museum, these 2½-hour tours offer a leisurely stroll around the city's main sights in the company of knowledgeable guides.

Hassle Free Tours
Bus

(📞03-385 5775; www.hasslefree.co.nz) Explore Christchurch in an open-top double-decker bus on a one-hour highlights tour ($35) or three-hour discovery tour ($69).

🛍 SHOPPING

Tannery
Shopping Centre

(www.thetannery.co.nz; 3 Garlands Rd, Woolston; ⊙10am-5pm) In a city mourning the loss of its heritage, this post-earthquake conversion of a 19th-century tannery couldn't be more welcome. The Victorian buildings have been beautifully restored, and are crammed with all manner of delightful boutiques.

New Regent St
Mall

(www.newregentstreet.co.nz) This pretty little stretch of pastel Spanish Mission–style shops was described as NZ's most beautiful street when it was completed in 1932. Fully restored post-earthquake, it's once again a delightful place to stroll and shop.

🍴 EATING

Supreme Supreme
Cafe $

(📞03-365 0445; www.supremesupreme.co.nz; 10 Welles St; mains breakfast $7-20, lunch $12-

22; ⊙7am-3pm Mon-Fri, 8am-3pm Sat & Sun; 🖥) With so much to love, where to start? Perhaps with a cherry and pomegranate smoothie, a chocolate-fish milkshake or maybe just an exceptional espresso, alongside a fresh bagel, a goji bowl or even pulled corn-beef hash. One of NZ's original and best coffee roasters comes to the party with a right-now cafe of splendid style, form and function.

Addington Coffee Co-op
Cafe $

(📞03-943 1662; www.addingtoncoffee.org. nz; 297 Lincoln Rd, Addington; meals $7-22; ⊙7.30am-4pm Mon-Fri, from 9am Sat & Sun; 🛜🖥) You will find one of Christchurch's biggest and best cafes packed to the rafters most days. A compact shop selling fair-trade gifts jostles for attention with delicious cakes, gourmet pies, legendary breakfasts (until 2pm) and, of course, excellent coffee. An on-site launderette completes the deal for busy travellers.

Canterbury Cheesemongers
Deli $

(📞03-379 0075; www.cheesemongers.co.nz; rear, 301 Montreal St; ⊙9am-5pm Tue-Fri, to 4pm Sat) Pop in to gather up artisanal cheese, bread and accompaniments, such as pickles and smoked salmon, then get your espresso to go and head down the road to the Botanic Gardens for the perfect picnic lunch.

Little High Eatery
Food Hall $$

(www.littlehigh.co.nz; 255 St Asaph St; dishes $5-20; ⊙7am-10pm Mon-Wed, 8am-midnight Thu-Sat, 8am-10pm Sun; 🛜) Can't decide whether you want sushi, pizza or Thai for dinner? At Little High, you won't have to choose – this stylish new food hall is home to eight different gourmet businesses, offering everything from dumplings to burgers. Stop in for your morning coffee or swing by for a late-night mojito in the beautifully outfitted space.

Twenty Seven Steps
Modern NZ $$$

(📞03-366 2727; www.twentysevensteps.co.nz; 16 New Regent St; mains $34-40; ⊙5pm-late) 🚣

Christchurch Combo Tickets

Christchurch Attractions (www. christchurchattractions.nz) is the company that runs the punting (p186), tram (p186) and gondola (p182). Combo tickets will save you some money if you're considering doing more than one activity. All of the above are included on the five-hour **Grand Tour** (adult/child $129/69).

Overlooking the pastel-coloured New Regent St strip, this elegant restaurant showcases locally sourced seasonal ingredients. Mainstays include modern renditions of lamb, beef, venison and seafood, as well as outstanding risotto. Delectable desserts and friendly waitstaff seal the deal; reservations are advised.

Gatherings   Modern NZ $$$

(☑021 02 93 5641; www.gatherings.co.nz; 2 Papanui Rd, Merivale; lunch mains $10-14, dinner 5-course tasting menu $65, with matched wines $110; ☺noon-2pm & 4-11pm Wed-Sat; ☑) ✔ Thoughtful, seasonal vegetarian dishes are the focus at this petite restaurant on the edge of the Papanui Rd dining strip. The set five-course tasting menu changes regularly, with a focus on sustainable, local produce and unique flavour combinations. At lunch, offerings include simple but well-executed staples like grilled cheese or soup.

🍷 DRINKING & NIGHTLIFE

Smash Palace   Bar

(☑03-366 5369; www.thesmashpalace.co.nz; 172 High St; ☺3pm-late Mon-Thu, from noon Fri-Sun) This deliberately downcycled and ramshackle beer garden is an intoxicating mix of grease-monkey garage, trailer-trash park and proto-hipster hang-out, complete with a psychedelic school bus, edible garden and blooming roses. There's craft beer,

chips, cheerios, and burgers made from scratch ($11 to $15).

Pomeroy's Old Brewery Inn   Pub

(☑03-365 1523; www.pomspub.co.nz; 292 Kilmore St; ☺3pm-late Tue-Thu, from noon Fri-Sun) For fans of great beer, Pomeroy's is perfect for supping a drop or two alongside a plate of proper pork crackling. Among this British-style pub's many endearing features are regular live music, a snug, sunny courtyard and **Victoria's Kitchen**, serving comforting pub food (mains $25 to $40). The newest addition, pretty **Little Pom's** cafe, serves excellent brunch fare ($9 to $25) until mid-afternoon.

Dux Central   Bar

(☑03-943 7830; www.duxcentral.co.nz; 6 Poplar St; ☺11am-late) Pumping a whole lot of heart back into the flattened High St precinct, the epic new Dux complex comprises a brew bar serving its own and other crafty drops, the Emerald Room wine bar, Upper Dux restaurant and the Poplar Social Club cocktail bar, all housed within the confines of a lovingly restored old building.

✪ ENTERTAINMENT

For live music and club listings, see www.undertheradar.co.nz and www.christchurchmusic.org.nz.

Isaac Theatre Royal   Theatre

(☑03-366 6326; www.isaactheatreroyal.co.nz; 145 Gloucester St; ☺box office 10am-5pm Mon-Fri) This century-old theatre survived the quakes and emerged restored to full glory in 2014. Its heritage features are enjoyed by patrons venturing inside for everything from opera and ballet to contemporary theatre and rock concerts.

darkroom   Live Music

(www.darkroom.bar; 336 St Asaph St; ☺7pm-late Thu-Sat) A hip combination of live-music venue and bar, darkroom has lots of Kiwi beers and great cocktails. Live gigs are frequent – and frequently free.

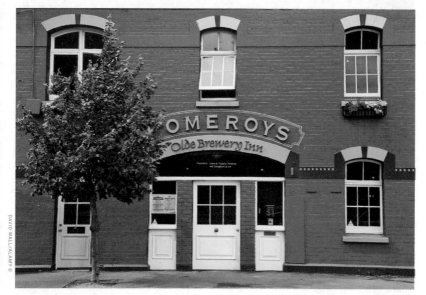

Pomeroy's Old Brewery Inn

🛈 INFORMATION

Airport i-SITE (📞03-741 3980; www.
christchurchnz.com; International Arrivals Hall;
🕑8am-6pm)

Christchurch i-SITE (📞03-379 9629; www.
christchurchnz.com; Arts Centre, 28 Worcester
Blvd; 🕑8.30am-5pm)

🛈 GETTING THERE & AWAY

AIR

Christchurch Airport (p405) The South Island's
main international gateway. **Air New Zealand**
(📞0800 737 000; www.airnewzealand.co.nz)
flies to/from Auckland, Wellington, Dunedin and
Queenstown.

Jetstar (📞0800 800 995; www.jetstar.com)
Flies to/from Auckland and Wellington.

BUS

Regular **InterCity** (📞03-365 1113; www.intercity.
co.nz; Lichfield St) buses connect 'ChCh' with the
rest of the nation, departing the **Bus Inter-change** (cnr Lichfield & Colombo Sts).

TRAIN

Christchurch Railway Station (www.greatjour
neysofnz.co.nz; Troup Dr, Addington; 🕑ticket
office 6.30am-3pm) is the terminus for the
TranzAlpine (📞03-341 2588, 0800 872 467;
www.kiwirailscenic.co.nz; one way from $119) to
Greymouth, and the *Coastal Pacific* to Picton,
scheduled to reopen in late 2018 (earthquake repairs). Contact **Great Journeys of New Zealand**
(📞0800 872 467; www.greatjourneysofnz.co.nz)
for updates.

🛈 GETTING AROUND

Christchurch's **Metro bus network** (📞03-366
8855; www.metroinfo.co.nz) is inexpensive, effi-
cient and comprehensive. Most buses run from
the inner-city Bus Interchange.

For a cab, try **Blue Star** (📞03-379 9799; www.
bluestartaxis.org.nz) or **First Direct** (📞03-377
5555; www.firstdirect.net.nz).

WESTLAND TAI POUTINI NATIONAL PARK

Westland Tai Poutini National Park at a Glance...

With colossal mountains, forests and glaciers, Westland Tai Poutini National Park clobbers visitors with its mind-bending proportions. Reaching from the West Coast to the razor peaks of the Southern Alps, the park's supreme attractions are twin glaciers Franz Josef and Fox: nowhere else at this latitude do glaciers descend so close to the ocean.

Just 23km apart, the towns bearing the glaciers' names are geared up for visitors, with plenty of good places to eat, drink and sleep. Not far away, the far-flung seaside hubs of Hokitika and Okarito deliver typically quirky west coast experiences.

Westland Tai Poutini National Park in One Day

Don't muck around: head straight to **Franz Josef Glacier** (p194) and get a good look at this monstrous icy beast, either via a helihike or scenic flight. Repair to the **Snake Bite Brewery** (p197) for dinner, with further imbibing at **Monsoon** (p197).

Westland Tai Poutini National Park in Two Days

Fox Glacier (p198) is bigger and longer than Franz Josef, which often makes for a less crowded ice encounter. If you're all iced-out, head to **Lake Matheson** (p199) for a hike, **Hokitika** (p201) for history and Māori culture, or **Okarito** (p200) for some wetland wildlife.

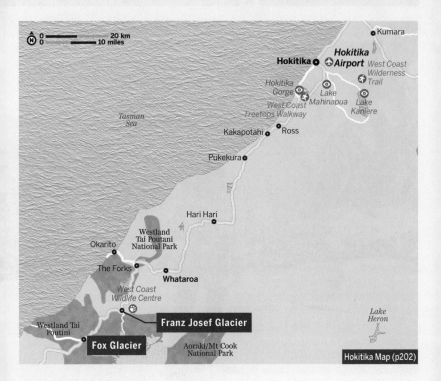

Arriving in Westland Tai Poutini National Park

Hokitika Airport (p205) is 1.5km east of the town centre. **Air New Zealand** (www.airnewzealand.com) has two flights most days to/from Christchurch.

Bus routes InterCity and Naked Bus service Franz Josef Glacier and Fox Glacier villages, with onward connections.

Sleeping

A big, all-budgets accommodation scene has sprung up to meet tourist demand in both glacier towns. Franz Josef has the biggest range (and the most luxurious options) while Fox is filled with motels and campgrounds. Booking ahead is recommended, particularly between November and March.

MATT MAKES PHOTOS/SHUTTERSTOCK ©

Franz Josef Glacier

Franz Josef's cloak of ice once flowed from the mountains right to the sea. Following millennia of gradual retreat, the glacier is now 19km inland and accessible only by helicopter.

Great For...

☑ **Don't Miss**

Landing on the ice at the head of the great glacier – pricey but priceless.

Swarms of small aircraft take off from Franz Josef village, 5km north of the glacier, lifting visitors to views of sparkling ice and toothy mountains. Many land on the glacier to lead groups into blue-tinged caves and crevasses. A glacier experience is the crowning moment for thousands of annual visitors, but walking trails, hot pools, and adventure sports from quad biking to clay target shooting keep adrenaline pulsing.

Geologist Julius von Haast led the first European expedition here in 1865, and named the glacier after the Austrian emperor. The dismal forecast of a rainier, warmer future spells more shrinkage for Franz Josef, whose trimlines (strips of vegetation on the valley walls) mark out decades of glacial retreat.

Independent Walks

A series of walks start from the glacier car park, 5km from the village. **Sentinel**

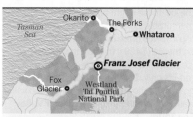

ⓘ Need to Know

Check out www.glaciercountry.co.nz for the low-down on both Franz Josef and Fox glaciers.

✕ Take a Break

Warm up with some glacier-sized pub grub at Landing Bar & Restaurant (p197).

★ Top Tip

Franz Josef has stacks of accommodation, but the town's popularity means booking ahead is recommended.

Rock (20 minutes return) reveals either impressive views of the glacier valley or a mysterious panorama swallowed by mist and cloud. **Kā Roimata o Hine Hukatere Track** (1½ hours return), the main glacier valley walk, leads you to the best permissible view of the terminal face.

Other walks include the **Douglas Walk** (one hour return), off the Glacier Access Rd, which passes moraine piled up by the glacier's advance in 1750, and **Peters Pool**, a small kettle lake. The **Terrace Track** (30 minutes return) is an easy amble over bushy terraces behind the village, with Waiho River views. Two good rainforest walks, **Callery Gorge Walk** and **Tatare Tunnels** (both around 1½ hours return), start from Cowan St – bring a torch for the latter.

Much more challenging walks, such as the five-hour **Roberts Point Track** and eight-hour **Alex Knob Track**, are detailed, along with all the others, in DOC's excellent *Glacier Region Walks* booklet ($2), which provides maps and illuminating background reading.

A rewarding alternative to driving to the glacier car park is the richly rainforested **Te Ara a Waiau Walkway/Cycleway**, starting from near the fire station at the south end of town. It's a one-hour walk (each way) or half that by bicycle. Leave your bikes at the car park – you can't cycle on the glacier walkways. When we passed through, bike hire wasn't easy to come by and folks were recommending rental from Fox Glacier Lodge (p198; per hour/half-day $5/15), 24km south. Ask in the **i-SITE** (☑0800 354 748; www.glaciercountry.co.nz; 63 Cron St; ☺8.30am-6pm) for the latest.

Guided Walks & Helihikes

Franz Josef Glacier Guides (☑03-752 0763, 0800 484 337; www.franzjosefglacier.com; 63 Cron St) runs small-group walks with experienced guides (boots, jackets and equipment supplied). With dazzling blue ice, photo ops in ice caves, and helicopter rides to and from the ice, these might be one of your most memorable experiences in NZ. The standard trip involves three hours of guided rambling on the ice ($459); the daring can seize an ice-pick for a five-hour ice-climbing tour (adults only, $575). If you don't need to get on the ice, choose a three-hour guided valley walk (adult/child $75/65). **Glacier Valley Eco Tours** (☑0800 925 586; www.glaciervalley. co.nz; 22 Main Rd; adult/child $75/37.50) ✿ offers a similar experience, a 3½-hour ramble by the river and into native forest. Conservation-focused commentary on local flora and geological forces enlivens the journey, which is rewarded by a steaming cuppa sipped in view of the glacier face.

Aerial Sightseeing

Forget sandflies and mozzies, the buzzing you're hearing is a swarm of small aircraft. The most affordable scenic flights involve 10 or 12 minutes in the air above Franz Josef Glacier (around $120 to $165) but it's worth paying for 20 minutes or more to get a snow landing or to view both Franz Josef and Fox glaciers (from $245). Pricier, 40-minute flights enjoy the most eye-popping views (around $370 to $460), swooping around Aoraki/Mt Cook. Fares for children under 12 years usually cost around 70% of the adult price. Shop around: most operators are situated on the main road.

Franz Josef on the Move

A town built on top of a fault line can't just up and leave. Or can it? A fault line slices right through Franz Josef, and fears of future earthquake damage and flooding from the ever-rising Waiho River have prompted regional council members to consider a lift

and shift: moving the township 10km north. Building an earthquake-resistant town next to Lake Mapourika has its appeal, though the price tag – an estimated $600m at last count – has sent town planners scrambling for alternatives.

Eating & Drinking

Snake Bite Brewery
Asian, Fusion $$

(📞03-752 0234; www.snakebite.co.nz; 28 Main Rd; mains $18-25; ⏱7.30am-10.30pm) Snake Bite's

> ★ **Did You Know?**
>
> The early Māori knew Franz Josef as Kā Roimata o Hine Hukatere (Tears of the Avalanche Girl). Legends tell of a woman persuading her lover to join her in the mountains only for him to die in a fall. Her flood of tears froze into the glacier.

MICHAEL R EVANS/SHUTTERSTOCK ©

motley Asian meals awaken taste buds after their long slumber through the West Coast's lamb-and-whitebait menus. Choices include nasi goreng (fried rice), Thai- and Malaysian-style curries, and salads of calamari and carrot that zing with fresh lime. Try the mussel fritters with wasabi mayo. Between courses, glug craft beers on tap or 'snakebite' (a mix of cider and beer).

Landing Bar & Restaurant
Pub Food $$

(📞03-752 0229; www.thelandingbar.co.nz; Main Rd; lunches $9-23, dinners $17-42; ⏱7.30am-late; 🛜) Portions are huge at the Landing Bar, from whopping whitebait patties to unfinishable nachos and bulky burgers. It gets busy but service meets demand admirably. The patio – complete with sunshine and gas heaters – is a good place to warm up after a day on the ice.

Monsoon
Bar

(📞03-752 0220; www.monsoonbar.co.nz; 46 Cron St; mains $15-33; ⏱11am-11pm) Sip drinks in the sunshine or within the cosy, chalet-style bar of the Rainforest Retreat, usually packed to the rafters with a sociable crowd of travellers. Bar snacks, burgers and posh pizzas (like chorizo and prawn pizzas) ensure you needn't move from your comfy spot by the fire.

> ★ **West Coast Wildlife Centre**
>
> The purpose of this feel-good **attraction** (📞03-752 0600; www.wildkiwi.co.nz; cnr Cron & Cowan Sts; day pass adult/child/family $38/20/85, incl backstage pass $58/35/145; ⏱8am-5pm) 🐾 is breeding two of the world's rarest kiwi – the rowi and the Haast tokoeka. The entry fee is well worthwhile by the time you've viewed the conservation, glacier and heritage displays, hung out with kiwi in their ferny enclosure, and met the five resident tuatara (native reptiles). The backstage pass into the incubating and rearing area is a rare opportunity to learn how a species can be brought back from the brink of extinction.

Fox Glacier

Impassable Fox Glacier seems to flow ominously towards the town below. But this 12km glacier (named for former New Zealand PM Sir William Fox) has been steadily retreating over the past century. Surrounded by farmland, the township's cafes and tour operators are strung along the main road.

Great For...

☑ Don't Miss

Pray the weather gods deliver the picture-perfect reflection of Aoraki (Mt Cook) on Lake Matheson.

Glacier Walks & Helihikes

The only way on to the ice is by taking a helihiking trip, run by the superb **Fox Glacier Guiding** (☎03-751 0825, 0800 111 600; www.foxguides.co.nz; 44 Main Rd). Independent walks offer a chance to explore the valley and get as close to the glacier's terminal face as safety allows (also a good option when unstable weather grounds the helicopters).

It's 1.5km from Fox Village to the glacier turn-off, and a further 2km to the car park, which you can reach under your own steam via **Te Weheka Walkway/Cycleway**, a pleasant rainforest trail starting just south of the Bella Vista motel. It's 2½ hours return on foot, or an hour by bike (leave your bikes at the car park – you can't cycle on the glacier walkways). Hire bikes from **Fox Glacier Lodge** (☎0800 369 800, 03-751 0888; www.

Hikers at Fox Glacier

foxglacierlodge.com; 41 Sullivan Rd; unpowered/powered sites $30/40, d $175-235; 🛜) (per hour/half-day $5/15).

From the car park, the terminal-face view point is around 40 minutes' walk, depending on current conditions. Obey all signs: this place is dangerously dynamic.

Short return walks near the glacier include the half-hour **Moraine Walk** (over a major 18th-century advance) and 20-minute **Minnehaha Walk**. The fully accessible **River Walk Lookout Track** (20 minutes return) starts from the Glacier View Rd car park.

Pick up a copy of DOC's excellent *Glacier Region Walks* booklet ($2), which provides maps and illuminating background reading.

Skydiving & Aerial Sightseeing

Short heliflights (10 to 20 minutes) offer a spectacular vantage point over Fox Glacier with a snow landing up top. On a longer flight (30 to 50 minutes) you can also enjoy sky-high sightseeing over Franz Josef Glacier and Aoraki/Mt Cook. Ten-minute joy flights cost from around $120, but we recommend 20 minutes or more in the air (from $245). Shop around: most operators are situated on the main road in Fox Glacier village.

What's Nearby

The famous 'mirror lake', **Lake Matheson** (www.doc.govt.nz) can be found 6km down Cook Flat Rd. Wandering slowly (as you should), it will take 1½ hours to complete the circuit. The best time to visit is early morning, or when the sun is low in the late afternoon, although the presence of the **Lake Matheson Cafe** (📞03-751 0878; www.lakematheson.com; Lake Matheson Rd; breakfast & lunch $10-21, dinner $29-35; ⏱8am-late Nov-Mar, to 3pm Apr-Oct) makes any time a good time.

Okarito

Huddled against a lagoon, the seaside hamlet of Okarito has a restorative air. Barely 10km from SH6, Okarito Lagoon is the largest unmodified wetland in NZ. More than 76 bird species preen and glide among its waterways, including gossamer-winged kōtuku (white heron). Hiding out in the forest are rowi kiwi, the rarest species of NZ's iconic land-bird – for a great chance of seeing one in the wild, hook up with the South Island's only licensed kiwi-tour operator, based in the village.

✪ ACTIVITIES

From a car park on the Strand you can begin the easy **Wetland Walk** (20 minutes), a longer mission along the **Three Mile Pack Track** (three hours, with the coastal return route tide dependent, so check in with the locals for tide times) and a jolly good

> *More than 76 bird species preen and glide among its waterways*

Birdwatcher near Okarito

puff up to **Okarito Trig** (1½ hours return), which rewards the effort with spectacular Southern Alps and Okarito Lagoon views (weather contingent).

🌀 TOURS

Okarito Kayaks   Kayaking
(✐03-753 4014, 0800 652 748; www.okarito.co.nz; 1 The Strand; kayak rental half-/full day $65/75; ⏲hours vary) This hands-on operator hires out kayaks for paddles across Okarito's shallow lagoon, in the company of strutting waterfowl and beneath a breathtaking mountainscape. Personalised guided kayaking trips (from $100) are ideal for getting to know the landscape; otherwise honest advice on weather, tides and paddling routes are gamely offered.

Okarito Boat Eco Tours   Wildlife
(✐03-753 4223; www.okaritoboattours.co.nz; 31 Wharf St; ⏲late Oct-May) Runs bird-spotting lagoon tours, the most fruitful of which is the 'early bird' ($80, 1½ hours, 7.30am). The popular two-hour 'ecotour' offers deeper insights into this remarkable natural

area ($90, 9am and 11.30am), or there's an afternoon 'wetlands tour' ($70, 2.30pm) if you aren't a morning person. Book at least 24 hours in advance.

Okarito Kiwi Tours Wildlife
(☏03-753 4330; www.okaritokiwitours.co.nz; 53 The Strand; 3-5hr tours $75) ✪ Spotting the rare kiwi in Okarito's tangle of native forest isn't easy, but bird-whisperer Ian has a 98% success rate for his small-group evening tours. Patience, tiptoeing and fine weather are essential. If you have your heart set on a kiwi encounter, book ahead and be within reach of Okarito for a couple of nights, in case of poor weather.

 INFORMATION

Okarito has no shops, limited visitor facilities and patchy phone reception, so stock up and book before you arrive.

 GETTING THERE & AWAY

Okarito is 10km north off SH6 between Franz Josef and Whataroa. You'll need your own wheels to get there.

Hokitika

This sweet seaside town has a glint in its eye: indigenous *pounamu* (greenstone), carved and buffed to a shine by a thriving community of local artists. Shopping for greenstone, glassware, textiles and other home-grown crafts inspires droves of visitors to dawdle along Hokitika's streets, which are dotted with grand buildings from its 1860s gold-rush days.

 SIGHTS

Hokitika Gorge Gorge
(www.doc.govt.nz) Water this turquoise doesn't come easy. Half a million years of glacial movement sculpted Hokitika's porcelain-white ravine; the rock 'flour' ground over millennia intensifies the water's dazzling hue. A lookout at the swingbridge is only 10

 West Coast Wilderness Trail

One of 22 NZ Cycle Trails (www.nzcycle trail.com), the 136km **West Coast Wilderness Trail** (www.westcoastwilder nesstrail.co.nz) stretches from Greymouth to Ross via Hokitika, following gold-rush trails, reservoirs, old tramways and railway lines, forging new routes cross-country. Suitable for intermediate riders, the trail reveals dense rainforest, glacial rivers, lakes and wetlands, and views from the snow-capped mountains of the Southern Alps to the wild Tasman Sea.

The trail is gently graded most of the way, and although the full shebang takes a good four days by bike, it can easily be sliced up into sections of various lengths, catering to every ability and area of interest.

Bike hire, transport and advice are available from the major setting-off points. In Hokitika, contact **Wilderness Trail Shuttle** (☏03-755 5042, 021 263 3299; www.wildernesstrailshuttle.co.nz).

ANDREW BAIN/ALAMY ©

minutes' walk from the car park. It's a scenic 35km drive south of Hokitika, well signposted from Stafford St (past the dairy factory).

Glowworm Dell Natural Feature
(SH6) At nightfall, bring a torch (or grope your way) into this grotto on the northern edge of town, signposted off the SH6. The dell is an easy opportunity to glimpse legions of glowworms (aka fungus gnat larvae), which emit an other-worldly blue light.

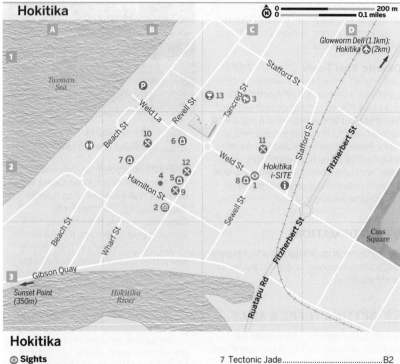

Hokitika

Lake Kaniere   Lake

(www.doc.govt.nz) Lying at the heart of a 7000-hectare scenic reserve, beautiful Lake Kaniere is 8km long, 2km wide, 195m deep, and freezing cold (as you'll discover if you swim). Undertake one of numerous walks, ranging from the 15-minute **Canoe Cove Walk** to the seven-hour return gut-buster up **Mt Tuhua**. It's 20km southeast of central Hokitika.

The historic **Kaniere Water Race Walkway** (3½ hours one way) forms part of the West Coast Wilderness Trail.

Lake Mahinapua   Lake

(www.doc.govt.nz; SH6, Ruatapu) Serene Lake Mahinapua and its diverse forests lie 10km south of Hokitika. The scenic reserve, gazetted in 1907, has a picnic area and DOC campsite that bask in mountain views, and the shallow, lagoon-fed water is warm enough for a paddle. There are several short walks (an hour return or less) signposted along the shore.

The starting point of the **Mahinapua Walkway** is 8km south of Hokitika. It's an easy four- to five-hour return walk following an old logging tramway.

Hokitika Museum   Museum

(www.hokitikamuseum.co.nz; 17 Hamilton St; gold coin donation; ☺10am-5pm Nov-Mar, 10am-2pm Apr-Oct) When we visited, most of the Hokitika Museum's excellent collection was inaccessible while the imposing Carnegie Building (1908) awaited assessment about its earthquake-strengthening needs. A small array of displays on jade, town history and whitebait fishing remained free to view. When it's restored to its former glory, expect to find it packed with intelligently curated exhibitions presented in a clear, modern style.

National Kiwi Centre Bird Sanctuary

(☏03-755 5251; www.thenationalkiwicentre. co.nz; 64 Tancred St; adult/child $24/12; ☺9am-5pm Dec-Feb, to 4.30pm Mar-Nov; ☝) Tiptoe through the darkened kiwi house to watch these iconic birds rummage for tasty insects, or stare a tuatara – a reptile unchanged for 225 million years – in its beady eyes.

Sunset Point   Viewpoint

(Gibson Quay) A visit to stunning Sunset Point is a quintessential Hokitika experience: watch the day's light fade away, observe whitebaiters casting nets, munch fish and chips, or stroll around the quayside shipwreck memorial.

✪ ACTIVITIES

Hokitika is a great base for walking and cycling. Download DOC's brochure *Walks in the Hokitika Area.*

Bonz 'N' Stonz   Art

(www.bonz-n-stonz.co.nz; 16 Hamilton St; carving per hour $30, full-day bone/jade workshop $80/180) Design, carve and polish your own *pounamu*, bone or paua (shellfish) masterpiece, with tutelage from Steve. Prices vary with materials and design complexity. Bookings recommended, and 'laughter therapy' included in the price.

 Required Reading

Sticking around in Hokitika for a while? Good, then you'll have time to read 800-page mystery *The Luminaries* by Eleanor Catton, a 2013 Man Booker Prize–winning novel set in Hokitika's gold-rush era.

West Coast Treetops Walkway   Outdoors

(☏0508 8733 8677, 03-755 5052; www. treetopsnz.com; 1128 Woodstock-Rimu Rd; adult/child $38/15; ☺9am-5pm Oct-Mar, 9am-4pm Apr-Sep) Visitors strolling along this wobbly steel walkway, 450m long and 20m off the ground, can enjoy an unusual perspective on the canopy of native trees, featuring many old rimu and kamahi. The highlight is the 40m-high tower, from which extend views across Lake Mahinapua, the Southern Alps and Tasman Sea. Wheelchair-friendly.

🛍 SHOPPING

Hokitika Craft Gallery Arts & Crafts

(☏03-755 8802; www.hokitikacraftgallery.co.nz; 25 Tancred St; ☺9.30am-5pm) The town's best one-stop shop, this co-op showcases a wide range of local work, including *pounamu*, jewellery, flax handbags, hand-coloured silk scarves, ceramics and woodwork.

Hokitika Glass Studio   Arts & Crafts

(☏03-755 7775; www.hokitikaglass.co.nz; 9 Weld St; ☺8.30am-5pm) Art and souvenirs from garish to glorious: glass eggs, multicoloured bowls and animal ornaments. And yes, the staff secure these fragile objects in oodles of protective wrapping. Watch the blowers at the furnace on weekdays.

Waewae Pounamu   Arts & Crafts

(☏03-755 8304; www.waewaepounamu.co.nz; 39 Weld St; ☺8am-5pm) This stronghold of NZ *pounamu* displays traditional and

From left: Lake Mahinapua (p202); Clock Tower; Hokitika Gorge (p201)

contemporary designs in its main-road gallery-boutique.

Tectonic Jade Arts & Crafts
(☏03-755 6644; www.tectonicjade.com; 67 Revell St; ☺9am-5pm) If you like your jade art and jewellery with a side order of spirituality, the lustrous *pounamu* (greenstone) carved by local artist Rex Scott will leave you entranced.

✖ EATING & DRINKING

Ramble + Ritual Cafe $
(☏03-755 6347; 51 Sewell St; snacks $3-8, meals $8-15; ☺7.30am-4pm Mon-Fri; 📷) Tucked away near the **Clock Tower** (cnr Weld & Sewell Sts), this gallery-cum-cafe is a stylish spot to linger while hobnobbing with friendly staff and punters. Let's see, will it be a Gruyère and mushroom slice, superfood salad, or a ginger oaty munched in between gulps of super-strength coffee?

In summer (December to February), the cafe opens its doors at weekends from 9am to 1pm.

Sweet Alice's Fudge Kitchen Sweets $
(☏03-755 5359; 27 Tancred St; fudge per slice $7; ☺10am-5pm, shorter hours Jun-Aug) Treat yourself with a slice of Alice's handmade fudge, real fruit ice cream or a bag of boiled lollies – or maybe all three. Jars of kiwifruit jam allow you to stash a little sweetness for later.

Aurora Modern NZ $$
(☏03-755 8319; http://aurorahoki.co.nz; 19 Tancred St; breakfast $10, mains $18-40; ☺8am-11pm) Breakfast egg-and-bacon ciabattas, Thai-style mussels, mid-afternoon tapas, desserts crowned with rich ice cream... from morning until closing time, everything at Aurora is beautifully plated and served with cheer.

Fat Pipi Pizza $$
(www.fatpipi.co.nz; 89 Revell St; pizzas $20-30; ☺noon-2.30pm Wed-Sun, 5-9pm daily; 📷) Purists might balk at flavour combos like smoked chicken and apricot, but Fat Pipi bakes Hokitika's best pizza. There

ROBERTHARDING/ALAMY ©

are versions for veggies and gluten-free diners, and garlicky whitebait pizza adds a local twist. Sweet tooth? Try dessert pizza heaped with blueberry, caramel and crumble. Enjoy it in the garden bar, or grab a takeaway and nibble at Sunset Point (p203).

West Coast Wine Bar   Wine Bar

(www.westcoastwine.co.nz; 108 Revell St; ⊙4pm-late Wed-Sat) Upping Hoki's sophistication factor, this weeny joint packs a fridge full of fine wine and craft beer. Sip it in the hidden-away back garden, laden with murals and dangling antlers.

ⓘ INFORMATION

Hokitika i-SITE (☑03-755 6166; www.hokitika. org; 36 Weld St; ⊙8.30am-5pm Mon-Fri, 10am-4pm Sat & Sun) One of NZ's best i-SITEs offers extensive bookings, including all bus services. Also holds DOC info, although you'll need to book online or at DOC visitor centres further afield.

See also www.westcoastnz.com.

ⓘ GETTING THERE & AWAY

AIR

Hokitika Airport (www.hokitikaairport.co.nz; Airport Dr, off Tudor St) is 1.5km east of the town centre. **Air New Zealand** (www.airnewzealand. com) has two flights most days to/from Christchurch.

BUS

InterCity (☑03-365 1113; www.intercity.co.nz) and **Naked Bus** (☑09-979 1616; https://naked bus.com) services leave from the i-SITE. For Christchurch, bus to Greymouth and take the **TranzAlpine** (☑04-495 0775, 0800 872 467; www.greatjourneysofnz.co.nz; one way adult/child from $119/83) train.

ⓘ GETTING AROUND

Greymouth's branch of **NZ Rent-a-Car** (☑03-768 0379; www.nzrentacar.co.nz; 170 Tainui St) can arrange vehicle pick-up/drop-off at Hokitika Airport.

Hokitika Taxis (☑03-755 5075)

QUEENSTOWN

Queenstown at a Glance...

Queenstown is as much a verb as a noun, a place of doing that likes to spruik itself as the 'adventure capital of the world'. It's famously the birthplace of bungy jumping, and the list of adventures you can throw yourself into here is encyclopaedic – alpine heliskiing to ziplining. It's rare that a visitor leaves without having tried something that ups their heart rate, but to pigeonhole Queenstown as just a playground is to overlook its cosmopolitan dining and arts scene, its fine vineyards, and the diverse range of bars that can make evenings as fun-filled as the days.

Queenstown in Two Days

Fuel up at **Bespoke Kitchen** (p228) before riding the **Skyline Gondola** (p224). Leap from **Kawarau Bridge Bungy** (p210) before drinks at **Atlas Beer Cafe** (p230) and dinner at **Public Kitchen & Bar** (p228).

The next day begin with breakfast at **Yonder** (p229) before a tour of the nearby **Gibbston Valley** (p218) wine region. Have dinner at **Blue Kanu** (p229) before winding down with a quiet fireside wine at **Bardeaux** (p230).

Queenstown in Four Days

Spend one day skiing the slopes (**the Remarkables** (p216) and **Coronet Peak** (p217) are on hand), and the next day maintaining the adrenaline with a ride on the **Shotover Jet** (p213). Or for something more low-key, a trip around **Lake Wakatipu** (p220) or to historic **Arrowtown** (p228). Finish up at **Zephyr** (p231) for some live tunes.

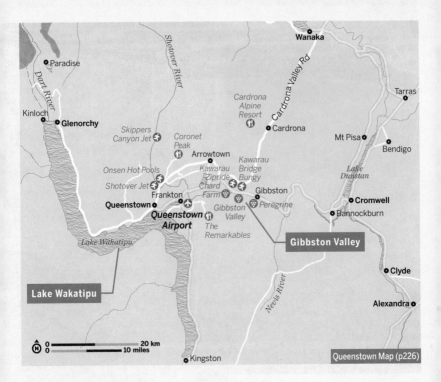

Arriving in Queenstown

Queenstown airport (p306) The airport lies 7km east of the town centre. Taxis charge $45 to $50 for the journey. Ritchies Connectabus (p221) runs every 15 minutes ($12). Super Shuttle (www. supershuttle.co.nz) runs a door-to-door shuttle ($20).

Buses Long-haul buses (to Christchurch, Te Anau, Dunedin, Franz Josef...) stop outside the Queenstown i-SITE.

Sleeping

Lakefront accommodation isn't difficult to come by in Queenstown, but mid-priced rooms are few and far between. Queenstown's hostels are competitive, however, often with an intriguing selection of extras – free GoPro hire, in-house saunas etc. Prices fluctuate widely with seasonal peaks (summer Christmas to February; winter June to September) so check hotel websites to see about discounts.

MOSEDALE/ALAMY ©

Extreme Queenstown

Many visitors who come to Queenstown try crazy things that they've never done before – often with a backdrop of stunning Central Otago scenery (...look forward to a good collection of 'I Did It!' souvenir T-shirts).

Shotover St, particularly the two blocks between Stanley and Brecon Sts, is wall-to-wall with adventure-tour operators selling their products, interspersed with travel agencies and 'information centres' hawking the very same products. Adding to the confusion is the fact that some stores change their name from summer to winter, while some tour operators list street addresses that are primarily their pick-up points rather than distinct shopfronts for the business.

Bungy Jumping & Swings

AJ Hackett Bungy (☑0800 286 4958, 03-450 1300; www.bungy.co.nz; The Station, cnr Camp & Shotover Sts), the bungy originator, now offers jumps from three sites in the Queenstown area, with giant swings available at two of them. It all started at the historic 1880 **Kawarau Bridge** (☑0800 286

Great For...

☑ **Don't Miss**

Leaping off the Kawarau Bridge, the site of the world's first commercial bungy jump (in 1988).

Kawarau Bridge bungy

4958; www.bungy.co.nz; Gibbston Hwy; adult/child $195/145), 23km from Queenstown, which became the world's first commercial bungy site in 1988. The 43m leap has you plunging towards the river, and is the only bungy site in the region to offer tandem jumps.

The Kawarau Bridge site also features the **Kawarau Zipride** (☑0800 286 4958; www.bungy.co.nz; Gibbston Hwy; adult/child $50/40, 3-/5-ride pack $105/150), a zipline along the riverbank that reaches speeds of 60km/h. Multiride packs can be split between groups, making it a far cheaper alternative to the bungy.

The closest options to Queenstown are the **Ledge Bungy** (☑0800 286 4958; www.bungy.co.nz; adult/child $195/145) and **Ledge Swing** (☑0800 286 4958; www.bungy.co.nz; adult/child $160/110), set just beneath the top station of the Skyline Gondola. The drop is 47m, but it's 400m above town. In winter you can even leap into the dark.

Last but most airy is the **Nevis Bungy** (☑0800 286 4958; www.bungy.co.nz; The Station, cnr Camp & Shotover Sts; $275), the highest leap in New Zealand. From Queenstown, 4WD buses will transport you onto private farmland where you can jump from a specially constructed bungy, 134m above the Nevis River. The **Nevis Swing** (☑0800 286 4958; www.bungy.co.nz; solo $195, tandem per person $175) starts 160m above the river and cuts a 300m arc across the canyon on a rope longer than a rugby field – yes, it's the world's biggest swing. If you're keen to try more than one AJ Hackett experience, enquire about the range of combo tickets.

Adventure Sports

The **Shotover Canyon Swing & Fox**
(☑03-442 6990; www.canyonswing.co.nz; 34 Shotover St; swing $229, fox $169, swing & fox combo $299) 🪂 sees you pick from any number of jump styles – backwards, in a chair, upside down – and then leap from a 109m cliff above the Shotover River, with 60m of free fall and a wild swing across the canyon at 150km/h. The Canyon Fox, new in 2016, can have you whizzing across the Shotover Canyon, more than 180m above

the river. The price includes transfer from the Queenstown booking office, and if you liked the swing the first time, you can go again for $45.

Jump, slide, zipline and abseil your way through a canyon with **Canyoning Queenstown** (☎03-441 3003; www.canyoning.co.nz; 39 Camp St) at Queenstown's edge ($219), or the remote Routeburn ($329) and Dart ($450) Canyons. Also operates via ferrata trips (adult/child $189/109), climbing cliffs that overlook Queenstown using metal rungs and safety cables.

Mountain Biking

Queenstown Bike Park (☎03-441 0101; www.skyline.co.nz; Skyline Gondola; half-/full day incl gondola $70/95; ☺Sep-May) has more than 30 different trails – from easy (green) to extreme (double black) – radiating out

from the top of the Skyline Gondola. Once you've descended the 400m of vertical, simply jump on the gondola and do it all over again. The best trail for novice riders is the 6km-long Hammy's Track, which is studded with lake views and picnic spots.

If you're serious about getting into mountain biking Queenstown-style, **Vertigo** (☎03-442 8378; www.vertigobikes. co.nz; 4 Brecon St; rental half-/full day from $39/59; ☺8am-7pm) is an essential first stop. Whether your fancy is trundling on the Queenstown Trail or bombing down the tracks of the Queenstown Bike Park, it hires out both hardtail and downhill bikes. Also runs skills-training clinics (from $159).

For a helibike epic barrelling down one of the peaks around Queenstown, **Heli Bike NZ** (☎0800 328 897; http://helibikenz.com; from $179) has tours to cater to any ability.

Shotover Jet boat rides

Water Sports

Queenstown Rafting (☑03-442 9792; www.queenstownrafting.co.nz; 35 Shotover St; rafting/helirafting $229/339) ☞ operates year-round on the churning Shotover River (Grades III to V) and calmer Kawarau River (Grades II to III). Half-day trips give you two to three hours on the water. Helirafting trips are an exciting alternative, and there are multiday trips on the Landsborough River. Rafters must be at least 13 years old and weigh more than 40kg.

Shotover Jet (☑03-442 8570; www.shotoverjet.com; Gorge Rd, Arthurs Point; adult/child $145/75) ☞ runs half-hour jetboat trips

through the narrow Shotover Canyon, with lots of thrilling 360-degree spins and reaching speeds of 85km/h.

Skippers Canyon Jet (☑03-442 9434; www.skipperscanyonjet.co.nz; Skippers Rd; adult/child $145/85) ☞ offers a 30-minute jetboat blast through the remote and hard-to-access Skippers Canyon, among the narrowest gorges on the Shotover River. Trips pick up from Queenstown, taking around three hours in total.

Paraflights

Queenstown Paraflights (☑03-441 2242; www.paraflights.co.nz; solo $159, tandem/triple per person $129/99) offers a solo, tandem or triple paraflight, zipping along 200m above the lake, pulled behind a boat. It departs from the town pier.

GForce Paragliding (☑03-441 8581; www.nzgforce.com; incl gondola $219) runs tandem paragliding from the top of the gondola (9am departures are $20 cheaper).

I VIEWFINDER/SHUTTERSTOCK ©

The Remarkables (p216)

Winter Slopes

New Zealand is a premier southern-hemisphere destination for snow bunnies. Wintry pursuits here span all levels, from family-friendly ski areas to daredevil snowboarding terrain and pulse-quickening heliskiing. Queenstown is the epicentre of the action.

Great For...

ⓘ Need to Know

The Queenstown ski season lasts from June til the snow starts to thaw in September.

★ **Top Tip**

For webcams and updates on snow conditions, see www.snow.co.nz and ww.nzski.com.

Skiing & Snowboarding

Queenstown has two excellent ski fields: the Remarkables and Coronet Peak. If you fancy a change of scenery, there's also **Cardrona Alpine Resort** (📞03-443 8880, snow report 03-443 7007; www.cardrona.com; Cardrona Skifield Access Rd; daily lift passes adult/child Jul & Aug $110/60, Jun, Sep & Oct $99/50; ⏰8.30am-4pm Jun-Oct) and **Treble Cone** (📞03-443 1406; www.treblecone.com; daily lift pass adult/child $110/55) nearby, accessed via Wanaka, an hour to the north of Queenstown. Coronet Peak is the only field to offer night skiing, which is an experience not to be missed if you strike a starry night. Roads around Queenstown become almost commuter busy on ski mornings and evenings, so taking the NZSki Snowline Express can mean one less vehicle holding up the show.

Outside the main ski season (June to September), heliskiing is an option for serious, cashed-up skiers; try **Harris Mountains Heli-Ski** (📞03-442 6722; www.heliski.co.nz; The Station, cnr Shotover & Camp Sts; from $990), **Alpine Heliski** (📞03-441 2300; www.alpineheliski.com; 37 Shotover St; 3-8 runs $940-1340; ⏰Jul-Sep) or **Southern Lakes Heliski** (📞03-442 6222; www.heliskinz.com; Torpedo 7, 20 Athol St; from $1050).

The Remarkables

Remarkable by name, and remarkable visually, this **ski field** (📞03-442 4615; www.nzski.com; daily lift pass adult/child $119/55) across the lake from Queenstown has a good smattering of intermediate, advanced and beginner runs. The access road is rough, but shuttles from Queenstown head

Coronet Peak

here during the ski season, so you don't have to worry about driving yourself.

Coronet Peak

New Zealand's oldest commercial ski field, opened in 1947, **Coronet Peak** (☑03-442 4620; www.nzski.com; Coronet Peak Rd; daily lift pass adult/child $119/55) offers excellent skiing and snowboarding for all levels thanks to its treeless slopes and multimillion-dollar snow-making system. It's also the only one

---

✕ Shuttles to the Snow

During the ski season, **NZSki Snow-line Express** (www.nzski.com) shuttles depart from outside the Snow Centre on Duke St every 20 minutes from 8am until 11.30am (noon for Coronet Peak), heading to both Coronet Peak and the Remarkables (return $20).

GLOBALTRAVELPRO/SHUTTERSTOCK ©

to offer night skiing, staying open until 9pm on Fridays and Saturdays at the peak of the season (and on Wednesdays through July).

Equipment Hire

In winter, shops throughout Queenstown are full of ski gear for purchase and hire; **Outside Sports** (☑03-441 0074; www.outsidesports.co.nz; 9 Shotover St; ⊗8.30am-8pm) and **Small Planet Outdoors** (☑03-442 5397; www.smallplanetsports.com; 15-17 Shotover St; ⊗9am-7pm Oct-May, 8am-9pm Jun-Sep) are reliable options.

Winter Festivals

LUMA Southern Light Project   Light Show

(http://luma.nz; Queenstown Gardens; ⊗Jun) Four nights of illumination throughout the Queenstown Gardens over the Queen's Birthday public-holiday weekend. It began in 2015 with four light installations, and had grown to 38 by 2017.

Queenstown Winter Festival   Sports

(www.winterfestival.co.nz; ⊗Jun) Four days of wacky ski and snowboard activities, live music, comedy, fireworks, a community carnival, parade, ball and plenty of frigid frivolity in late June.

Gay Ski Week   LGBT

(www.gayskiweekqt.com; ⊗Aug/Sep) The South Island's biggest and best gay-and-lesbian event, held in late August/ early September.

✕ Take a Break

Warm up with a hot aprés-ski rum at rustic **Rhino's Ski Shack** (☑03-441 3329; www.rhinosskishack.com; Cow Lane; ⊗3pm-late).

Gibbston Valley

Queenstown's adrenaline junkies might be happiest dangling off a giant rubber band, but they might not realise they're in the heart of one of Central Otago's main wine subregions.

Great For...

☑ Don't Miss

The drive to picturesque Chard Farm along a steep 2km road.

Wineries

Strung along Gibbston Hwy (SH6) is an interesting and beautiful selection of vineyards. Almost opposite the Kawarau Bridge, a precipitous 2km gravel road leads to **Chard Farm** (📞03-442 6110; www.chardfarm.co.nz; Chard Rd, Gibbston; ⊙10am-5pm Mon-Fri, 11am-5pm Sat & Sun), the most picturesque of the wineries. A further 1km along SH6 is **Gibbston Valley** (📞03-442 6910; www.gibbstonvalley.com; 1820 Gibbston Hwy/SH6, Gibbston; ⊙10am-5pm), the area's oldest commercial winery. As well as tastings, it has a restaurant, cheesery, tours of NZ's largest wine cave and bike hire. It also operates its own bus from Queenstown – you could always take the bus and then hire a bike to get between cellar doors.

Another 3km along SH6, **Peregrine** (📞03-442 4000; www.peregrinewines.co.nz;

Chard Farm

Ask at the Queenstown i-SITE (p231) for maps and info about touring the valley.

✖ **Take a Break**

The earthy **Gibbston Tavern** (☑03-409 0508; www.gibbstontavern.co.nz; 8 Coalpit Rd, Gibbston; ☺11am-8pm) stocks Gibbston wines and plates up good pizzas.

★ **Top Tip**

Gibbston comes to Queenstown in March with the **Gibbston Wine & Food Festival** (www.gibbstonwineandfood.co.nz; ☺Mar).

Beach on the Kawarau River, with views of Nevis Bluff.

2127 Gibbston Hwy/SH6, Gibbston; ☺11am-5pm) has an impressive, award-winning cellar door – a bunker-like building with a roof reminiscent of a falcon's wing in flight. As well as tastings, you can take a stroll through the adjoining barrel room.

Gibbston River Trail

The Gibbston River Trail, part of the Queenstown Trail, is a walking and cycling track that follows the Kawarau River for 11km from the Kawarau Bridge, passing all of the wineries. From Peregrine, walkers (but not cyclists) can swing onto the Peregrine Loop (one hour, 2.7km), which crosses over old mining works on 11 timber and two steel bridges, one of which passes through the branches of a willow tree. A 30-minute loop trail from Waitiri Creek Wines heads to Big

Tours

Appellation Central Wine Tours (☑03-442 0246; www.appellationcentral.co.nz; tours $199-265) Take a tipple at four or five wineries in Gibbston, Bannockburn and Cromwell, including platter lunches at a winery restaurant.

Cycle de Vine (☑0800 328 897; http://m. queenstown-trails.co.nz; tour $155; ☺Oct–mid-May) Cruise around Gibbston on a retro bicycle. Tours take in three different wineries and a picnic snack beside the Kawarau River. Pick-ups from your Queenstown accommodation.

New Zealand Wine Tours (☑0800 666 778; www.nzwinetours.co.nz; from $235) Small-group (maximum seven people) or private winery tours, including lunch – platter, degustation or à la carte, depending on the tour – and an 'aroma room' experience.

Lake Wakatipu

Shaped like a perfect cartoon thunderbolt and framed on its southeastern edge by the spectacular Remarkables mountain range, beautiful Lake Wakatipu offers lake cruises, and easy-going adventures at sleepy Glenorchy.

Great For...

<details about map area>
Fiordland
National
Park

● Glenorchy

Queenstown ●   *Queenstown*
       ◎   ✈ *Airport*
  Lake
  Wakatipu

● Kingston

● **Need to Know**

Glenorchy Information Centre & Store (☎03-409 2049; www.glenorchy-nz. co.nz; 42-50 Mull St; ⊘8.30am-9pm)

★ **Top Tip**

DOC's *Head of Lake Wakatipu* and *Wakatipu Walks* brochures detail day walks in the area.

This gorgeous lake has a 212km shoreline and reaches a depth of 379m (the average depth is over 320m). Five rivers flow into it but only one (the Kawarau) flows out, making it prone to sometimes quite dramatic floods.

If the water looks clean, that's because it is. Scientists have rated it as 99.9% pure – making it the second-purest lake water in the world. In fact, you're better off dipping your glass in the lake than buying bottled water. It's also very cold. That beach by Marine Pde may look tempting on a scorching day, but trust us, you won't want to splash about in water that hovers at around 10°C year-round.

Legend of the Lake

Māori tradition sees the lake's shape as the burnt outline of the evil giant Matau sleeping with his knees drawn up. Local lad Matakauri set fire to the bed of bracken on which the giant slept in order to rescue his beloved Manata, a chief's daughter who was kidnapped by the giant. The fat from Matau's body created a fire so intense that it burnt a hole deep into the ground.

Boat Trips

KJet
Boating

(☏03-442 6142; www.kjet.co.nz; adult/child $129/69) Skim, skid and spin around Lake Wakatipu and the Kawarau and Lower Shotover Rivers on these one-hour trips, leaving from the main town pier.

TSS Earnslaw
Boating

(☏0800 656 501; www.realjourneys.co.nz; Steamer Wharf, Beach St) The stately, steam-powered TSS *Earnslaw* was built

Routeburn Track

in the same year as the *Titanic* (but with infinitely better results). Climb aboard for the standard 1½-hour Lake Wakatipu tour (adult/child $65/22), or take a 3½-hour excursion to the high-country Walter Peak Farm for $80/22, where there are sheepdog and shearing demonstrations.

Hydro Attack
Boating

(☏0508 493 762; www.hydroattack.co.nz; Lapsley Butson Wharf; $149; ⊗9am-6pm Nov-Mar, 10am-4.30pm Apr-Oct) That shark you see buzzing about Lake Wakatipu is the Hydro Attack – jump inside, strap yourself in and

take a ride. This 'Seabreacher X' watercraft can travel at 80km/h on the water, dive 2m underneath and then launch itself nearly 6m into the air. It's mesmerising to watch, let alone travel inside.

Looking at the Lake

Ben Lomond Track
Tramping

(www.doc.govt.nz) The popular track to Ben Lomond (1748m, six to eight hours return) culminates in probably the best accessible view in the area, stretching over Lake Wakatipu and as far as Tititea/Mt Aspiring.

Underwater Observatory
Viewpoint

(☏03-442 6142; www.kjet.co.nz; Marine Pde; adult/child $10/5; ⊗8.30am-dusk) Six windows showcase life under the lake in this reverse aquarium (the people are behind glass) beneath the KJet office. Large brown trout abound, and look out for freshwater eels and scaup ducks, which dive past the windows. A KJet trip gets you free entry.

Glenorchy

The small town of Glenorchy sits on a rare shelf of flat land at the head of Lake Wakatipu. The tramping around here is sensational, and the town is also a base for horse treks, jetboat rides, helicopter flights and skydives. It's Queenstown on sedatives.

Two good short tracks here are the **Routeburn Flats** walk (three hours), which follows the first section of the famous Routeburn Track, and **Lake Sylvan** (one hour 40 minutes). If you like birds, the **Glenorchy Walkway** starts in the town centre and loops around Glenorchy Lagoon, switching to boardwalks for the swampy bits.

> ✕ **Take a Break**
>
> Glenorchy has a few cafes and a pub, and there's also a cafe-bistro at **Kinloch Lodge** (☏03-442 4900; www.kinlochlodge. co.nz; Kinloch Rd, Kinloch; dm $39, d with/ without bathroom from $175/115; ☏) ✿.

MILAN SOMMER/SHUTTERSTOCK ©

> ☑ **Don't Miss**
>
> The scenic 40-minute (46km) drive to Glenorchy, at the head of the lake northwest of Queenstown.

⊙ SIGHTS

Queenstown Gardens
Park

(Park St) Set on its own tongue of land framing Queenstown Bay, this pretty park is the perfect city escape right within the city. Laid out in 1876, it features an 18-'hole' **frisbee golf course** (www.queenstowndiscgolf.co.nz) **FREE**, an **ice-skating rink** (☑03-441 8000; www.queenstownicearena.co.nz; 29 Park St; entry incl skate hire $19; ⊙10am-5pm mid-Apr–mid-Oct), skate park, lawn-bowls club, tennis courts, mature exotic trees (including large sequoias and some fab monkey puzzles by the rotunda) and a rose garden. To stroll a loop around the peninsula and gardens should take about 30 minutes.

Skyline Gondola
Cable Car

(☑03-441 0101; www.skyline.co.nz; Brecon St; adult/child return $35/22; ⊙9am-9pm) Hop aboard for fantastic views as the gondola squeezes through pine forest to its grandstand location 400m above Queenstown. At the top there's the inevitable cafe, restaurant, souvenir shop and observation deck, as well as the Queenstown Bike Park

(p212), **Skyline Luge** (2/3/5 rides incl gondola adult $49/52/56, child $37/42/46; ⊙from 10am, closing times vary btwn 6pm & 9pm) 🏃, Ledge Bungy (p211), Ledge Swing (p211) and **Ziptrek Ecotours** (☑03-441 2102; www.ziptrek.co.nz) 🏃. At night there are Māori culture shows from **Kiwi Haka** (adult/child incl gondola $77/52) and stargazing tours (including gondola adult/child $93/49).

Kiwi Birdlife Park
Zoo

(☑03-442 8059; www.kiwibird.co.nz; Brecon St; adult/child $49/24; ⊙9am-5pm, shows 11am, 1.30pm & 4pm) These 2 hectares are home to 10,000 native plants, tuatara (reptiles) and scores of birds, including kiwi, kea, NZ falcons, parakeets and extremely rare black stilts. Stroll around the aviaries, watch the conservation show and tiptoe quietly into the darkened kiwi houses. Kiwi feedings take place five times a day.

⊕ ACTIVITIES

Ultimate Hikes
Tramping

(☑03-450 1940; www.ultimatehikes.co.nz; The Station, Duke St entrance; ⊙Nov-Apr) 🏃 If you

Chairlift to the Skyline Luge

BEATRICE SIRINUNTANANON/SHUTTERSTOCK ©

like your adventure with a little comfort, Ultimate Hikes offers three-day guided tramps on the Routeburn (from $1375) and Milford (from $2130) tracks, staying in its own well-appointed private lodges. It also runs day walks on both tracks (from $179) and a couple of combinations of tracks. Prices include transfers from Queenstown, meals and accommodation.

In winter the office is rebranded as Snowbiz and rents skis and snowboards.

Guided Walks
New Zealand Tramping

(☏03-442 3000; www.nzwalks.com; unit 29, 159 Gorge Rd) Guided walks ranging from half-day nature walks near Queenstown (adult/child $109/69) to a day on the Routeburn Track ($199/140) and the full three-day Hollyford Track (from $1895/1495). Also offers snowshoeing in winter.

Family Adventures Rafting

(☏03-442 8836; www.familyadventures.co.nz; adult/child $189/120; ۞Oct-Apr; ⊞) Gentle (Grades I to II) rafting trips on the Shotover River, suitable for children three years and older. Trips depart from Browns Ski Shop (39 Shotover St).

NZone Adventure Sports

(☏03-442 5867; www.nzoneskydive.co.nz; 35 Shotover St; from $299) Jump out of a perfectly good airplane from 9000, 12,000 or 15,000ft...in tandem with someone who actually knows what they're doing.

Climbing Queenstown Climbing

(☏027 477 9393; www.climbingqueenstown. com; 9 Shotover St; from $179) Rock climbing, mountaineering and guided trekking and snowshoeing trips in the Remarkables. Trips depart from (and can be booked at) Outside Sports (p217).

 TOURS

Nomad Safaris Driving

(☏03-442 6699; www.nomadsafaris.co.nz; 37 Shotover St; adult/child from $185/90) Runs 4WD tours into hard-to-get-to backcountry destinations such as Skippers Canyon

 Soothing the Strains

After days of adventure and activity, your body might well be craving a break in the pace. Here's our pick of the best ways to slow down and recharge in Queenstown.

Onsen Hot Pools (☏03-442 5707; www.onsen.co.nz; 160 Arthurs Point Rd, Arthurs Point; 1/2/3/4 people $75/95/129/152; ۞10am-11pm) has private Japanese-style hot tubs with mountain views.

Let the goodness come to you with in-room massage and spa treatments with the **Mobile Massage Company** (☏0800 426 161; 2c Shotover St; 1hr from $125; ۞9am-9pm).

Check into **Hush Spa** (☏03-442 9656; www.hushspa.co.nz; 1st fl, 32 Rees St; 30/60min massage from $70/129; ۞9am-6pm Fri-Mon, to 9pm Tue-Thu) for a massage or pedicure.

and Macetown, as well as a trip through Middle-earth locations around Glenorchy and the Wakatipu Basin.

Queenstown Heritage Tours Bus

(☏03-409 0949; www.queenstown-heritage. co.nz; adult/child from $140/70) Scenic but hair-raising 4WD minibus tours into Skippers Canyon along a narrow, winding road built by gold miners in the 1800s. Wine tours to Gibbston are also available, as is a combination of the canyon and the wineries.

🔒 SHOPPING

Romer Gallery Photography

(☏021 171 1771; www.romer-gallery.com; 15 Earl St; ۞8.30am-5pm) Stunning gallery of large-format, Perspex-finished NZ land-scapes from renowned Queenstown-based photographer Stephan Romer. Images are up to $15,000 a pop, but they display a rare beauty.

Vesta Arts & Crafts

(☏03-442 5687; www.vestadesign.co.nz; 19 Marine Pde; ۞10am-5.30pm) Arguably

Queenstown

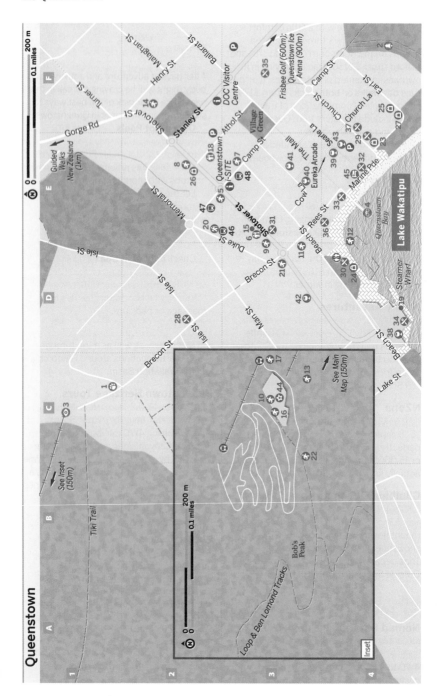

Lake Wakatipu

Queenstown Bay

Steamer Wharf

Inset

Bob's Peak

Loop & Ben Lomond Tracks

See Main Map (150m)

See Inset (150m)

Tiki Trail

Guided Walks New Zealand (2km)

Frisbee Golf (600m); Queenstown Ice Arena (900m)

Queenstown

Queenstown's most interesting store, inside inarguably the town's oldest building. Vesta sells a collection of prints, glassware, jewellery and homewares as fascinating as the original wallpaper and the floorboards warped by time in the 1864 wooden cottage.

Artbay Gallery   Art
(☏03-442 9090; www.artbay.co.nz; 13 Marine Pde; ⏰10am-9pm) Occupying an attractive 1863-built Freemason's Hall on the lakefront, Artbay is always an interesting place to peruse, even if you don't have $10,000 to drop on a painting. It showcases the

work of contemporary NZ artists, most of whom have a connection to the region.

It's now both the oldest and newest art gallery in town, after opening an exhibition space across the road (above Louis Vuitton) in 2016, from where the lake view is as good as the art.

Creative Queenstown
Arts & Crafts Market   Market
(www.queenstownmarket.com; Earnslaw Park; ⏰9am-4.30pm Sat Nov-Apr, 9.30am-3.30pm May-Oct) Gifts and souvenirs crafted from around the South Island; on the lakefront beside Steamer Wharf.

 **Arrowtown**

Beloved by day-trippers, exceedingly quaint Arrowtown, just 20km northeast of Queenstown, sprang up in the 1860s following the discovery of gold in the Arrow River. Today its pretty, tree-lined avenues retain more than 60 of their original gold-rush buildings, and history is so ingrained here that even the golf course wraps around the ruined cottages and relics of the town's gold-mining heyday.

But don't be fooled by the rustic facades; Arrowtown has a thriving contemporary scene, with chic modern dining, a cool cinema and a couple of drinking dens to rival the finest in Queenstown. Don't miss lunch at **Chop Shop** (☏03-442 1116; www.facebook.com/thechopshopfoodmerchants; 7 Arrow Lane; mains $20-30; ⊙8am-3pm) and a drink at **Blue Door** (☏03-442 0415; www.facebook.com/TheBlueDoorBar; 18 Buckingham St; ⊙4pm-late; 🛜).

Arrowtown Visitor Information Centre (☏03-442 1824; www.arrowtown.com; 49 Buckingham St; ⊙8.30am-5pm) has local info.

Buckingham St
GRACETHANG2/SHUTTERSTOCK ©

😋 EATING

Fergbaker   Bakery $
(40 Shotover St; items $5-10; ⊙6.30am-4.30am) Fergburger's sweeter sister bakes all manner of tempting treats – and though most things look tasty with 3am beer goggles on, it withstands the daylight test admirably.

Goodies include inventive pies (venison and portobello mushroom) and breads (pinot, fig and cranberry), filled rolls and a sugary wealth of sweet treats. If you're after gelato, call into Mrs Ferg next door.

Empanada Kitchen   Fast Food $
(☏021 0279 2109; www.theempanadakitchen.com; 60 Beach St; empanadas $5.50; ⊙10am-5pm) Yes, this little hole-in-the-wall kiosk is built into a public toilet, but that's far from a statement about its food. The empanadas are absolutely delicious, with flavours that change daily and include savoury and sweet options.

Patagonia   Sweets $
(☏03-409 2465; www.patagoniachocolates.co.nz; 2 Rees St; ice cream $5-8, breakfast $8-13; ⊙9am-9pm; 🛜) Its popularity is its only detraction, but fight your way in and you'll find 24 superb ice-cream flavours, a host of chocolate and the truly Patagonian touch of *churros* (Spanish doughnuts) and *dulce de leche*–flavoured ice cream.

Bespoke Kitchen   Cafe $$
(☏03-409 0552; www.bespokekitchen.co.nz; 9 Isle St; mains $11-19; ⊙8am-5pm; 🛜) Occupying a light-filled corner site near the gondola, Bespoke delivers everything you'd expect of a smart Kiwi cafe. There's a good selection of counter food, beautifully presented cooked options, a range of outside seating in sight of the mountains and, of course, great coffee. In 2015, within six months of opening, it was named NZ's cafe of the year.

**Public Kitchen
& Bar**   Modern NZ $$
(☏03-442 5969; www.publickitchen.co.nz; Steamer Wharf, Beach St; dishes $12-46; ⊙11am-late; 🛜) You can't eat closer to the water than at this excellent lakefront eatery where local is law: Cardrona lamb, Fiordland wild venison, Geraldine pork, South Island fish. Grab a group and order a selection of plates of varying sizes from the menu. The meaty dishes, in particular, are excellent.

Vudu Cafe & Larder   Cafe $$
(☏03-441 8370; www.vudu.co.nz; 16 Rees St; breakfast $15-23, lunch $19-23; ⊙7.30am-6pm)

Excellent home-style baking combines with great coffee and the sort of breakfasts that make bacon and eggs seem very passé (try the French-toast pudding) at this ever-popular cafe. Admire the huge photo of a far less populated Queenstown from an inside table, or head outside to graze by the lake. Service can be slow, but that's the weight of numbers.

Yonder
Cafe $$

(☏03-409 0994; www.yonderqt.co.nz; 14 Church St; brunch $9-23; ⏰7.30am-late; 🛜) With a menu inspired 'by the things we've loved around our travels', this new cafe brings to the table a cosmopolitan assortment of dishes: bacon butties, kimchi bowls, tuna poke bowls. There are power points and USB ports by many of the indoor tables, but when the sun's out you'll want to be on the outdoor patio.

Blue Kanu
Modern NZ $$

(☏03-442 6060; www.bluekanu.co.nz; 16 Church St; mains $28-38; ⏰4pm-late) Disproving the rule that all tiki houses are inherently tacky, Blue Kanu serves up a food style it calls 'Polynasian' – bibimbap in one hand, fried chicken pineapple buns in the other. It's relaxed and personable, capable of making you feel like a regular in minutes. The marriage of the Polynesian decor and the chopsticks sounds impossible to pull off, but it works.

Rata
Modern NZ $$$

(☏03-442 9393; www.ratadining.co.nz; 43 Ballarat St; mains $35-44, 2-/3-course lunch $28/38; ⏰noon-late) After gaining Michelin stars for restaurants in London, New York and LA, chef-owner Josh Emett now wields his exceptional but surprisingly unflashy cooking back home in this upmarket but informal back-lane eatery. Native bush, edging the windows and in a large-scale photographic mural, sets the scene for a short menu showcasing the best seasonal NZ produce.

Gantley's
Modern NZ $$$

(☏03-442 8999; www.gantleys.co.nz; 172 Arthurs Point Rd, Arthurs Point; 2-/3-course dinner $65/75, 6-/8-course degustation $95/130, with paired wines $160/215; ⏰6-10pm) Gantley's French-influenced menu and highly regarded wine list justify the 7km journey

Patagonia

Al fresco diners at a restaurant

from Queenstown. The atmospheric dining experience is showcased in a stone-and-timber building, built in 1863 as a wayside inn and surrounded by beautiful gardens. The degustation options are the menu's centrepiece. Reservations are essential, and free pick-up from Queenstown is available by arrangement.

Grille by Eichardt's Modern NZ $$$
(☏03-441 0444; www.eichardtsdining.com; Eichardt's Private Hotel, Marine Pde; mains $25-54; ☺noon-late) At this Grille – the newest arrival on the dining scene from Eichardt's Private Hotel – steak unsurprisingly gets star billing, but you can also order share boards or burgers. It's remarkably good value given the swanky setting and the in-your-lap view of the lake.

DRINKING & NIGHTLIFE

Atlas Beer Cafe Bar
(☏03-442 5995; www.atlasbeercafe.com; Steamer Wharf, Beach St; ☺10am-late) There are usually around 20 beers on tap at this pint-sized lakefront bar, headlined by brews

from Dunedin's Emerson's Brewery and Queenstown's Altitude. There are tasting paddles (with tasting notes) with four beers of your choice available. It serves excellent cooked breakfasts ($10 to $20) and simple substantial fare such as steaks, burgers and chicken parmigiana ($20).

**Smiths Craft
Beer House** Craft Beer
(☏03-409 2337; www.smithscraftbeer.co.nz; 53 Shotover St; ☺noon-late) It's back to basics in everything but the taps, with bare concrete floors and industrial tables and chairs, but up to 20 creative craft beers on tap. The folks behind the bar will chat brews as long as you'll listen, and there's a menu (mains $17 to $20) of burgers and po' boys to mop up the suds.

Bardeaux Wine Bar
(☏03-442 8284; www.goodgroup.co.nz; Eureka Arcade, Searle Lane; ☺4pm-4am) This small, cavelike wine bar is all class. Under a low ceiling are plush leather armchairs and a fireplace made from Central Otago schist. Whisky is king here, but the wine list is

extraordinary, especially if you're keen to drop $4500 on a bottle once in your life. It's surprisingly relaxed for a place with such lofty tastes.

Zephyr
Bar

(☎03-409 0852; www.facebook.com/zephyrqt; Searle Lane; ☺7pm-4am) Queenstown's coolest indie rock bar is located – as all such places should be – in a dark, grungy, concrete-floored space off a back lane. There's a popular pool table and live bands on Wednesday nights. Beer comes only in bottles, and there's a permanently rockin' soundtrack.

Vinyl Underground
Club

(www.facebook.com/Vinylundergroundqt; 12 Church St; ☺8pm-late) Enter the underworld, or at least the space under the **World Bar** (☎03-450 0008; www.theworldbar.co.nz; 12 Church St; ☺11.30am-2.30am), to find the heartbeat of Queenstown's nightlife. Inside the concrete bunker – the bar alone must weigh several tonnes – projectors screen dance clips onto a faux brick wall, and DJs spin from 10pm. There's a pool table in the back room.

Bunker
Cocktail Bar

(☎03-441 8030; www.thebunker.co.nz; 14 Cow Lane; ☺5pm-4am) Bunkered upstairs rather than down, this chichi little bar clearly fancies itself the kind of place that Sean Connery's James Bond might frequent, if the decor is anything to go by. Best of all is the outside terrace, with couches, a fire in winter and a projector screening classic movies onto the wall of a neighbouring building.

ENTERTAINMENT

Pick up a copy of *The Source* (www.source-mag.nz), a free monthly publication with articles and details of goings-on around Queenstown.

Sherwood
Live Music

(☎03-450 1090; www.sherwoodqueenstown.nz; 554 Frankton Rd) The faux-Tudor architecture

might have you expecting lutes and folk ballads, but the Sherwood is Queenstown's go-to spot for visiting musos. Many of NZ's bigger names have performed here; check the website for upcoming gigs.

ℹ️ INFORMATION

DOC Visitor Centre (☎03-442 7935; www.doc. govt.nz; 50 Stanley St; ☺8.30am-4.30pm) Head here to pick up Routeburn Track bookings and backcountry hut passes. Posts weather and tramper alerts, has good day-walk advice and sells maps.

Queenstown i-SITE (☎03-442 4100; www. queenstownisite.co.nz; cnr Shotover & Camp Sts; ☺8.30am-8pm) Friendly and informative despite being perpetually frantic, the saintly staff here can help with bookings and information on Queenstown, Gibbston, Arrowtown and Glenorchy.

ℹ️ GETTING THERE & AWAY

AIR

Air New Zealand (☎0800 737 000; www. airnewzealand.co.nz) flies direct to Queenstown from Auckland, Wellington and Christchurch. **Jetstar** (☎0800 800 995; www.jetstar.com) also flies the Auckland route.

Various airlines offer direct flights to Queenstown from Sydney, Melbourne, Brisbane and the Gold Coast in Australia.

BUS

Most buses and shuttles stop on Athol St or opposite the i-SITE; check when you book. Destinations include Christchurch, Franz Josef, Te Anau and Dunedin.

ℹ️ GETTING AROUND

Ritchies Connectabus (☎03-441 4471; www. connectabus.com) has various colour-coded routes, including one to Arrowtown.

Green Cabs (☎0800 464 7336; www.greencabs. co.nz)

FIORDLAND

Fiordland at a Glance...

Brace yourself for sublime scenery on a breathtaking scale. In New Zealand's far southwest, Fiordland National Park's mountains, forests and mirror-smooth waters hold visitors in thrall. Framed by kilometre-high cliffs, Milford Sound was clawed away by glaciers over millennia. Leading here is the Milford Hwy, which reveals a magnificent alpine view at every bend; and the epic Milford Track, one of NZ's (and arguably, the planet's) best tramping trails. Shying away from attention is Doubtful Sound, the pristine 'place of silence', which leaves many admiring visitors speechless (doubtfulness doesn't often enter into it).

Fiordland in Two Days

Kick-start your Fiordland adventures with a day trip to **Milford Sound** (p240), along the astonishingly photogenic **Milford Highway** (p244). Explore by boat, or to really experience the area's watery expanses, soaring cliffs and lush forest, consider a kayaking excursion. Kayaking is also popular on **Doubtful Sound** (p246), a much less-visited destination (if you feel like sidestepping the crowds).

Fiordland in Five Days

For an extended Fiordland experience, undertake one of New Zealand's Great Walks for three days and four nights. Once you've conquered the **Milford Track** (p236), take time to explore **Milford Sound** (p240) by boat, before returning to lakeside **Te Anau** (p248). You'll really have earned something delicious at the **Sandfly Cafe** (p250), or an ice-cold beer at the local pub. Cheers!

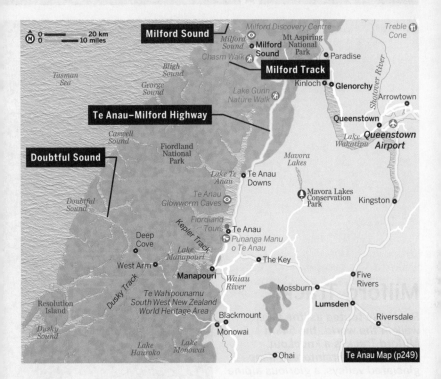

Te Anau Map (p249)

Arriving in Fiordland

Te Anau Fiordland is a long way from anywhere, but Te Anau has direct bus connections with Queenstown, Dunedin and Christchurch.

Queenstown Tour companies run return day trips to Milford Sound from Queenstown, but it's a long day in the saddle with just a couple of hours at Milford.

Sleeping

Te Anau has a decent array of motels, B&Bs and tramper-friendly hostels. Accommodation can get booked out in the peak season when hiker numbers soar (December to February), so book early if possible. Closer to Doubtful Sound, Manapouri also has some good places to stay.

Milford Track

Routinely touted as 'the finest walk in the world', the 54km Milford Track is a knockout, complete with rainforest, deep glaciated valleys, a glorious alpine pass and rampaging waterfalls.

Great For...

❶ Need to Know

See www.doc.govt.nz/milfordtrack for essential pre-trip planning and booking guidelines.

★ **Top Tip**

Between late October and mid-April, hut passes must be pre-booked, online via **Great Walks Bookings** (☏ 0800 694 732; www.greatwalks.co.nz) or at a DOC visitor centre. Book early!

The Milford track is hugely popular: almost 7500 trampers complete the 54km-long track each summer. Soon after bookings open (sometime between February and May, for the summer season starting in October), this Great Walk becomes fully booked – keep an eye on www.doc.govt.nz/milfordtrack to time it right.

During the Great Walks season (late October through April), the track can only be walked in one direction, starting from Glade Wharf. You must stay at Clinton Hut the first night, despite it being only one hour from the start of the track, and you must complete the trip in the prescribed three nights and four days. This is perfectly acceptable if the weather is kind, but when the weather turns sour you'll still have to push on across the alpine Mackinnon Pass

and may miss some rather spectacular views. It's all down to the luck of the draw.

During the Great Walk season, the track is also frequented by guided tramping parties, which stay at cosy, carpeted lodges with hot showers and proper food. If that sounds appealing, contact Ultimate Hikes, the only operator permitted to run guided tramps on the Milford.

The track is covered by 1:70,000 *Parkmap 335-01 (Milford Track)*.

Bookings & Transport

The Milford Track is officially a Great Walk. Between late October and mid-April, you need to book each of your three nights in the huts ($70): Clinton Hut, Mintaro Hut and Dumpling Hut. Hut passes must be obtained in advance, either online via

Boat at Glade Wharf

DOC's **Great Walks Bookings** (📞0800 694 732; www.greatwalks.co.nz) or in person at a DOC visitor centre. Book early to avoid disappointment as the entire season books up very quickly.

DOC advises against tackling the Milford Track between early May and late October because of the significant risk of avalanches and floods, and the fact that bridges at risk of avalanche are removed. It's wet, very cold, and snow conceals trail markers. If you're a well-equipped tramping pro considering the Milford Track out of season, get DOC advice on weather conditions. During this low season, huts revert to the 'serviced' category ($15), and restrictions on walking the track in four days are removed.

The track starts at Glade Wharf, at the head of Lake Te Anau, accessible by a 1½-hour boat trip from Te Anau Downs, itself 29km from Te Anau on the road to Milford Sound. The track finishes at Sandfly Point, a 15-minute boat trip from Milford Sound village, from where you can return by road to Te Anau, around two hours away. You will be given options to book this connecting transport online, at the same time as you book your hut tickets.

Tracknet (p252) offers transport from Queenstown and Te Anau to meet the boats at Te Anau Downs and Milford Sound. There are other options for transport to and from the track, including a float-plane hop from Te Anau to Glade Wharf with Wings & Water (p248). Fiordland i-SITE and the Fiordland National Park Visitor Centre can advise on options to best suit you. **Safer Parking** (📞03-249 7198; www.saferparking.co.nz; 48 Caswell Rd; per day per motorbike/car/motorhome $4/9/10) is a good option for stashing your vehicle while you hike.

Tours

Real Journeys (p248) You can count on sharp service and well-organised tours from this major player, which offers guided day walks on the Milford Track.

Ultimate Hikes (📞03-450 1940, 0800 659 255; www.ultimatehikes.co.nz; 5-day tramps incl food dm/s/d $2295/3330/5390; ⊙Nov–mid-Apr) ✔ Booking yourself onto a guided tramp of the Milford Track with Queenstown-based Ultimate Hikes puts route planning and logistics in the capable hands of an experienced operator. The guides' expert knowledge of fauna and flora enhances the journey, and walkers will overnight in lodges with hot showers and proper food.

HARRY GREEN/SHUTTERSTOCK ©

✕ Take a Break

Back in Te Anau, celebrate completing the Milford Track with dinner at Kepler's (p251).

Milford Sound

The iconic image of Mitre Peak amid Milford Sound has long dominated New Zealand tourism marketing. Opportunities to explore the fabled body of water include boat cruises, kayaking and flight-seeing.

Great For...

☑ Don't Miss

At least one moment alone on the sound, just you and nature's beautiful oblivion.

The pot of gold at the end of Milford Hwy (SH94) is sublime Milford Sound (Piopiotahi). Rising above the fiord's indigo water is Mitre Peak (Rahotu), the deserved focal point of millions of photographs. Tapering to a cloud-piercing summit, the 1692m-high mountain appears sculpted by a divine hand.

In truth, it's the action of glaciers that carved these razor-edge cliffs. Scoured into the bare rock are pathways from tree avalanches, where entangled roots dragged whole forests down into the darkly glittering water. When rain comes (and that's often), dozens of temporary waterfalls curtain the cliffs. Stirling and Lady Bowen Falls gush on in fine weather, with rainbows bouncing from their mists when sunlight strikes just right.

Milford Sound receives an estimated one million annual visitors – it's an almighty

ⓘ Need to Know

Fill your tank in Te Anau before driving to Milford (no petrol stations en route). Bring snow chains in winter.

✕ Take a Break

At **Milford Sound Lodge** (☎03-249 8071; www.milfordlodge.com; SH94; powered camp-ervan sites $60, dm $40, chalets $415-465; 🛜), travellers convene at the on-site Pio Pio Cafe for breakfast, dinner and good espresso.

★ Top Tip

Raining? Fear not: cruises on rainy Milford days have views of innumerable temporary waterfalls.

challenge to keep its beauty pristine. But out on the water, all human activity – cruise ships, divers, kayakers – seems dwarfed into insignificance.

Cruises

Fiordland's most accessible experience is a cruise on Milford Sound, usually lasting 90 minutes or more. A slew of companies have booking desks in the flash cruise terminal, a 10-minute walk from the main car park, but it's always wiser to book ahead.

Each cruise company claims to be quieter, smaller, bigger, cheaper or in some way preferable to the rest. What really makes a difference is timing. Most bus tours aim for 1pm sailings, so if you avoid that time of day there will be fewer people on the boat, fewer boats on the water and fewer buses on the road.

If you're particularly keen on wildlife, opt for a cruise with a nature guide on board. These are usually a few minutes longer than the standard 'scenic' cruises, and often on smaller boats. Most companies offer coach transfers from Te Anau for an additional cost. Day trips from Queenstown make for a very long 13-hour day.

Arrive 20 minutes before departure. All cruises visit the mouth of the sound, just 15km from the wharf, poking their prows into the choppy waves of the Tasman Sea. Shorter cruises visit fewer en route 'highlights', which include Bowen Falls, Mitre Peak, Anita Bay and Stirling Falls.

Only visitable on trips run by Southern Discoveries and Mitre Peak Cruises, **Milford Discovery Centre** (www.southern discoveries.co.nz; Harrison Cove; adult/child $36/18; ⊗9am-4pm), New Zealand's only floating underwater observatory, showcases interactive displays on the natural environment of the fiord. The centre offers a chance to view corals, tube anemones and bottom-dwelling sea perch from 10m below the waterline.

Operators

Real Journeys (☎03-249 7416, 0800 656 501; www.realjourneys.co.nz) ⚓ Milford's biggest and most venerable operator runs a popular 1¾-hour scenic cruise (adult/child from $76/22). More specialised is the 2½-hour nature cruise (adult/child from $88/22), which hones in on wildlife with commentary from a nature guide. Overnight cruises are also available, from which you can kayak and take nature tours in small boats en route. Gilded with a long list of awards since it was founded in 1954, Real Journeys continues to be involved in local conservation efforts, from its minimal-impact cruises to fundraisers and charitable donations.

Cruise Milford (☎0800 645 367; www.cruisemilfordnz.com; adult/child from $95/18; ⊙10.45am, 12.45pm & 2.45pm) Offering a more personal touch than some of the big-boat tours, Cruise Milford's smaller vessels head out three times a day on 1¾-hour cruises, divulging great info from tectonics to wildlife.

Mitre Peak Cruises (☎03-249 8110, 0800 744 633; www.mitrepeak.com; adult/child from $70/17) Two-hour cruises in smallish boats (maximum capacity 75), allowing closer waterfall and wildlife viewing than larger vessels. The 4.30pm cruise is a good choice because many larger boats are heading back at this time.

Kayakers in Milford Sound

Kayaking

Getting out on the water offers one of the best perspectives of Milford Sound. The following operators both have booking offices in Te Anau and offer excursions for experienced paddlers and total beginners.

Rosco's Milford Kayaks (📞0800 476 726, 03-249 8500; www.roscosmilfordkayaks.com; 72 Town Centre, Te Anau; trips $99-199; ⊙Nov-Apr) Rosco, a colourful character seasoned by decades of kayaking experience, leads guided, tandem-kayak trips such as the 'Morning Glory' ($199), a challenging paddle the full length of the fiord to Anita Bay,

and the 'Stirling Sunriser' ($195), which ventures beneath the 151m-high Stirling Falls. Beginners can take it easy on a two-hour paddle on the sound ($109).

Go Orange Kayaks (📞03-442 7340; www.goorangekayaks.co.nz; ⊙Sep-Apr) Options with this good-value operator include 'Milford Must Do' ($149, four hours kayaking), 'Milford Magic' ($205, two-hour kayak and two-hour cruise combo) and 'Milford Track Taster' ($118, paddle up to Sandfly Point followed by a two-hour guided walk).

Diving

For total immersion in Milford Sound's wildlife, a dive with **Descend Scubadiving** (📞027 337 2363; www.descend.co.nz; dives incl gear $345) plunges you amid black coral and more than 150 species of fish. Descend's six-hour trips include a cruise in a 7m catamaran and two dives along the way. It offers excursions for experienced divers and novices. Transport, equipment, hot drinks and snacks included.

VIEWFINDER/SHUTTERSTOCK ©

Te Anau–Milford Highway

Milford Sound is deservedly famous, but the road linking Te Anau to the sound is also a world standout – wonderfully scenic and travelling deep into the heart of true wilderness.

Great For...

☑ **Don't Miss**

Hiking along one of the excellent tracks off the main road to hidden lakes and rivers.

Sometimes the journey is the destination, and that's certainly true of the 119km stretch of road between Te Anau and Milford Sound (SH94). The Milford Hwy offers the most easily accessible experience of Fiordland in all its diversity, taking in expanses of beautiful beech forest, gentle river valleys, mirror-like lakes, exquisite alpine scenery and ending at arguably New Zealand's most breathtaking vista, Milford Sound.

The journey should take 2½ hours each way, but expect to spend time dawdling along walking trails and maxing out your camera's memory card. Most travellers embark on the Milford Hwy as a day trip from Te Anau, with a cruise on Milford Sound to break up the return journey. But the prospect of longer tramps or camping beneath jagged mountains might entice you to stay.

Peking Youth Hostel 北平国际青年旅舍

Restaurant 美食 *Wine* 美酒 *Flowers* 鲜花   Email: pekinghostel@vip.163.com

■首都国际机场 / Beijing International Airport
Take the Airport Express to Dongzhimen, then transfer to Line 2 to Chaoyangmen, from there transfer to Line 6 to Nanluoguxiang, takes Exit E. Then walk to North around 200 meters on your left hand you will find our hostel in Yu'er Hutong.
乘坐机场快轨至东直门，换乘2号线至朝阳门，再换乘6号线至南锣鼓巷，E口出站，往北走约200米到雨儿胡同即是。

■北京站 / Beijing Railway Station:
Take the subway Line 2 to Chaoyangmen, then

transfer to Line 6 to Nanluoguxiang and take Exit E.
乘坐地铁2号线至朝阳门，换乘6号线至南锣鼓巷，E口出。

■北京西站 / Beijing West Railway Station
Take the subway Line 9 to Baishiqiao South, then transfer to Line 6 to Nanluoguxiang, take Exit E.
乘坐地铁9号线至白石桥南站，换乘6号线至南锣鼓巷站，E口出。

■北京南站 / Beijing South Railway Station
Take the subway Line 4 to Ping' anli, then transfer to Line 6 to Nanluoguxiang, take Exit E.
乘坐地铁4号线至平安里，换乘6号线至南锣鼓巷站，E口出，往北走约200米到雨儿胡同即是。

请送我去Please Take Me To
东城区地安门东大街南锣鼓巷113-2号（南锣鼓巷南口向北第三个胡同，雨儿胡同左拐）

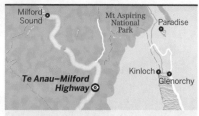

❶ Need to Know

Fill up with petrol in Te Anau. Allow at least 2½ hours to drive the full length of the highway.

✕ Take a Break

There are no eateries along the highway and only average ones in Milford Sound. Fill your hamper in Te Anau.

★ Top Tip

Kea (alpine parrots) hang around the Homer Tunnel. Don't feed them as it's bad for their health.

Tapara, and served as a stopover for parties heading to Anita Bay in search of *pounamu* (greenstone).

Hiking

Chasm Walk (SH94) About 9km before the end of the Te Anau–Milford Hwy, the 20-minute Chasm Walk affords staggering views over the churning Cleddau River. Pebbles caught in its frenetic currents have hollowed boulders into shapes reminiscent of a Salvador Dalí scene, while deep falls and thrashing waters give an unmistakable glimpse of nature's might. Wheelchair- and pram-friendly.

Lake Gunn Nature Walk (SH94) An easy 45-minute return walk loops through tall red beech forest at this bewitching spot along the Milford Hwy, 77km north of Te Anau. Moss-clung logs and a chorus of birdsong create a fairy-tale atmosphere, and side trails lead to quiet lakeside beaches. The area was known to Māori as O

Milford Highway Checklist

Set your alarm clock Aim to leave Te Anau early (by 8am) or later in the morning (11am) to avoid the tour buses heading for midday sound cruises.

Read up Pick up DOC's *Fiordland National Park Day Walks* brochure ($2) from the Fiordland i-SITE (p252) or Fiordland National Park Visitor Centre (p252), or download it at www.doc.govt.nz. Otherwise you risk zooming past the loveliest spots.

Allow loads of time The trip takes two to 2½ hours if you drive straight through, but take time to pull off the road and explore the many view points and nature walks along the way.

Doubtful Sound

Milford Sound gets all the attention, but the misty expanse of Doubtful Sound is even more spectacular. The area's remoteness is especially enhanced during an overnight stay on the water.

Remote Doubtful Sound is humbling in size and beauty. Carved by glaciers, it's one of New Zealand's largest fiords – almost three times the length of more popular Milford. Boats gliding through this maze of forested valleys have good chances of encountering fur seals and Fiordland penguins. Aside from haunting birdsong, Doubtful Sound deserves its Māori name, Patea, the 'place of silence'.

Until relatively recently, Doubtful Sound was isolated from all but intrepid explorers. Even Captain Cook only observed it from off the coast in 1770, because he was 'doubtful' whether winds would be sufficient to blow the ship back to sea. Access improved when the road over Wilmot Pass opened in 1959 to facilitate construction of West Arm power station.

Great For...

☑ **Don't Miss**

Dipping your kayak blades into mirror-flat water as you explore Doubtful Sound's mystic coves.

① Need to Know

Doubtful Sound is a one-hour boat trip from Manapouri to West Arm power station, followed by a 22km drive to Deep Cove.

✕ Take a Break

Manapouri's The Church (p252) is a merry pub (...formerly a church) with very welcoming staff.

★ Top Tip

Manapouri makes a logical base, although Te Anau (20km) and Queenstown (170km) pick-ups can be organised through cruise-boat operators.

Boat and coach transfers from Manapouri to Deep Cove are easily organised through tour operators, but time-consuming enough to deter some travellers...ideal for those who want to enjoy the silence.

Cruises

Day cruises allow about three hours on the water (once you've factored in transport time to the sound). Overnight cruises are pricey but preferable; they include meals plus the option of fishing and kayaking, depending on the weather.

Operators

Real Journeys (☑0800 656 501; www.real journeys.co.nz) 🌀 One-day 'wilderness cruis-es' (adult/child from $250/65) include a three-hour journey aboard a modern catamaran with a specialist nature guide. The overnight cruise (September to May) is aboard the *Fiordland Navigator*, which sleeps 70 in en suite cabins (quad-share per adult/child from $419/210, single/double from $1171/1338).

Fiordland Expeditions (☑0508 888 656, 03-249 9005; www.fiordlandexpeditions.co.nz; dm/s/d/tr from $645/1340/1420/2130; 🚣) A classy operator offering overnight cruises on the *Tutoko II* (maximum 14 passengers). It's a standard Doubtful Sound program plus fishing for your dinner and a welcome drink of bubbly.

Deep Cove Charters (☑03-249 6828; https://doubtfulsoundcruise.nz; s $550, cabins tw/d $1300/1400) Overnight cruises on board the *Seafinn* (maximum 12 passengers) run by home-grown crew. There are options to kayak and fish but it had us at 'crayfish lunch and venison supper included'.

Te Anau

Picturesque Te Anau is the main gateway to Milford Sound and three Great Walks: the Milford, Kepler and Routeburn tracks. Far from being a humdrum stopover, Te Anau is stunning in its own right. The township borders Lake Te Anau, New Zealand's second-largest lake, and while Te Anau doesn't party as hard as Queenstown, there are plenty of places to eat, sleep and sink a few beers here (all the tastier after a long day of tramping, kayaking or driving the Milford Hwy).

fringed by forest and towered over by the impressive Thomson and Livingstone Mountains, whose peaks rise to more than 1600m. Trampers can overnight at **Mavora Lakes Campsite** (adult/child $8/4), an unpowered 60-site camping space in a sublime setting in the heart of the park. The campsite is the starting point of the four-day, 50km Mavora–Greenstone Walkway.

The park, part of the Te Wāhipounamu (Southwest New Zealand) World Heritage Area, served as a *Lord of the Rings* filming location to represent Silverlode and Nen Hithoel.

◎ SIGHTS

Te Anau Glowworm Caves   Cave
(📞0800 656 501; www.realjourneys.co.nz; adult/child $83/22) Stare up at constellations of glowworms on an underground boat ride. Once present only in Māori legends, this 200m-long cave system was rediscovered in 1948. Its sculpted rocks, waterfalls and whirlpools are impressive by themselves, but the bluish sparkle of glowworms, peculiar territorial larvae that lure prey with their come-hither lights, is the main draw.

Reach the caves on a 2¼-hour guided tour with Real Journeys, via a lake cruise, walkway and a short boat ride. Tours depart from its office on Lakefront Dr.

**Punanga Manu
o Te Anau**   Bird Sanctuary
(Te Anau Bird Sanctuary; www.doc.govt.nz; Te Anau-Manapouri Rd; ⊙dawn-dusk) FREE By the lake, this set of outdoor aviaries offers a chance to see native bird species difficult to spot in the wild, including the precious icon of Fiordland, the extremely rare takahe. Arrive for the feeding time of this royal-blue flightless bird at 9.30am (October to March) or 10.30am (April to September).

Mavora Lakes Conservation Park
Nature Reserve
(www.doc.govt.nz; Centre Hill Rd) Within the Snowdon State Forest, this conservation park's huge golden meadows sit alongside two lakes – North and South Mavora –

✪ ACTIVITIES

Hollyford Track   Tramping
(📞03-442 3000; www.hollyfordtrack.com; adult/child from $1895/1495; ⊙late Oct-late Apr) 🦶 Brimming with insight into Māori history and Fiordland wildlife, this Ngāi Tahu–owned operator leads small-group (less than 16 people) three-day guided trips on the Hollyford staying at private huts/lodges. The journey is shortened with a jetboat trip down the river and Lake McKerrow on day two, and ends with a scenic flight to Milford Sound.

Fiordland Jet   Adventure Sports
(📞0800 253 826; www.fjet.nz; 84 Lakefront Dr; adult/child $139/70) Thrilling 90-minute jet-boating trips on the Upper Waiau River (in *Lord of the Rings*, the River Anduin), zipping between mountain-backed beech forest, with commentary on the area's natural (and fictional) highlights.

Wings & Water   Scenic Flights
(📞03-249 7405; www.wingsandwater.co.nz; Lakefront Dr) Take a scenic 20-minute flight over the Kepler Track (adult/child $225/130), or soar over Dusky, Doubtful and Milford Sounds (from $349/210) on longer joyrides of 40 minutes or more.

⊛ TOURS

Real Journeys   Tours
(📞0800 656 501; www.realjourneys.co.nz; 85 Lakefront Dr; ⊙7.30am-8.30pm Sep-May,

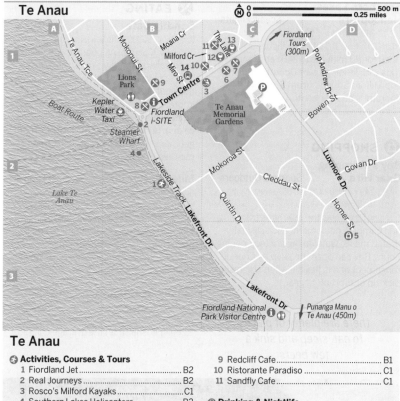

Te Anau

8am-7pm Jun-Aug) ✒ You can count on sharp service and well-organised tours from this major player, which offers cruises on Doubtful and Milford Sounds on its big menu of tours, walks and outdoor activities – always with sensitivity to local wildlife. Other highlights are guided day walks on the Milford Track and tours of the Te Anau Glowworm Caves.

Fiordland Tours   Tours

(☑ 0800 247 249; www.fiordlandtours.co.nz; 208 Milford Rd; adult/child from $149/69) Runs small-group bus and Milford Sound cruise tours (15 passengers or less), departing from Te Anau and stopping at scenic view points along the way. It also provides track transport and guided day walks on the Kepler Track.

Southern Lakes Helicopters
Scenic Flights

(📞03-249 7167; www.southernlakeshelicopters.co.nz; Lakefront Dr) Offering flights over Te Anau for 30 minutes ($240) and longer trips with landings over Doubtful, Dusky and Milford Sounds (from $685), this operator's quarter-century of experience in Fiordland will reassure nervous flyers.

🔒 SHOPPING

Bev's Tramping Gear Hire
Sports & Outdoors

(📞03-249 7389, 027 249 7389; www.bevs-hire.co.nz; 16 Homer St; ⊙9am-noon & 6-7pm Mon-Fri Oct-Apr) Bev walks the talk, hires tramping and camping equipment, and sells dehydrated meals. Outside the limited opening hours, Bev can open the shop by prior arrangement and is flexible when organising pick-up or drop-off of gear.

there are plenty of places to eat, sleep and sink a few beers

Stores in Te Anau

❌ EATING

Sandfly Cafe
Cafe $

(📞03-249 9529; 9 The Lane; mains $7-20; ⊙7am-4.30pm; 🛜) As popular with locals as travellers, Sandfly serves the town's best espresso alongside breakfasts, light meals of pasta or club sandwiches, and an impressive rack of sweet treats from caramel slices to berry friands (almond-flour cakes). Sun yourself on the lawn, or try to get maximum mileage out of the free 15 minutes of wi-fi.

Miles Better Pies
Fast Food $

(📞03-249 9044; www.milesbetterpies.co.nz; 19 Town Centre; pies $5-6.50; ⊙6am-6pm Oct-May, to 3pm Jun-Sep) The bumper selection here includes venison, lamb and mint, and fruit pies. There are a few pavement tables, but sitting and munching beside the lake is nicer.

Mainly Seafood
Fish & Chips $

(📞027 516 5555; www.facebook.com/mainlyseafood; 106 Town Centre; mains $5-27; ⊙11.30am-8.30pm) Posher than the average chippie,

DAVID L. MOORE / NZL/ALAMY ©

this commendable fast-food joint serves great fish and chips, homemade venison and vegie burgers, as well as deep-fried scallops and manuka-smoked salmon specials. Sound a bit too heavy? We refer you to their health boasts about using only rice bran oil.

Ristorante Paradiso Italian $$

(Pizzeria da Toni; ☑03-249 4305; www.paradiso pizzeria.co.nz; 1 Milford Cres; mains $20-29; ⊙4-9pm; ☑) Wood-fired pizzas with simple, high-quality toppings and homemade pastas are the stars of the show at this surprisingly authentic Italian restaurant. Red-gingham tablecloths and the odd splash of Italian art don't quite transport you to Rome but the marinara sauce comes close.

Kepler's South American $$$

(☑03-249 7909; 90 Town Centre; mains $29-40; ⊙5-9pm) Mountains of crayfish, mouth-watering ceviche and perfectly seared steaks are whisked to tables at this efficient but friendly family-run place. South American flair permeates the menu (quinoa-crusted orange roughy, Chilean malbec); we suggest the whopping roast lamb with a generous pour of merlot.

Redcliff Cafe Modern NZ $$$

(☑03-249 7431; www.theredcliff.co.nz; 12 Mokonui St; mains $38-41; ⊙4-10pm) Housed in a replica settler's cottage, relaxed Redcliff offers well-executed locally sourced food amid nostalgic decor (think old photos and antique sewing machines). We liked the succulent slow-roasted pork and wild hare on barley risotto, but Redcliff is just as good for a drink in the antique bar (or the adjoining outdoor terrace, which catches the sun).

🍷 DRINKING & NIGHTLIFE

Black Dog Bar Bar

(☑03-249 9089; www.blackdogbar.co.nz; 7 The Lane; ⊙10am-late; ☎) Cocktails, Kiwi-style tapas, a smooth soundtrack and plump black sofas by an open fire...they all

Short Walks Around Te Anau

Te Anau's **Lakeside Track** makes for a very pleasant stroll or cycle in either direction – north to the marina and around to the Upukerora River (about an hour return), or south past the Fiordland National Park Visitor Centre and on to the control gates and start of the Kepler Track (50 minutes).

Day tramps in the national park are readily accessible from Te Anau. **Kepler Water Taxi** (☑027 249 8365, 03-249 8364; www.keplerwatertaxi.co.nz; one way $25) and **Fiordland Outdoors Company** (☑0800 347 4538; www.fiordlandoutdoors. co.nz) can scoot you over to Brod Bay, from where you can walk back along the Lakeside Track to Te Anau (two to three hours). During summer, **Trips & Tramps** (☑03-249 7081, 0800 305 807; www.tripsandtramps.com) offers small-group, guided day hikes on the Kepler and Routeburn, among other tracks (as well as shuttles to and from trailheads). Real Journeys (p247) runs guided day hikes (adult/child $195/127, November to mid-April) along an 11km stretch of the Milford Track. Various day walks can also be completed by linking with regular bus services run by Tracknet (p252).

For self-guided adventures, pick up DOC's *Fiordland National Park Day Walks* brochure ($2) from the Fiordland i-SITE or Fiordland National Park Visitor Centre, or download it at www.doc.govt.nz.

Lake Te Anau
TAROMON/SHUTTERSTOCK ©

conspire to make Black Dog the most sophisticated watering hole in Te Anau. It's attached to the Fiordland Cinema.

Ranch Bar & Grill   Pub
(☑03-249 8801; www.theranchbar.co.nz; 111 Town Centre; ☺8am-late) An open fire and chalet-style eaves heighten the appeal of this popular local pub, most loved for its hefty Sunday roast dinners ($15), Thursday jam nights and sports matches on big screens. Show up for big pancake breakfasts (until 11.30am) or generous schnitzels and mostly meaty mains ($20 to $42) at other times.

⭐ ENTERTAINMENT
Fiordland Cinema   Cinema
(☑03 249 8844; www.fiordlandcinema.co.nz; 7 The Lane; 🛜) In between regular showings of the excellent *Ata Whenua/Fiordland on Film* (adult/child $10/5), essentially a 32-minute advertisement for Fiordland scenery, Fiordland Cinema serves as the local movie house.

ℹ️ INFORMATION
Fiordland i-SITE (☑03-249 8900; www.fiord land.org.nz; 19 Town Centre; ☺8.30am-8pm Dec-Mar, to 5.30pm Apr-Nov) The official information centre, offering activity, accommodation and transport bookings.

Fiordland National Park Visitor Centre (DOC; ☑03-249 7924; www.doc.govt.nz; cnr Lakefront Dr & Te Anau-Manapouri Rd; ☺8.30am-4.30pm) Can assist with Great Walks bookings, general hut tickets and information, with the bonus of a natural-history display and a shop stocking tramping supplies and essential topographical maps for backcountry trips.

ℹ️ GETTING THERE & AWAY
InterCity (☑03-442 4922; www.intercity.co.nz; Miro St) Services to Milford Sound ($22 to $44, three hours, two to three daily) and Queenstown ($21 to $49, 3¼ hours, four daily).

Naked Bus (https://nakedbus.com) Has daily bus services to Queenstown (from $30, 2¾ hours) and one daily morning bus to Milford Sound (from $32, 2¼ hours).

Tracknet (☑0800 483 262; www.tracknet.net) From November to April Te Anau–based Tracknet has at least three daily scheduled buses to/from Milford Sound ($53, 2¼ hours), one bus to/from Manapouri ($25, 30 minutes) and four daily to Queenstown ($47, 2¾ hours).

Topline Tours (☑03-249 8059; www.topline tours.co.nz; 32 Caswell Rd) Offers year-round shuttles between Te Anau and Manapouri ($20).

Manapouri

Manapouri, 20km south of Te Anau, is the jumping-off point for cruises to Doubtful Sound. But little Manapouri has a few other tricks up its sleeve. The town can't compete with Te Anau's restaurants and motels but it has mountain-backed lake views easily as lovely as those enjoyed by its bigger, more popular sibling.

🎯 ACTIVITIES
By crossing the Waiau River at **Pearl Harbour** (Waiau St, Manapouri) you can embark on day walks as detailed in DOC's *Fiordland Day Walks* brochure. A classic circuit with glimmering lake views (and occasional steep parts) is the **Circle Track** (3½ hours). Cross the river aboard a hired rowing boat or water taxi from **Adventure Manapouri** (☑03-249 8070, 021 925 577; www.adventurema napouri.co.nz; rowing boat hire per day $40, water taxi per person return $20), which also offers guided walks and fishing tours.

Running between the northern entrance to Manapouri township and Pearl Harbour, the one-hour **Frasers Beach** walk offers picnic and swimming spots as well as fantastic views across the lake.

❌ EATING & DRINKING
The Church   Pub Food $$
(☑03-249 6001; www.facebook.com/pg/ manapouri.co.nz; 23 Waiau St; mains $17-25;

Pearl Harbour

🕑11am-10pm Sun-Thu, to midnight Fri & Sat) No need to head up to Te Anau for a satisfying feed and a few beers, hurrah! Plates heavy with steaks, burgers and butter chicken are hauled to tables in this converted church building, now a merry pub with exceptionally welcoming staff.

Lakeview Cafe & Bar   Pub Food **$$**
(📞03-249 6652; www.manapouri.com; 68 Cathedral Dr; mains $16-34; 🕑11am-9pm; 🛜) The motor inn's cafe serves substantial meals (pizzas, schnitzels, venison stew and a token veggie dish) with a generous side order of lake views from the front lawn. The adjacent bar is well located for a drink as you sigh over Lake Manapouri flushing pink with the setting sun.

❶ GETTING THERE & AWAY

Topline Tours Offers year-round shuttles between Te Anau and Manapouri ($20).

Tracknet One daily bus to/from Te Anau ($25, 30 minutes) from November to April, and on demand at other times of the year.

OTAGO
PENINSULA

Otago Peninsula at a Glance...

It's hard to believe that the Otago Peninsula – a picturesque haven of rolling hills, secluded bays, sandy beaches and clifftop vistas – is only half an hour's drive from downtown Dunedin. This small sliver of land is home to the South Island's most accessible diversity of wildlife, including albatrosses, penguins, fur seals and sea lions. The peninsula's only town is the petite Portobello, and despite a host of tours exploring the region, it maintains its quiet rural air.

Back in Dunedin (aka the 'Edinburgh of the South'), New Zealand's oldest university provides plenty of student energy to sustain the local bars.

Otago Peninsula in One Day

Fuel-up for a day trip: grab breakfast with a Dunedin view at **No 7 Balmac** (p265) before exploring the peninsula. Must-sees include the **Penguin Place** (p260) and the big birds at the **Royal Albatross Centre** (p260). Back in Dunedin, dinner at **Bracken** (p265) awaits.

Otago Peninsula in Two Days

Next morning, grab your caffeine hit at Dunedin's **Insomnia by Strictly Coffee** (p266) or **Allpress** (p266) before trucking out to the peninsula again. **Nature's Wonders Naturally** (p259) wildlife reserve hosts yellow-eyed penguins, NZ fur seals and beautiful beaches. Back in the city, tour **Emerson's Brewery** (p263), rolling on to the bars around The Octagon.

Dunedin Map (p264)

Arriving on the Otago Peninsula

Dunedin Airport (p405) There's no public transport to the airport, located 27km southwest of the city. A taxi to/from the city costs around $90. Pre-booked shuttle buses run door-to-door ($20).

Cumberland St Bus Stop Dunedin's GoBus (p267) network extends to the Otago Peninsula (adult/child $6/3.60, one hour), or it's a 20km drive.

Sleeping

The Otago Peninsula is easily visited on a day trip from Dunedin, where there are myriad places to stay. There are some good accommodation options on the peninsula too (notably a motel, B&B and hostel) – worth considering if you don't fancy a drive back to the city after a wild evening with the penguins.

MICHAEL W NZ/SHUTTERSTOCK ©

Wildlife Watching

The Otago Peninsula is one of the best places on the South Island for wildlife spotting. Jagging into the ocean east of Dunedin, the peninsula provides safe, sheltered harbours for resident penguins and albatrosses, and nomadic sea lions. You might also spot a few passing whales or dolphins.

Great For...

☑ Don't Miss

Spying some slow-circling albatrosses at Taiaroa Head, the world's only mainland royal albatross colony.

Yellow-Eyed Penguins

One of the world's rarest penguins, the endangered hoiho (yellow-eyed penguin) is found along the Otago coast. It's estimated that fewer than 4000 of these penguins remain in the wild, with around 150 breeding pairs resident on deserted beaches in the southeast of the South Island during the 2016/17 breeding season.

The encroachment of humans on their habitat is one of the main causes of the penguins' decline. Penguins have been badly distressed by tourists using flash photography or traipsing through the nesting grounds; under no circumstances should you approach one. Even loud voices can disturb them. For this reason, the best way to see a hoiho in the wild is through an organised tour onto private land, such

Little penguins

Blue Penguins

Nowhere near as rare as their yellow-eyed cousins, little penguins sometimes pop up in the oddest places (window-shopping in Oamaru's Victorian Precinct, for instance). Also known as blue penguins, little blue penguins, kororā (in Māori) and fairy penguins (in Australia), these little cuties can spend days out at sea before returning to their colony just before dusk in batches known as rafts.

Although you might chance upon one at night, the best places to see them arrive en masse are at the Royal Albatross Centre (p260) on the Otago Peninsula.

as through Nature's Wonders Naturally or Penguin Place (p260).

ℹ️ Need to Know

Visit the Dunedin i-SITE (p266) for maps, directions, tour info and DOC walking guides.

✕ Take a Break

Portobello is the peninsula's only town, home to the reliable **Portobello Hotel & Bistro** (☏03-478 0759; www.portobellohotelandbistro.co.nz; 2 Harington Point Rd; mains lunch $13-23, dinner $23-36; ⊙11.30am-11.30pm).

★ Top Tip

The peninsula can be easily tackled as a day trip (or two) from Dunedin.

Sea Lions

Sea lions are most easily seen on a tour, but are regularly present at Sandfly Bay, Allans Beach and Victory Beach on the Otago Peninsula. They are predominantly bachelor males vacationing from Campbell Island or the Auckland Islands. Give them plenty of space, as these powerful beasts can really motor over the first 20m.

Sanctuaries & Sights

Nature's Wonders Naturally
Wildlife Reserve

(☏03-478 1150; www.natureswonders.co.nz; Taiaroa Head; adult/child Argo $99/45, coach $45/22.50; ⊙tours from 10.15am) What makes the improbably beautiful beaches of this coastal sheep farm different from other important wildlife habitats is that (apart from pest eradication and the like) they're left completely alone. Many of the multiple private beaches haven't suffered a human footprint in years. The result is that yellow-eyed penguins can often be spotted (through binoculars) at any time of the day, and NZ fur seals laze around rocky swimming holes, blissfully unfazed by tour groups passing by.

Depending on the time of year, you might also see whales and little penguin chicks.

The tour is conducted in 'go-anywhere' Argo vehicles by enthusiastic guides, at least some of whom double as true-blue Kiwi farmers. A less bumpy coach option is also available, though you won't see as much.

Penguin Place — Bird Sanctuary
(☏03-478 0286; www.penguinplace.co.nz; 45 Pakihau Rd, Harington Point; adult/child $54/16; ⏱tours from 10.15am Oct-Mar, 3.45pm Apr-Sep) On private farmland, this reserve protects nesting sites of the rare yellow-eyed penguin/hoiho. The 90-minute tours focus on penguin conservation and close-up viewing from a system of hides. Bookings are recommended.

Royal Albatross Centre & Fort Taiaroa — Bird Sanctuary
(☏03-478 0499; www.albatross.org.nz; Taiaroa Head; adult/child albatross $50/15, fort $25/10, combined $55/20; ⏱10.15am-dusk) Taiaroa Head, at the peninsula's northern tip, has the world's only mainland royal albatross colony, along with a late 19th-century military fort. The only public access to the area is by guided tour. There's an hour-long albatross tour and a 30-minute fort tour available, or the two can also be combined. Otherwise you can just call into the centre to look at the displays and have a bite in the cafe.

Albatrosses are present on Taiaroa Head throughout the year, but the best time to see them is from December to March, when one parent is constantly guarding the young while the other delivers food throughout the day. Sightings are most common in the afternoon when the winds

Sea lion

pick up; calm days don't see as many birds in flight.

Little penguins swim ashore at Pilots Beach (just below the car park) around dusk to head to their nests in the dunes. For their protection, the beach is closed to the public every evening, but viewing is possible from a specially constructed wooden platform (adult/child $35/10). Depending on the time of year, 50 to 300 penguins might waddle past.

Fort Taiaroa was built in 1885 in response to a perceived threat of Russian invasion. Its **Armstrong Disappearing Gun** was designed to be loaded and aimed underground, then popped up like the world's slowest jack-in-the-box to be fired.

Tours

Back to Nature Tours Bus

(☑0800 286 000; www.backtonaturetours. co.nz) ✎ The full-day Royal Peninsula tour (adult/child $193/125) heads to points of interest around Dunedin before hitting the Otago Peninsula. Stops include Larnach Castle's gardens (castle entry is extra), Penguin Place and the Royal Albatross Centre. There's also a half-day option that visits various beaches ($83/55) and another tackling the Lovers Leap walking track ($89/55). Will pick up from your accommodation.

Elm Wildlife Tours Wildlife

(☑03-454 4121; www.elmwildlifetours.co.nz; tours from $103) ✎ Well-regarded, small-group, wildlife-focused tours, with options to add the Royal Albatross Centre or a Monarch Cruise. Pick-up and drop-off from Dunedin is included.

Wild Earth Adventures Kayaking

(☑03-489 1951; www.wildearth.co.nz; per person $115) Offers guided tours in double sea kayaks, with wildlife often sighted en route. Tours take between three hours and a full day, with pick-ups from The Octagon in Dunedin.

Dunedin

Two words immediately spring to mind when Kiwis think of their seventh-largest city: 'Scotland' and 'students'. Dunedin is immensely proud of its Scottish heritage, never missing an opportunity to break out the haggis and bagpipes on civic occasions. The city even has its own tartan.

Just like the Scots, Dunedin locals love a drink, and none more so than the Otago University students who dominate Dunedin in term time.

◎ SIGHTS

Olveston   House

(☏03-477 3320; www.olveston.co.nz; 42 Royal Tce, Roslyn; adult/child $20/11; ⊘tours 9.30am, 10.45am, noon, 1.30pm, 2.45pm & 4pm) Although it's a youngster by European standards, this spectacular 1906 mansion provides a wonderful window into Dunedin's past. Entry is via fascinating guided tours; it pays to book ahead. There's also a pretty little garden to explore (entry free).

Toitū Otago
Settlers Museum   Museum

(☏03-477 5052; www.toituosm.com; 31 Queens Gardens; ⊘10am-5pm) FREE Storytelling is the focus of this excellent interactive museum which traces the history of human settlement in the South Island. The engrossing Māori section is followed by a large gallery where floor-to-ceiling portraits of Victorian-era settlers stare out from behind their whiskers and lace. Other displays include a recreated passenger-ship cabin, an impressive vintage car collection and a fascinating array of obsolete technology, like the first computer used to draw the lottery in Dunedin.

Otago Museum   Museum

(☏03-474 7474; www.otagomuseum.nz; 419 Great King St, North Dunedin; ⊘10am-5pm) ✐FREE The centrepiece of this august institution is Southern Land, Southern People, showcasing Otago's cultural and physical past and present, from geology and dinosaurs to the modern day. The *Tāngata Whenua* Māori gallery houses an impressive *waka taua* (war canoe), won-

Dunedin Railway Station

BANGKOKFLAME/SHUTTERSTOCK ©

derfully worn old carvings, and some lovely *pounamu* (greenstone) weapons, tools and jewellery.

Emerson's Brewery   Brewery
(✑03-477 1812; www.emersons.co.nz; 70 Anzac Ave; tour per person $28; ✆tours 10.30am, 12.30pm, 3.30pm & 5.30pm, restaurant 10am-late, cellar door 10am-6pm Sun-Wed, to 8pm Thu-Sat) Opened in 2016, this impressive brick-and-glass structure is the flash new home of Emerson's, the microbrewery founded by local-boy-made-good Richard Emerson in 1992. Forty-five-minute tours take you behind the scenes of the brewing process, ending with the all-important tasting.

Dunedin Railway
Station   Historic Building
(22 Anzac Ave) Featuring mosaic-tile floors and glorious stained-glass windows, Dunedin's striking bluestone railway station (built between 1903 and 1906) claims to be NZ's most photographed building. Head upstairs for the **New Zealand Sports Hall of Fame** (✑03-477 7775; www.nzhalloffame. co.nz; adult/child $6/2; ✆10am-4pm), a small museum devoted to the nation's obsession, and the **Art Station** (✑03-477 9465; www. otagoartsociety.co.nz; ✆10am-4pm) FREE, the local Art Society's gallery and shop.

⊕ ACTIVITIES
Tunnel Beach Walkway   Walking
(Tunnel Beach Rd, Blackhead) This short but extremely steep pathway (15 minutes down, 30 back up) brings you to a dramatic stretch of coast where the wild Pacific has carved sea stacks, arches and unusual formations out of the limestone. Strong currents make swimming here dangerous, but the views are spectacular.

Esplanade Surf School   Surfing
(✑0800 484 141; www.espsurfschool.co.nz; 1 Esplanade, St Clair; 90min group lesson $60, private instruction $120) Operating from a van parked at St Clair Beach in summer whenever the surf is up (call at other times), the

---

📖 Dunedin Bookshops

Dunedin is a bookish sort of town, whether you're reading one, writing one or buying one. It was designated a UNESCO City of Literature in 2014, in recognition of the profound creative energy of this small southern city. If you'd like to explore Dunedin's literary side during your stay, check out the City of Literature office's website (www. cityofliterature.co.nz) for information about readings, launches and other literary events.

University Book Shop (✑03-477 6976; www.unibooks.co.nz; 378 Great King St, North Dunedin; ✆8.30am-5.30pm Mon-Fri, 10am-4pm Sat, 11am-3pm Sun) Dunedin's best bookshop is perfect for browsing, with lots of Māori, Pacific and NZ titles in stock.

Dead Souls (✑021 0270 8540; www. deadsouls.co.nz; 393 Princes St; ✆10am-6pm) Crammed to the rafters with interesting volumes. Worth a peek just for the ceiling, which is papered with old book covers.

Hard to Find Books (✑03-471 8518; www.hardtofind.co.nz; 20 Dowling St; ✆10am-6pm) Bookworms will spend hours prowling the shelves of this sprawling store. If you can't find it here, it probably doesn't exist.

Scribes (✑03-477 6874; 546 Great King St; ✆10am-5pm Mon-Fri, to 4.30pm Sat & Sun) Stacks upon stacks of treasures await at this excellent secondhand bookshop.

---

experienced crew provide board hire and lessons to suit all levels.

🛍 SHOPPING
Gallery De Novo   Art
(✑03-474 9200; www.gallerydenovo.co.nz; 101 Stuart St; ✆9.30am-5.30pm Mon-Fri, 10am-3pm Sat & Sun) This interesting, contemporary,

Central Dunedin

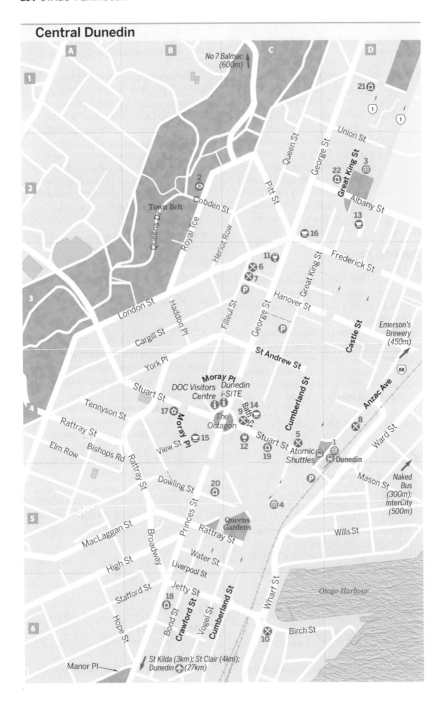

No 7 Balmac (600m)

Town Belt

Queens Dr

Royal Tce

Cobden St

Heriot Row

Queen St

George St

Pitt St

Union St

Great King St

Albany St

21

22

3

13

16

11

6

7

Hanover St

Frederick St

Great King St

Castle St

Emerson's Brewery (450m)

London St

Haddon Pl

Filleul St

George St

Cargill St

St Andrew St

Cumberland St

Anzac Ave

88

York Pl

Stuart St

Moray Pl

DOC Visitors Centre

Dunedin i-SITE

Tennyson St

Moray Pl

17

The Octagon

9

14

Bath St

5

1

8

Ward St

Rattray St

Elm Row

Bishops Rd

Rattray St

View St

15

12

Stuart St

Atomic Shuttles

19

Dunedin

Mason St

Naked Bus (300m); InterCity (500m)

Dowling St

20

Princes St

4

MacLaggan St

Broadway

High St

Rattray St

Queens Gardens

Water St

Wills St

Stafford St

Liverpool St

Jetty St

Crawford St

Cumberland St

Wharf St

Otago Harbour

18

Bond St

Vogel St

Birch St

10

Hope St

Manor Pl

St Kilda (3km); St Clair (4km); Dunedin (27km)

Central Dunedin

fine-art gallery is worth a peek whether you're likely to invest in a substantial piece of Kiwi art or not.

 EATING

Otago Farmers Market   Market $

(www.otagofarmersmarket.org.nz; Dunedin Railway Station; ⊙8am-12.30pm Sat) This thriving market is all local, all edible (or drinkable) and mostly organic. Grab a freshly baked pastry and a flat white to sustain you while you browse, and stock up on fresh meat, seafood, veggies and cheese for your journey. Sorted.

Best Cafe   Fish & Chips $

(www.facebook.com/bestcafedunedin; 30 Stuart St; takeaways $6-10, mains $11-26; ⊙11am-2.30pm & 5-8pm Mon-Sat) Serving up fish and chips since 1932, this local stalwart has its winning formula down pat, complete with vinyl tablecloths, hand-cut chips and curls of butter on white bread.

Perc   Cafe $

(🖉03-477 5462; www.perc.co.nz; 142 Stuart St; brunch $8-20; ⊙7am-4pm Mon-Fri, from 8am Sat & Sun; 🛜) Hanging plants, flower-filled vases and large art deco windows give this central cafe a creative, artsy vibe. The well-executed brunch options, fresh salads and counter full of tempting baked goods woo local students and office workers alike,

who set up camp here all day long for the flat whites and free wi-fi.

Miga   Korean $$

(🖉03-477 4770; www.facebook.com/migadunedin; 4 Hanover St; mains lunch $10-15, dinner $16-42; ⊙11.30am-2pm & 5pm-late Mon-Sat) Settle into a booth at this attractive brick-lined eatery, and order claypot rice or noodle dishes from the extensive menu. Japanese dishes include tempura, katsu and incredible ramen soups, made with fresh noodles. Otherwise go for broke and cook a Korean barbecue right at your table.

No 7 Balmac   Cafe $$

(🖉03-464 0064; www.no7balmac.co.nz; 7 Balmacewen Rd, Maori Hill; mains brunch $14-26, dinner $29-45; ⊙7am-late Mon-Fri, 8.30am-late Sat, 8.30am-5pm Sun; 🛜) We wouldn't recommend walking to this sophisticated cafe at the top of Maori Hill, but luckily it's well worth the price of a cab. The fancy cafe fare stretches from smashing brunches to the likes of confit duck and slow-braised lamb. If you're on a diet, avoid eye contact with the cake cabinet.

Bracken   Modern NZ $$$

(🖉03-477 9779; www.brackenrestaurant.co.nz; 95 Filleul St; 5-/7-/9-course menu $79/99/120, with matched wines $134/164/200; ⊙6-9pm Tue-Sat) 🌿 Bracken's seasonal tasting menus offer a succession of pretty little plates

 Just Give Me the Coffee & No One Will Get Hurt

Dunedin has some excellent coffee bars in which you can refuel and recharge:

The Fix (www.thefixcoffee.co.nz; 15 Frederick St; ⏰7am-4pm Mon-Fri, 8am-noon Sat)

Mazagran Espresso Bar (36 Moray Pl; ⏰8am-6pm Mon-Fri, to 2pm Sat)

Insomnia by Strictly Coffee (☎03-479 0017; www.strictlycoffee.co.nz; 23 Bath St; ⏰7am-4pm Mon-Fri)

Allpress (☎03-477 7162; www.nz.allpress espresso.com; 12 Emily Siedeberg Pl; ⏰8am-4pm Mon-Fri)

JOHN GEERE/SHUTTERSTOCK ©

bursting with flavour. While the dishes are intricate, nothing's overly gimmicky, and the setting, in an old wooden house, is classy without being too formal.

Plato   Modern NZ $$$

(☎03-477 4235; www.platocafe.co.nz; 2 Birch St; mains lunch $20-28, dinner $29-38; ⏰noon-2pm Wed-Sat, from 11am Sun, plus 6pm-late daily) The kooky decor (including collections of toys and beer tankards) gives little indication of the seriously good food on offer at this relaxed eatery by the harbour. Fresh fish and shellfish feature prominently in a lengthy menu full of international flavours and subtle smoky elements. Servings are enormous.

DRINKING & NIGHTLIFE

Aika + Co   Bar

(www.facebook.com/aikaandcompany; 357 George St; ⏰10am-late Mon-Sat) With a new name but the same tiny space, 'Dunedin's littlest bar' might only be 1.8m wide, but it's still big enough to host regular live bands. There are just six bar stools, so patrons spill out into an adjacent laneway. By day, it's a handy caffeine-refuelling spot, as well as offering juices, milkshakes, baked goods and simple bar snacks.

Albar   Bar

(☎03-479 2468; 135 Stuart St; ⏰11am-late) This former butcher is now a bohemian bar, with a dark, atmospheric interior and cosy booths, illuminated by a single chandelier. Punters are drawn in by the many single-malt whiskies and interesting tap beers, as well as the cheap tapas-style snacks (from $7).

Carousel   Cocktail Bar

(☎03-477 4141; www.carouselbar.co.nz; 141 Stuart St; ⏰5pm-late Wed-Sat) Monochrome tartan wallpaper, a roof deck and great cocktails leave the classy clientele looking pleased to be seen somewhere so deadly cool. DJs spin deep house until late from Thursday through to Saturday, and there's often live jazz on Friday evenings from 8.30pm. It's upstairs.

ENTERTAINMENT

Fortune Theatre   Theatre

(☎03-477 8323; www.fortunetheatre.co.nz; 231 Stuart St; adult/child $45/17.50; ⏰box office 10.30am-5pm Mon-Fri, 4.30-7.30pm Sat, 1.30-4pm Sun) The world's southernmost professional theatre company has been staging dramas, comedies, pantomimes, classics and contemporary NZ productions for over 40 years. Shows are performed – watched over by the obligatory theatre ghost – in an old Gothic-style Wesleyan church.

ℹ INFORMATION

The **Dunedin i-SITE** (☎03-474 3300; www.isite dunedin.co.nz; 50 The Octagon; ⏰8.30am-5pm Apr-Oct, to 6pm Nov-Mar) incorporates the **DOC**

Visitors Centre (Department of Conservation; ☑03-474 3300; www.doc.govt.nz; 50 The Octagon; ⊙8.30am-5.30pm), providing a one-stop shop for all of your information needs, including Great Walks and hut bookings.

❶ GETTING THERE & AWAY

AIR

Air New Zealand (☑0800 737 000; www.airnewzealand.co.nz) Flies to/from Auckland, Wellington and Christchurch.

Jetstar (☑0800 800 995; www.jetstar.com) Flies to/from Auckland and Wellington.

Virgin Australia (☑0800 670 000; www.virginaustralia.com) Flies to/from Brisbane, Australia.

BUS

Atomic Shuttles (☑03-349 0697; www.atomictravel.co.nz) Buses to/from Christchurch ($35, six hours) and Queenstown ($45, 4½ hours).

InterCity (☑03-471 7143; www.intercity.co.nz) Coaches to/from Christchurch (from $42, six hours), Queenstown (from $26, 4¼ hours) and Te Anau (from $38, 4½ hours) at least daily.

Naked Bus (https://nakedbus.com) Daily buses head to/from Christchurch (six hours, prices vary).

❶ GETTING AROUND

Dunedin's **GoBus** (☑03-474 0287; www.orc.govt.nz; adult $2.60-15.30) network extends across the city.

Port Chalmers

Little Port Chalmers is only 13km from central Dunedin but it feels a world away. Somewhere between working class and bohemian, Port Chalmers has a history as a port town but has long attracted Dunedin's arty types. The main drag, George St, is home to a handful of cafes, design stores and galleries, perfect for a half-day's worth of wandering, browsing and sipping away from the city crush.

⊙ SIGHTS

Orokonui Ecosanctuary   Wildlife Reserve
(☑03-482 1755; www.orokonui.org.nz; 600 Blueskin Rd; adult/child $19/9.50; ⊙9.30am-4.30pm) From the impressive visitors centre there are great views over this 307-hectare predator-free nature reserve, which encloses cloud forest on the mountainous ridge above Port Chalmers and stretches to the estuary on the opposite side. Its mission is to provide a mainland refuge for species usually exiled to offshore islands for their own protection. Visiting options include self-guided explorations, hour-long 'highlights' tours (adult/child $35/17.50; 11am and 1.30pm daily) and two-hour 'forest explorer' tours (adult/child $50/35; 11am daily).

Rare bird species finding sanctuary here include kiwi, takahe and kaka, while reptiles include tuatara and Otago skinks.

Orokonui is a well-signposted 6km drive from the main road into Port Chalmers.

❽ EATING

Union Co.   Cafe $
(2 George St; mains $8-15; ⊙8am-3pm) Great coffee, delicious baked goods and a sunny corner position make this the pick for your morning caffeine fix.

Carey's Bay Hotel   Pub Food $$
(☑03-472 8022; www.careysbayhotel.co.nz; 17 Macandrew Rd, Carey's Bay; mains $19-30; ⊙10am-late) Just around the corner from Port Chalmers you'll find this historic pub, popular with locals for its hearty meals and unbeatable location – on sunny days grab a table out the front for first-class views over the sparkling water.

❶ GETTING THERE & AWAY

On weekdays buses (adult/child $6/3.60, 30 minutes, half-hourly) travel between Dunedin and Port Chalmers between 6.30am and 9.30pm (11.30pm on Friday). On weekends buses run hourly between 8.30am and 11.30pm on Saturday, and 9.30am and 5.30pm on Sunday.

Performers at Tamaki Māori Village (p90)

In Focus

Queens Wharf, Auckland (p35)

CHAMELEONSEYE/SHUTTERSTOCK ©

New Zealand Today

Despite a decade marred by disasters – earthquakes and mining and helicopter tragedies – New Zealand never loses its nerve. The country remains a titan on both the silver screen and the sports field, there's a new prime minister at the helm, and change is afoot in the realms of housing affordability and conservation.

Jacinda-Mania

In 2010 she was NZ's youngest sitting MP, by 2017 she was running the country. The swift rise of Jacinda Ardern has been touted as part of a global political shift. Ardern became the youngest ever Labour Party leader in 2017, only a few weeks ahead of the election that propelled her to the role of prime minister at the age of 37 – making her NZ's youngest PM for 150 years. Passionate about climate change, unabashedly feminist and an ardent supporter of gay rights, Ardern's ability to win support with her energetic style was dubbed 'Jacinda-mania'. The final polls gave Labour a less-than-maniacal 37% of the vote, but resulted in a coalition government led by Labour.

Ardern's articulacy and verve have seen her aligned with other youthful, socially progressive world leaders like Justin Trudeau and Emmanuel Macron, part of a youth-powered

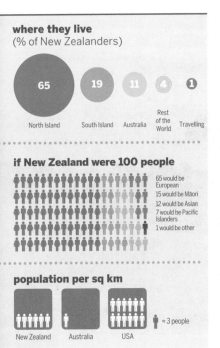

where they live
(% of New Zealanders)

65 — North Island
19 — South Island
11 — Australia
4 — Rest of the World
1 — Travelling

if New Zealand were 100 people

65 would be European
15 would be Māori
12 would be Asian
7 would be Pacific Islanders
1 would be other

population per sq km

New Zealand
Australia
USA

♦ ≈ 3 people

political sea change. But Ardern's style remains quintessentially Kiwi: unpretentious and accessible.

Cultural & Sporting Colossus

For a small country, New Zealand has enjoyed plenty of time on the world stage lately. Cementing NZ's reputation as a primo movie set, movie director James Cameron has been working out of Wellington on his long-awaited four *Avatar* sequels. They're slated for staggered release between 2020 and 2025...good thing New Zealanders are a patient bunch. Meanwhile, director Taika Waititi has been enjoying a wave of global adulation. His works *Boy* (2010) and *Hunt for the Wilderpeople* (2016) broke records in NZ, and vampire flat-sharing mockumentary *What We Do in the Shadows* (2014), a horror-comedy co-directed with Jemaine Clement, ensnared a cult following. But Waititi went stratospheric as the director of *Thor: Ragnarok* (2017), injecting distinctly Kiwi humour into a Marvel franchise that had lost its zest.

In the world of sport, NZ remains a force to be reckoned with. Following the All Blacks' success at the 2011 Rugby World Cup at home, the beloved national team beat arch-rivals Australia in 2015, becoming the first country ever to win back-to-back Rugby World Cups. The pressure is on for the 2019 World Cup, especially with stalwarts Richie McCaw and Dan Carter announcing retirement from the national team. After the Black Caps made the final of the Cricket World Cup for the first time in 2015, they were deprived of glory in a stinging loss to their trans-Tasman rivals Australia. The 2019 World Cup is their chance to seize victory. Out on the water, Emirates Team New Zealand scored a victory in 2017 at venerable sailing race the America's Cup. Auckland 2021, anyone?

The Big Issues

Being a dream destination has its challenges, especially when tourist numbers boom and property investors swoop. Aussie and Asian buyers are increasingly wise to NZ property: cue a spiralling housing crisis, and the IMF ranking NZ's housing as the most unaffordable in the OECD in 2016. With Auckland's population expected to increase by one million in the next 30 years, the fixes can't come swiftly enough.

The ever-increasing number of visitors to NZ – now an annual 3.54 million – is also a hot issue. In response to the enormous popularity of the Tongariro Alpine Crossing, the DOC has placed a time limit at the car park at the beginning of the track, forcing tourists to use traffic-reducing shuttle services. Meanwhile tourism hubs like Te Anau, gateway to world-famous Milford Sound, are seeing their peak season start ever earlier. A country beloved for being wild, green and beautiful faces the challenge of keeping it that way.

ANUPAM HATUI/SHUTTERSTOCK ©

History

Historians continue to unravel New Zealand's early history...with much of what they discover confirming traditional Māori narratives. In less than a thousand years NZ produced two new peoples: the Polynesian Māori and European New Zealanders (also known by their Māori name, 'Pākehā'). NZ shares some of its history with the rest of Polynesia, and with other European settler societies. This cultural intermingling has created unique features along the way.

AD 1280	1642	1769
Based on evidence from archaeological digs, the most likely arrival date of east Polynesians in NZ, now known as Māori.	First European contact: Abel Tasman arrives from the Dutch East Indies (Indonesia) but leaves after a sea skirmish with Māori.	European contact recommences via James Cook and Jean de Surville. Despite violence, both communicate with Māori.

Waitangi Treaty Grounds (p68)

Māori Settlement

The first settlers of NZ were the Polynesian forebears of today's Māori. Archaeologists and anthropologists continue to search for the details but the most widely accepted evidence suggests they arrived in the 13th century. Most historians now agree on 1280 as the Māori's most likely arrival date. Scientists have sequenced the DNA of settlers buried at the Wairau Bar archaeological site on the South Island, and confirmed the settlers as originating from east Polynesia (though work is ongoing to pinpoint their origins more precisely). The genetic diversity of the buried settlers suggests a fairly large-scale settlement – a finding consistent with Māori narratives about numerous vessels reaching the islands.

Prime sites for first settlement were warm coastal gardens for the food plants brought from Polynesia (kumara or sweet potato, gourd, yam and taro); sources of workable stone for knives and adzes; and areas with abundant big game. NZ has no native land mammals apart from a few species of bat, but 'big game' is no exaggeration: the islands were home to a dozen species of moa (a large flightless bird), the largest of which weighed up to

1790s	1818–45	1840
Whaling ships and sealing gangs arrive. Europeans depend on Māori contacts for essentials such as food, water and protection.	Intertribal Māori 'Musket Wars' take place: tribes acquire muskets and win bloody victories against tribes without them.	On 6 February around 500 chiefs countrywide sign the Treaty of Waitangi. NZ becomes a nominal British colony.

240kg, about twice the size of an ostrich...preyed upon by *Harpagornis moorei*, a whopping 15kg eagle. Other species of flightless birds and large sea mammals, such as fur seals, were easy game for hunters from small Pacific islands. The first settlers spread far and fast, from the top of the North Island to the bottom of the South Island within the first 100 years. High-protein diets are likely to have boosted population growth.

By about 1400, however, with big-game supply dwindling, Māori economics turned from big game to small game – forest birds and rats – and from hunting to gardening and fishing. A good living could still be made, but it required detailed local knowledge, steady effort and complex communal organisation, hence the rise of the Māori tribes. Competition for resources increased, conflict did likewise, and this led to the building of increasingly sophisticated *pā* (fortified villages), complete with wells and food storage pits. Vestiges of *pā* earthworks can still be seen around the country (on the hilltops of Auckland, for example).

Enter Europe

The first authenticated contact between Māori and European explorers took place in 1642. Seafarer Abel Tasman had just claimed Van Diemen's Land (Tasmania) for the Dutch when rough winds steered his ships east, where he sighted New Zealand. Tasman's two ships were searching for southern land and anything valuable it might contain. Tasman was instructed to pretend to any natives he might meet 'that you are by no means eager for precious metals, so as to leave them ignorant of the value of the same'.

When Tasman's ships anchored in the bay, local Māori came out in their canoes to make the traditional challenge: friends or foes? The Dutch blew their trumpets, unwittingly challenging back. When a boat was lowered to take a party between the two ships, it was attacked and four crewmen were killed. Having not even set foot on the land, Tasman sailed away and didn't return; nor did any other European for 127 years. But the Dutch did leave a name: initially 'Statenland', later changed to 'Nova Zeelandia' by cartographers.

English & French Arrivals

Contact between Māori and Europeans was renewed in 1769, when English and French explorers arrived, under James Cook and Jean de Surville – Cook narrowly pipped the latter to the post, naming Doubtless Bay before the French party dropped anchor there. The first French explorations ended sourly, with misunderstandings and violence; later expeditions were more fruitful. Meanwhile Cook made two more visits between 1773 and 1777. Exploration continued, motivated by science, profit and political rivalry.

Unofficial visits, by whaling ships in the north and sealing gangs in the south, began in the 1790s (though Māori living in New Zealand's interior remained largely unaffected). The first Christian missionaries established themselves in the Bay of Islands in 1814, followed by dozens of others: Anglican, Methodist and Catholic. Europe brought such things as pigs and potatoes, which benefited Māori and were even used as currency. Trade in flax and timber generated small European–Māori settlements by the 1820s. Surprisingly, the most

1844	**1860–69**	**1861**
Young Ngāpuhi chief Hōne Heke challenges British sovereignty. The ensuing Northland war continues until 1846.	The Taranaki wars, starting with the controversial swindling of Māori land by the government at Waitara.	Gold discovered in Otago, the local population climbing from less than 13,000 to over 30,000 in six months.

numerous category of European visitor was probably American. New England whaling ships favoured the Bay of Islands for rest and recreation, which meant sex and drink. Their favourite haunt, the little town of Kororāreka (now Russell), was known as 'Gomorrah, the scourge of the Pacific'. New England visitors today might well have distant relatives among the local Māori.

Māori–European Trade

One or two dozen bloody clashes dot the history of Māori–European contact before 1840 but, given the number of visits, inter-racial conflict was modest. Europeans needed Māori protection, food and labour, and Māori came to need European articles, especially muskets. Whaling stations and mission stations were linked to local Māori groups by intermarriage, which helped keep the peace.

The Māori population for 1769 has been estimated as between 85,000 and 110,000. The Musket Wars killed perhaps 20,000,

The Musket Wars

Most warfare was between Māori and Māori: the terrible intertribal 'Musket Wars' of 1818–36. Because Northland had the majority of early contact with Europe, its Ngāpuhi tribe acquired muskets first. Under their great general Hongi Hika, Ngāpuhi then raided south, winning bloody victories against tribes without muskets. Once they acquired muskets, these tribes then saw off Ngāpuhi, but also raided further south in their turn. The domino effect continued to the far south of the South Island in 1836. The missionaries claimed that the Musket Wars then tapered off through their influence, but the restoration of the balance of power through the equal distribution of muskets was probably more important.

and new diseases (including typhoid, tuberculosis and venereal disease) did considerable damage, too. Fortunately NZ had the natural quarantine of distance: infected Europeans often recovered or died during the long voyage, and smallpox, for example, which devastated indigenous North Americans, never arrived. By 1840 Māori had been reduced to about 70,000, a decline of at least 20%. Māori bent under the weight of European contact, but they certainly did not break.

Growing Pains

Māori tribes valued the profit and prestige brought by the Pākehā and wanted both, along with protection from foreign powers. Accepting nominal British authority was the way to get them. NZ was appointed its first British Resident, James Busby, in 1833, though his powers were largely symbolic. Busby selected the country's first official flag and established the Declaration of the Independence of New Zealand. But Busby was too ineffectual to curb rampant colonisation.

By 1840 the British government was overcoming its reluctance to undertake potentially expensive intervention in NZ. The British were eager to secure their commercial interests

1863–64	**1867**	**1893**
Waikato Land War. Despite surprising successes, Māori are defeated and much land is confiscated.	All Māori men (rather than individual land owners) are granted the right to vote.	NZ becomes the first country in the world to grant the vote to women, following a campaign led by Kate Sheppard.

and they also believed, wrongly but sincerely, that Māori could not handle the increasing scale of unofficial European contact. In 1840 the two peoples struck a deal, symbolised by the treaty first signed at Waitangi on 6 February that year. The Treaty of Waitangi now has a standing not dissimilar to that of the Constitution in the US, but is even more contested. The original problem was a discrepancy between British and Māori understandings of it. The English version promised Māori full equality as British subjects in return for complete rights of government. The Māori version also promised that Māori would retain their chieftainship, which implied local rights of government. The problem was not great at first, because the Māori version applied outside the small European settlements. But as those settlements grew, conflict brewed.

Mass Migration

In 1840 there were only about 2000 Europeans in NZ, with the shanty town of Kororāreka as the capital and biggest settlement. By 1850 six new settlements had been formed with 22,000 settlers between them. About half of these had arrived under the auspices of the New Zealand Company and its associates. The company was the brainchild of Edward Gibbon Wakefield, who also influenced the settlement of South Australia. Wakefield hoped to short-circuit the barbarous frontier phase of settlement with 'instant civilisation', but his success was limited. From the 1850s his settlers, who included a high proportion of upper-middle-class gentlefolk, were swamped by succeeding waves of immigrants that continued to wash in until the 1880s. These people were part of the great British and Irish diaspora that also populated Australia and much of North America, but the NZ mix was distinctive. Lowland Scots settlers were more prominent in NZ than elsewhere, for example, with the possible exception of parts of Canada. NZ's Irish, even the Catholics, tended to come from the north of Ireland. NZ's English tended to come from the counties close to London. Small groups of Germans, Scandinavians and Chinese made their way in, though the last faced increasing racial prejudice from the 1880s, when the Pākehā population reached half a million.

Māori Resistance

The Māori tribes did not go down without a fight. Indeed, their resistance was one of the most formidable ever mounted against European expansion. The first clash took place in 1843 in the Wairau Valley, now a wine-growing district. A posse of settlers set out to enforce the myth of British control, but encountered the reality of Māori control. Twenty-two settlers were killed, including Wakefield's brother, Arthur, along with about six Māori. In 1845 more serious fighting broke out in the Bay of Islands, when Hōne Heke sacked a British settlement. Heke and his ally Kawiti baffled three British punitive expeditions, using a modern variant of the traditional pā fortification. Vestiges of these innovative earthworks can still be seen at Ruapekapeka (south of Kawakawa). Governor Grey claimed victory in the north, but few were convinced at the time. Grey had more success in the south, where he arrested the formidable Ngāti Toa chief Te Rauparaha, who until then wielded great

1901	**1908**	**1914–18**
New Zealand politely declines the invitation to join the new Commonwealth of Australia (...but thanks for asking).	NZ physicist Ernest Rutherford is awarded the Nobel Prize in chemistry for 'splitting the atom'.	For a country of just over one million, about 100,000 NZ men serve overseas in WWI. Some 60,000 become casualties.

influence on both sides of Cook Strait. Pākehā were able to swamp the few Māori living in the South Island, but the fighting of the 1840s confirmed that the North Island at that time comprised a European fringe around an independent Māori heartland.

In the 1850s settler population and aspirations grew, and fighting broke out again in 1860. The wars burned on sporadically until 1872 over much of the North Island. In the early years the King Movement, seeking to establish a monarchy that would allow Māori to assume a more equal footing with the European settlers, was the backbone of resistance. In later years some remarkable prophet-generals, notably Titokowaru and Te Kooti, took over. Most wars were small-scale, but the Waikato war of 1863–64 was not. This conflict, fought at the same time as the American Civil War, involved armoured steamships, ultramodern heavy artillery, telegraph and 10 proud British regular regiments. Despite the odds, Māori forces won several battles, such as that at Gate Pā, near Tauranga, in 1864. But in the end they were ground down by European numbers and resources. Māori political, though not cultural, independence ebbed away in the last decades of the 19th century. It finally expired when police invaded its last sanctuary, the Urewera Mountains, in 1916.

From Gold Rush to Welfare State

From the 1850s to the 1880s, despite conflict with Māori, the Pākehā economy boomed. A gold rush on the South Island made Dunedin NZ's biggest town, and a young, mostly male population chased their fortunes along the West Coast. Fretting over the imbalance in this frontier society, the British government tried to entice women to settle in NZ. Huge amounts of wool were exported and there were unwise levels of overseas borrowing for development of railways and roads. By 1886 the population reached a tipping point: the population of non-Māori people were mostly born in NZ. Many still considered Britain their distant home, but a new identity was taking shape.

Depression followed in 1879, when wool prices slipped and gold production thinned out. Unemployment pushed some of the working population to Australia and many of those who stayed suffered miserable working conditions. There was still cause for optimism: NZ successfully exported frozen meat in 1882, raising hopes of a new backbone for the economy. Forests were enthusiastically cleared to make way for farmland.

In 1890 the Liberals, NZ's first organised political party, came to power. They stayed there until 1912, helped by a recovering economy. For decades, social reform movements such as the Woman's Christian Temperance Union (WCTU) had lobbied for women's freedom and NZ became the first country in the world to give women the vote in 1893. (Another major WCTU push, for country-wide prohibition, didn't take off.) Old-age pensions were introduced in 1898 but these social leaps forward didn't bring universal good news. Pensions only applied for those falling within a very particular definition of 'good character', and the pension reforms deliberately excluded the population of Chinese settlers who had arrived to labour in the goldfields. Meanwhile, the Liberals were obtaining more and more Māori land for settlement. By now, the non-Māori population outnumbered the Māori by 17 to one.

1931	1939–45	1953
A massive earthquake in Napier and Hastings kills at least 256 people.	NZ troops back Britain and the Allies during WWII; from 1942 around 45,000 Americans arrive to protect NZ from the Japanese.	New Zealander Edmund Hillary and Nepalese Tenzing Norgay become the first men to reach the summit of Mt Everest.

Te Papa (p134)

MOLLY NZ/SHUTTERSTOCK ©

Nation-Building

NZ had backed Britain in the Boer War (1899–1902) and WWI (1914–18), with dramatic losses in WWI. However, the bravery of Anzac (Australian and New Zealander Army Corps) forces in the failed Gallipoli campaign endures as a nation-building moment for NZ. In the 1930s NZ's experience of the Great Depression was as grim as any. The derelict farmhouses still seen in rural areas often date from this era. In 1935 a second reforming government took office, campaigning on a platform of social justice: the First Labour government, led by Australian-born Michael Joseph Savage. In WWII NZ formally declared war on Germany: 140,000 or so New Zealanders fought in Europe and the Middle East, while at home, women took on increasing roles in the labour force.

By the 1930s giant ships were regularly carrying frozen meat, cheese and butter, as well as wool, on regular voyages from NZ to Britain. As the NZ economy adapted to the feeding of London, cultural links were also enhanced. NZ children studied British history and literature, not their own. NZ's leading scientists and writers, such as Ernest Rutherford and Katherine Mansfield, gravitated to Britain. Average living standards in NZ were normally better than in Britain, as were the welfare and lower-level education systems. New Zealanders had access to British markets and culture, and they contributed their share to the latter as equals. The list of 'British' writers, academics, scientists, military leaders, publishers and the like who were actually New Zealanders is long.

NZ prided itself on its affluence, equality and social harmony. But it was also conformist, even puritanical. The 1953 Marlon Brando movie, *The Wild One,* was banned until 1977. Full Sunday trading was not allowed until 1989. Licensed restaurants hardly existed in 1960, nor did supermarkets or TV. Notoriously, from 1917 to 1967, pubs were obliged to shut at 6pm (which, ironically, paved the way for a culture of fast, heavy drinking before closing time). Yet puritanism was never the whole story. Opposition to Sunday trading stemmed, not so much from belief in the sanctity of the Sabbath, but from the belief that workers should have weekends, too. Six o'clock closing was a standing joke in rural areas. There was always something of a Kiwi counterculture, even before imported countercultures took root from the 1960s onward.

1981	1985	2010
Springbok rugby tour divides the nation. Many New Zealanders show a strong anti-apartheid stance by protesting the games.	*Rainbow Warrior* sunk in Auckland Harbour by French government agents.	A cave-in at Pike River coalmine on the South Island's West Coast kills 29 miners.

In 1973 'Mother England' ran off and joined the budding EU. NZ was beginning to develop alternative markets to Britain, and alternative exports to wool, meat and dairy products. Wide-bodied jet aircraft were allowing the world and NZ to visit each other on an increasing scale. Women were beginning to penetrate first the upper reaches of the workforce and then the political sphere. Gay people came out of the closet, despite vigorous efforts by moral conservatives to push them back in. University-educated youths were becoming more numerous and more assertive.

The Modern Age

From the 1930s, Māori experienced both a population explosion and massive urbanisation. Life expectancy was lengthening, the birth rate was high, and Māori were moving to cities for occupations formerly filled by Pākehā servicemen. Almost 80% of Māori were urban dwellers by 1986, a staggering reversal of the status quo that brought cultural displacement but simultaneously triggered a movement to strengthen pride in Māori identity. Immigration was broadening, too, first allowing in Pacific Islanders for their labour, and then (East) Asians for their money.

Then, in 1984, NZ's next great reforming government was elected – the Fourth Labour government, led nominally by David Lange, and in fact by Roger Douglas, the Minister of Finance. This government adopted a more-market economic policy (dubbed 'Rogernomics'), delighting the right, and an antinuclear foreign policy, delighting the left. NZ's numerous economic controls were dismantled with breakneck speed. Middle NZ was uneasy about the antinuclear policy, which threatened NZ's Anzus alliance with Australia and the US. But in 1985 French spies sank the antinuclear protest ship *Rainbow Warrior* in Auckland Harbour, killing one crewman. The lukewarm American condemnation of the French act brought middle NZ in behind the antinuclear policy, which became associated with national independence. Other New Zealanders were uneasy about the more-market economic policy, but failed to come up with a convincing alternative. Revelling in their new freedom, NZ investors engaged in a frenzy of speculation, and suffered even more than the rest of the world from the economic crash of 1987.

From the 1990s, a change to points-based immigration was weaving an increasingly multicultural tapestry in NZ. Numbers of incoming Brits fell but new arrivals increased, particularly from Asia but also from North Africa, the Middle East and various European countries. By 2006 more than 9% of the population was Asian.

By 2017 NZ had a new face to the world. Helmed by Jacinda Ardern, a coalition government was formed by Labour and NZ First, with support from the Green Party. NZ's third woman prime minister is faced with a balancing act between her governing parties while tackling the housing crisis and effecting bigger investment in education and health. It's no wonder that Ardern's ascendancy has been touted as the dawn of a new period of major reform.

2011	**2013**	**2015**
A severe earthquake strikes Christchurch, killing 185 people and badly damaging the central business district.	New Zealand becomes one of just 15 countries in the world to legally recognise same-sex marriage.	New Zealand's beloved All Blacks win back-to-back Rugby World Cups in England, defeating arch-rivals Australia 34-17 in the final.

Mt Taranaki

JAN KOZAK/SHUTTERSTOCK ©

Environment

New Zealand's landforms have a diversity that you would expect to find across an entire continent: snow-dusted mountains, drowned glacial valleys, rainforests, dunelands and an otherworldly volcanic plateau. Straddling the boundary of two great colliding slabs of the earth's crust – the Pacific plate and the Indian/Australian plate – NZ is a plaything for nature's strongest forces.

The Land

New Zealand is a young country – its present shape is less than 10,000 years old. Having broken away from the supercontinent of Gondwanaland (which included Africa, Australia, Antarctica and South America) some 85 million years ago, it endured continual uplift and erosion, buckling and tearing, and the slow fall and rise of the sea as ice ages came and went.

Evidence of NZ's tumultuous past is everywhere. The South Island's mountainous spine – the 650km-long ranges of the Southern Alps – grew from the clash between plates at a rate of 20km over three million years...in geological terms, that's a sprint. Despite NZ's highest peak, Aoraki/Mt Cook, losing 10m from its summit overnight in a 1991 landslide (and a couple of dozen more metres to erosion), the Alps are overall believed to be some of the fastest-growing mountains in the world.

Volcanoes

The North Island's most impressive landscapes have been wrought by volcanoes. Auckland is built on an isthmus peppered by some 48 scoria cones (cinder cones, or volcanic vents). The city's biggest and most recently formed volcano, 600-year-old Rangitoto Island, is a short ferry ride from the downtown wharves. Some 300km further south, the classically shaped cone of snowcapped Mt Taranaki overlooks tranquil dairy pastures.

But the real volcanic heartland runs through the centre of the North Island, from the restless bulk of Mt Ruapehu in Tongariro National Park, northeast through the Rotorua lake district out to NZ's most active volcano, White Island, in the Bay of Plenty. Called the Taupo Volcanic Zone, this great 350km-long rift valley – part of a volcano chain known as the 'Pacific Ring of Fire' – has been the seat of massive eruptions that have left their mark on the country physically and culturally. The volcano that created Lake Taupo last erupted 1800 years ago in a display that was the most violent anywhere on the planet within the past 5000 years.

You can experience the aftermath of volcanic destruction on a smaller scale at **Te Wairoa** (The Buried Village; ☏07-362 8287; www.buriedvillage.co.nz; 1180 Tarawera Rd; adult/child $35/10; ⊙9am-5pm), near Rotorua on the shores of Lake Tarawera. Here, partly excavated and open to the public, lie the remains of a 19th-century Māori village overwhelmed when nearby Mt Tarawera erupted without warning. The famous Pink and White Terraces, spectacular naturally formed pools (and one of several claimants to the title 'eighth wonder of the world'), were destroyed overnight by the same upheaval.

Born of geothermal violence, Waimangu Volcanic Valley (p87) is the place to go to experience hot earth up close and personal amid geysers, silica pans, bubbling mud pools and the world's biggest hot spring. Alternatively, wander around Rotorua's Whakarewarewa village (p86), where descendants of Māori displaced by the eruption live in the middle of steaming vents and prepare food for visitors in boiling pools.

The South Island can also see some evidence of volcanism – if the remains of the old volcanoes of Banks Peninsula weren't there to repel the sea, the vast Canterbury Plains, built from alpine sediment washed down the rivers from the Alps, would have eroded long ago.

Earthquakes

Not for nothing has New Zealand been called 'the Shaky Isles'. Earthquakes are common, but most only rattle the glassware. A few have wrecked major towns. In 1931 an earthquake measuring 7.9 on the Richter scale levelled the Hawke's Bay city of Napier, causing huge damage and loss of life. Napier was rebuilt almost entirely in then-fashionable art deco architectural style.

Over on the South Island, in September 2010 Christchurch was rocked by a magnitude 7.1 earthquake. Less than six months later, in February 2011, a magnitude 6.3 quake destroyed much of the city's historic heart and claimed 185 lives, making it the country's second-deadliest natural disaster. Then in November 2016 an earthquake measuring 7.8 on the Richter scale struck Kaikoura, resulting in two deaths and widespread damage to local infrastructure.

Flora & Fauna

New Zealand's long isolation has allowed it to become a veritable warehouse of unique and varied plants. Separation of NZ's landmass occurred before mammals appeared on the scene, leaving birds and insects to evolve in spectacular ways. As one of the last places on earth to be colonised by humans, NZ was for millennia a safe laboratory for risky

A tui

RYAN YEE/SHUTTERSTOCK ©

★ Native Birds

Kea Big cheeky parrot

Kereru The New Zealand pigeon

Kiwi Famously flightless national icon

Pukeko Elegant swamp hen

Tui Beautiful songbird

evolutionary strategies. But the arrival of Māori, and later Europeans, brought new threats and sometimes extinction.

The now-extinct flightless moa, the largest of which grew to 3.5m tall and weighed over 200kg, browsed open grasslands much as cattle do today (skeletons can be seen at Auckland Museum), while the smaller kiwi still ekes out a nocturnal living rummaging among forest leaf litter for insects and worms. One of the country's most ferocious-looking insects, the mouse-sized giant weta, meanwhile, has taken on a scavenging role elsewhere filled by rodents.

Many endemic creatures, including moa and the huia, an exquisite songbird, were driven to extinction, and the vast forests were cleared for their timber and to make way for agriculture. Destruction of habitat and the introduction of exotic animals and plants have taken a terrible environmental toll and New Zealanders are now fighting a rearguard battle to save what remains.

Trees

Distinctive native trees you're likely to spy on your travels include the colourful kowhai, a small-leaved tree growing to 11m, which in spring has drooping clusters of bright-yellow flowers (informally considered NZ's national flower); the pohutukawa, a beautiful coastal tree of the northern North Island that bursts into vivid red flower in December, earning the nickname 'Christmas tree'; and a similar crimson-flowered tree, the rata. Rata species are found on both islands; the northern rata starts life as a climber on a host tree (that it eventually chokes).

The few remaining pockets of mature centuries-old kauri are stately emblems of former days. Their vast trunks and towering, epiphyte-festooned limbs reach well over 50m high, reminders of why they were sought after in colonial days for spars and building timber.

Other native timber trees include the distinctive rimu (red pine) and the long-lived totara (favoured for Māori war canoes). NZ's perfect pine-growing conditions encouraged one of the country's most successful imports, *Pinus radiata,* which grow to maturity in 35 years (and sometimes less). Plantation forests are now widespread through the central North Island – the southern hemisphere's biggest, Kaingaroa Forest, lies southeast of Rotorua.

NZ also has an impressive 200 species of ferns and almost half grow nowhere else on the planet. Most easily recognised are the mamaku (black tree fern) – which grows to 20m and can be seen in damp gullies throughout the country – and the 10m-high ponga (silver tree fern) with its distinctive white underside. The silver fern is a national symbol and adorns sporting and corporate logos, as well as shop signs, clothing and jewellery.

Environmental Issues

New Zealand's reputation as an Eden, replete with pristine wilderness and ecofriendly practices, has been repeatedly placed under the microscope. The industry most visible to visitors, tourism, appears studded in green accolades, with environmental best practices employed in areas as broad as heating insulation in hotels to minimum-impact wildlife watching. But mining, offshore oil and gas exploration, pollution, biodiversity loss, conservation funding cuts and questionable urban planning have provided endless hooks for bad-news stories.

An Ancient Lizard

The largest native reptile in NZ is the tuatara, a crested lizard that can grow up to 50cm long. Thought to be unchanged for more than 220 million years, these endearing creatures can live for up to a century. Meet them at Auckland Zoo (p47), Hokitika's National Kiwi Centre (p203), and other zoos and sanctuaries around NZ.

Water quality is arguably the most serious environmental issue faced by New Zealanders. More than a quarter of the country's lakes and rivers have been deemed unsafe for swimming, and research from diverse sources confirms that the health of waterways is in decline. The primary culprit is 'dirty dairying' – cow effluent leaching into freshwater ecosystems, carrying with it high levels of nitrates, as well as bacteria and parasites such as E. coli and giardia. A 2017 report by the Ministry for the Environment and Statistics showed that nitrate levels in water were worsening at 55% of monitored river sites, and that urban waterways were in an especially dire state – with levels of harmful bacteria more than 20 times higher than in forest areas. A government push to make 90% of rivers and lakes swimmable by 2040 was met with initial scepticism about the metrics involved, but it's hoped that it will provide an impetus to make NZ's waterways worthy of the country's eco-conscious reputation.

Another ambitious initiative is Predator Free 2050, which aims to rid NZ of introduced animals that prey on native flora and fauna. The worst offenders are possums, stoats and rats, which eat swathes of forest and kill wildlife, particularly birds. Controversy rages at the Department of Conservation (DOC) use of 1080 poison (sodium fluoroacetate) to control these pests, despite it being sanctioned by prominent environmental groups, such as Forest & Bird, as well as the Parliamentary Commissioner for the Environment. Vehement opposition to 1080 is expressed by such diverse camps as hunters and animal-rights activists, who cite detriments such as by-kill and the potential for poison passing into waterways. Proponents of its use argue that it's biodegradable and that aerial distribution of 1080 is the only cost-effective way to target predators across vast, inaccessible parts of NZ. Still, 'Ban 1080' signs remain common in rural communities and the controversy is likely to continue.

As well as its damaging impact on NZ waterways, the $12 billion dairy industry – the country's biggest export earner – generates 48% of NZ's greenhouse gas emissions. And it's not just the dairy industry: NZ might be a nation of avid recyclers and solar-panel enthusiasts, but it also has the world's fourth-highest ratio of motor vehicles to people.

But with eco-conscious Jacinda Ardern leading a coalition government from 2017, New Zealanders have reason to be hopeful of a greener future – Ardern has pledged an ambitious goal of reducing net greenhouse gas emissions to zero by 2050. More trains, 100% renewable energy sources and planting 100 million trees per year...goals worthy of NZ's clean, green reputation.

Waitangi Day (p22) celebratiions at the Waitangi Treaty Grounds (p68)

Māori Culture

'Māori' once just meant 'common' or 'everyday', but Māori today are a diverse people. Some are engaged with traditional cultural networks and pursuits; others are occupied with adapting tradition and placing it into a dialogue with globalising culture.

People of the Land

Māori are New Zealand's *tangata whenua* (people of the land), and the Māori relationship with the land has developed over hundreds of years of occupation. Once a predominantly rural people, many Māori now live in urban centres, away from their traditional home base. But it's still common practice in formal settings to introduce oneself by referring to home: an ancestral mountain, river, sea or lake, or an ancestor.

The Māori concept of *whanaungatanga* – family relationships – is central to the culture: families spread out from the *whānau* (extended family) to the *hapū* (subtribe) and *iwi* (tribe), and even, in a sense, beyond the human world and into the natural and spiritual worlds.

If you're looking for a Māori experience in NZ you'll find it – in performance, in conversation, in an art gallery, on a tour...

Māori Then

Some three millennia ago people began moving eastward into the Pacific, sailing against the prevailing winds and currents (hard to go out, easier to return safely). Some stopped at Tonga and Samoa, and others settled the small central East Polynesian tropical islands.

The Māori colonisation of Aotearoa began from an original homeland known to Māori as Hawaiki. Skilled navigators and sailors travelled across the Pacific, using many navigational tools – currents, winds, stars, birds and wave patterns – to guide their large, double-hulled ocean-going craft to a new land. The first of many was the great navigator Kupe, who arrived, the story goes, chasing a giant octopus named Muturangi. But the distinction of giving NZ its well-known Māori name – Aotearoa – goes to his wife, Kuramarotini, who cried out, '*He ao, he ao tea, he ao tea roa!*' (A cloud, a white cloud, a long white cloud!).

Kupe and his crew journeyed around the land, and many places around Cook Strait (between the North and South Islands) and the Hokianga in Northland still bear the names that the crew gave them and the marks of their passage. Kupe returned to Hawaiki, leaving from (and naming) Northland's Hokianga. He gave other seafarers valuable navigational information. And then the great *waka* (ocean-going craft) began to arrive.

What would it have been like making the transition from small tropical islands to a much larger, cooler land mass? There was land, lots of it. There was an untouched, massive fishery. There were great seaside mammalian convenience stores – seals and sea lions – as well as a fabulous array of birds.

The early settlers went on the move, pulled by love, by trade opportunities and greater resources; pushed by disputes and threats to security. When they settled, Māori established *mana whenua* (regional authority), whether by military campaigns, or by the peaceful methods of intermarriage and diplomacy. Looking over tribal history it's possible to see the many alliances, absorptions and extinctions that went on.

Māori lived in *kainga* (small villages), which often had associated gardens. Housing was quite cosy by modern standards – often it was hard to stand upright while inside. From time to time people would leave their home base and go to harvest seasonal foods. When peaceful life was interrupted by conflict, the people would withdraw to *pā* (fortified dwelling places).

And then Europeans began to arrive.

Visiting Marae

As you travel around NZ, you will see many *marae* complexes. Often *marae* are owned by a descent group. They are also owned by urban Māori groups, schools, universities and church groups, and they should only be visited by arrangement with the owners.

Marae complexes include a *wharenui* (meeting house), which often embodies an ancestor. Its ridge is the backbone, the rafters are ribs, and it shelters the descendants. There is a clear space in front of the *wharenui*, the *marae ātea*. Sometimes there are other buildings: a *wharekai* (dining hall); a toilet and shower block; perhaps even classrooms, play equipment and the like.

Hui (gatherings) are held at *marae*. Issues are discussed, classes conducted, milestones celebrated and the dead farewelled. Te reo Māori (the Māori language) is prominent, and sometimes the only language used.

Māori Today

Today's culture is marked by new developments in the arts, business, sport and politics. Many historical grievances still stand, but some *iwi* (Ngāi Tahu and Tainui, for example) have settled major historical grievances and are significant forces in the NZ economy.

Otago Museum (p262)

Māori have also addressed the decline in Māori language use by establishing *kōhanga reo, kura kaupapa Māori* and *wānanga* (Māori-medium preschools, schools and universities). There is now a generation of people who speak Māori as a first language. There is a network of Māori radio stations, and Māori TV attracts a committed viewership. A recently revived Māori event is becoming more and more prominent – Matariki (Māori New Year). The constellation Matariki is also known as the Pleiades. It begins to rise above the horizon in late May or early June and its appearance traditionally signals a time for learning, planning and preparing as well as singing, dancing and celebrating. Watch out for talks and lectures, concerts, dinners and even formal balls.

Religion

Christian churches and denominations are prominent in the Māori world, including televangelists, mainstream churches for regular and occasional worship, and two major Māori churches (Ringatū and Rātana). But in the (non-Judeo-Christian) beginning there were the *atua Māori,* the Māori gods, and for many Māori the gods are a vital and relevant force still. It is common to greet the earth mother and sky father when speaking formally at a *marae* (meeting house). The gods are represented in art and carving, sung of in *waiata* (songs), and invoked through *karakia* (prayer and incantation) when a meeting house is opened, when a *waka* is launched, even (more simply) when a meal is served. They are spoken of at the *marae* and in wider Māori contexts. The traditional Māori creation story is well known and widely celebrated.

Arts & Media

You can stay up to date with what's happening in the Māori arts by listening to *iwi* stations (www.irirangi.net) or tuning into Māori TV (www.maoritelevision.com) for regular features on the Māori arts. Māori TV went to air in 2004, an emotional time for many Māori who could at last see their culture, their concerns and their language in a mass medium. Over 90% of content is NZ made, and programs are in both Māori and English: they're subtitled and accessible to everyone. If you want to really get a feel for the rhythm and meter of spoken Māori from the comfort of your own chair, switch to Te Reo (www.maoritelevision. com/tv/te-reo-channel), a Māori-language-only channel.

When we wrote this, production of Māori lifestyle magazine *Mana* (www.manaonline. co.nz) had stopped, but there were hopes of a relaunch down the line.

Seafood dish

DAVID WALL/ALAMY ©

Food & Drink

Travellers, start your appetites! Eating in New Zealand is a highlight of any visit, from fresh seafood and gourmet burgers to farmers market fruit-and-veg and crisp-linen fine dining. Eateries range from fish and chip shops and pub bistros to retro cafes and ritzy dining rooms. Drinking here, too, presents boundless opportunities to have a good time, with Kiwi coffee, craft beer and wine at the fore.

Modern NZ

Once upon a time in a decade not so far away, New Zealand subsisted on a modest diet of 'meat and three veg'. Though small-town country pubs still serve their unchanging menu of roasted meats and battered fish, overall NZ's culinary sophistication has evolved dramatically. In larger towns, kitchens thrive on bending conventions and absorbing gastronomic influences from around the planet, all the while keeping local produce central to the menu.

Immigration has been key to this culinary rise – particularly the post-WWII influx of migrants from Europe, Asia and the Middle East – as has an adventurous breed of local restaurant-goers and the elevation of Māori and Pacific Islander flavours and ingredients to the mainstream.

Restaurants on New Regent St, Christchurch (p175)

★ **Best Restaurants**

Bistronomy (p126), Napier

Noble Rot (p147), Wellington

Cassia (p53), Auckland

Twenty Seven Steps (p187), Christchurch

Public Kitchen & Bar (p228), Queenstown

In order to wow the socks off increasingly demanding diners, restaurants must now succeed in fusing contrasting ingredients and traditions into ever more innovative fare. The phrase 'Modern NZ' has been coined to classify this unclassifiable technique: a melange of East and West, a swirl of Atlantic and Pacific Rim, and a dash of authentic French and Italian.

Traditional staples still hold sway (lamb, beef, venison, green-lipped mussels), but dishes are characterised by interesting flavours and fresh ingredients rather than fuss, clutter or snobbery. Spicing ranges from gentle to extreme, seafood is plentiful and meats are tender and full flavoured.

For up-to-date online restaurant reviews and listings around NZ, see www.menus.co.nz. Enjoy!

Cafes & Coffee

Somewhere between the early 2000s and now, New Zealand cottoned on to coffee culture in a big way. Caffeine has become a nationwide addiction: there are Italian-style espresso machines in virtually every cafe, boutique roasters are de rigueur and, in urban areas, a qualified barista (coffee maker) is the norm. Auckland, Christchurch and student-filled Dunedin have borne generations of coffee aficionados, but Wellington takes top billing as NZ's caffeine capital. The cafe and bean-roasting scene here rivals the most vibrant in the world, and is very inclusive and family friendly. Join the arty local crew and dunk yourself into it over a late-night conversation or an early-morning recovery.

Vegetarians & Vegans

More than 10% of New Zealanders are vegetarian (more in the North than the South Island), and numbers are rising. Most large urban centres have at least one dedicated vegetarian cafe or restaurant: see the Vegetarians New Zealand website (www.vegetarians. co.nz) for listings. Beyond this, almost all restaurants and cafes offer some vegetarian menu choices (although sometimes only one or two). Many eateries also provide gluten-free and vegan options.

Pubs, Bars & Beer

Kiwi pubs were once male bastions with dim lighting, smoky air and beer-soaked carpets – these days they're more of a family affair. Sticky floors and pie-focused menus still abound in rural parts of NZ but pubs are generally where parents take their kids for lunch, friends mingle for sav blanc and tapas, and locals of all ages congregate to roar at live sports screenings. Food has become integral to the NZ pub experience, along with the inexorable rise of craft beer in the national drinking consciousness.

Myriad small, independent breweries have popped up around the country in the last decade. Wellington, in particular, offers dozens of dedicated craft-beer bars, with revolving beers on tap and passionate bar staff who know all there is to know about where the beers have come from, who made them and what's in them. A night on the tiles here has become less about volume and capacity, more about selectivity and virtue.

But aside from the food and the fancy beer, the NZ pub remains a place where all Kiwis can unite with a common purpose: to watch their beloved All Blacks play rugby on the big screen – a raucous experience to say the least!

To Market, to Market

There are more than 50 farmers markets held around NZ. Most happen on weekends and are upbeat local affairs, where visitors can meet local producers and find fresh regional produce. Mobile coffee is usually present, and tastings are offered by enterprising and innovative stallholders. Bring a carrier bag, and get there early for the best stuff! Check out www.farmersmarkets.org.nz for major market locations, and ask locally about smaller, and seasonal, markets.

At the bar, 'shouting' is a revered custom, where people take turns to pay for a round of drinks. Disappearing before it's your shout won't win you many friends. Once the drinks are distributed, a toast of 'Cheers!' is standard practice: look each other in the eye and clink glasses.

Wine Regions

Like the wine industry in neighbouring Australia, the New Zealand version has European migrants to thank for its status and success – visionary visitors who knew good soils and good climate when they saw them, and planted the first vines around Hawke's Bay.

But it wasn't until the 1970s that things really got going, with traditional agricultural exports dwindling, Kiwis travelling more and the introduction of BYO ('Bring Your Own' wine) restaurant licensing conspiring to raise interest and demand for local wines.

Since then, New Zealand cool-climate wines have conquered the world, a clutch of key regions producing the lion's share of bottles. Organised day tours via minivan or bicycle are a great way to visit a few select wineries.

Marlborough NZ's biggest and most widely known wine region sits at the top of the South Island, where a microclimate of warm days and cool nights is perfect for growing sauvignon blanc.

Hawke's Bay The North Island's sunny East Coast is the cradle of the NZ wine industry and second-largest producer – chardonnay and syrah are the mainstays.

The Wairarapa Just an hour or two over the hills from Wellington, the Wairarapa region is prime naughty-weekender territory, and produces winning pinot noir.

Central Otago Reaching from Cromwell in the north to Alexandra in the south and Gibbston Valley near Queenstown in the west, the South Island's Central Otago region produces sublime riesling and pinot noir.

Waipara Valley Not to be left out of proceedings, Christchurch has its own nearby wine region – the Waipara Valley just north of the city – where divine riesling and pinot noir come to fruition.

Waiheke Island In the middle of the Hauraki Gulf, a short ferry ride from Auckland, Waiheke has a hot, dry microclimate that just happens to be brilliant for growing reds and rosés.

Musicians in Wellington (p131)

NATALIA RAMIREZ ROMAN/SHUTTERSTOCK ©

Arts & Music

*Māori music and art extends back to New Zealand's
early, unrecorded history but its motifs endure today.
European settlers imported artistic styles, but it took
a century for postcolonial NZ to hone its distinctive
artistic identity. In the first half of the 20th century it
was writers and visual artists who led the charge, but
in following decades music and movies catapulted
the nation's creativity into the world's consciousness.*

Literature

In 2013 28-year-old Eleanor Catton became only the second NZ writer to ever win the
Man Booker Prize for her epic historical novel *The Luminaries* set on the West Coast. Lloyd
Jones came close in 2007 when his novel *Mister Pip* was shortlisted, but it had been a long
wait between drinks since Keri Hulme took the prize in 1985 for her haunting novel *The
Bone People*.

Katherine Mansfield's work had begun a Kiwi tradition in short fiction, and for years the
standard was carried by novelist Janet Frame, who won the Commonwealth Writers' Prize
in 1989 for *The Carpathians*.

Less recognised internationally, Maurice Gee has gained the nation's annual top fiction
gong six times, most recently with *Blindsight* in 2006. A new author on New Zealanders'

must-read lists is Catherine Chidgey: look for her heart-rending novel *The Wish Child* (2016).

Cinema & TV

Sir Peter Jackson's NZ-made *The Lord of the Rings* and *The Hobbit* trilogies were the best thing to happen to NZ tourism since Captain Cook. The uniting factor in NZ film and TV is the landscape, which provides a haunting backdrop. Jane Campion's *The Piano* (1993) and *Top of the Lake* (2013), Brad McGann's *In My Father's Den* (2004) and Jackson's *Heavenly Creatures* (1994) all use magically lush scenery to couch disturbing violence.

Exporting NZ comedy hasn't been easy, yet the HBO-produced TV musical parody *Flight of the Conchords* – featuring a mumbling, bumbling Kiwi folk-singing duo trying to get a break in New York – found surprising international success. Also packaging offbeat NZ humour for an international audience, Taika Waititi, who directed *Thor: Ragnarok* (2017), is a household name.

The Brothers Finn

There are certain tunes that all Kiwis can sing along to, given a beer and the opportunity. A surprising proportion of these were written by Tim and Neil Finn, many of which have been international hits. Tim Finn first came to prominence in the 1970s group Split Enz, who amassed a solid following in Australia, NZ and Canada before disbanding in 1985. Neil then formed Crowded House with two Australian musicians (Paul Hester and Nick Seymour) and one of their early singles, 'Don't Dream It's Over', hit number two on the US charts. Tim and Neil have both released a number of solo albums, as well as releasing material together as the Finn Brothers.

Visual Arts

Traditional Māori art has a distinctive visual style with well-developed motifs that have been embraced by NZ artists of every race. In the painting medium, these include the cool modernism of Gordon Walters and the more controversial pop-art approach of Dick Frizzell's *Tiki* series. Also look for the intricate, collage-like paintings of Niuean-born, Auckland-raised John Pule.

Charles Frederick Goldie painted a series of controversial, realist portraits of Māori, who were feared to be a dying race. Recalibrating the ways in which Pacific Islander and Māori people are depicted in art, Lisa Reihana wowed the Venice Biennale in 2017 with her multimedia work *In Pursuit of Venus*.

Music

New Zealand music began with the *waiata* (singing) developed by Māori following their arrival in the country. These days, the liveliest place to see Māori music being performed is at traditional *kapa haka* song-and-dance competitions.

Rock & Metal

New Zealand's most acclaimed rock exports are the music of the Finn Brothers and the revered indie label Flying Nun. Started in 1981 by Christchurch record-store owner Roger Shepherd, many of Flying Nun's early groups came from Dunedin, where local musicians produced lo-fi indie-pop.

Something heavier? Hamilton heavy-metal act Devilskin's 2014 debut album hit the top spot on NZ's charts, as did their punchy 2016 follow-up *Be Like the River*. We're not worthy.

Hobbiton movie set (p62), where *The Lord of the Rings* and *The Hobbit* trilogies were filmed

PHOTO COURTESY OF HOBBITON MOVIE SET TOURS ©

★ New Zealand Oscar Winners

Anna Paquin Best Supporting Actress, 1993; *The Piano*

Peter Jackson Best Director, 2003; *The Lord of the Rings: The Return of the King*

Bret McKenzie Best Music – Original Song, 2011; 'Man or Muppet,' *The Muppets*

Reggae, Hip-Hop & Dance

Reggae (in the 1970s) and hip-hop (in the 1980s) have been adopted enthusiastically by Māori and Polynesian New Zealanders. In Wellington, a thriving jazz scene took on a reggae influence to spawn a funky dub/roots/jazz scene – most notably played by Fat Freddy's Drop.

The local hip-hop scene has its heart in the suburbs of South Auckland, which have a high concentration of Māori and Pacific Island residents. This area is home to one of New Zealand's foremost hip-hop labels, Dawn Raid. Savage sold a million copies of his single 'Swing' after it was featured in the movie *Knocked Up*. Other well-known hip-hop acts are Scribe, Che Fu and Smashproof.

Dance music gained a foothold in Christchurch in the 1990s, spawning dub/electronica outfit Salmonella Dub and its offshoot act, Tiki Taane.

Classical & Opera

In the 1950s Douglas Lilburn became one of the first internationally recognised NZ classical composers. More recently the country has produced a number of world-renowned musicians in this field, including legendary opera singer Dame Kiri Te Kanawa, million-selling classic-to-pop singer Hayley Westenra, composer John Psathas and composer/percussionist Gareth Farr (who also performs in drag under the name Lilith LaCroix).

Movers & Shakers

Rock groups such as Shihad, the Feelers, the Datsuns, D4 and Opshop thrived since 2000, as did soulful female solo artists Bic Runga, Anika Moa and Brooke Fraser.

Current Kiwis garnering international recognition include the incredibly gifted song-stress Kimbra; electro-rockers the Naked and Famous; multitalented singer-songwriter Ladyhawke; arty Lawrence Arabia; and the semi-psychedelic Unknown Mortal Orchestra. R&B singer Aaradhna made a splash with her album *Treble & Reverb*.

But the biggest name in Kiwi music today is Lorde, a singer-songwriter from Devonport on Auckland's North Shore. Known less regally to her friends as Ella Yelich-O'Connor, Lorde was 16 years old when she cracked the number-one spot on the US Billboard charts in 2013 with her magical, schoolyard-chant-evoking, Grammy-winning hit 'Royals'. Her debut album *Pure Heroine* spawned a string of hits and sold millions of copies worldwide, while moody follow-up *Melodrama* instantly topped charts in NZ and the US upon its release in 2017.

Redwoods Whakarewarewa Forest (p93)

ELENA YAKUSHEVA/SHUTTERSTOCK ©

Survival Guide

Directory A–Z

Accommodation

Book beds well in advance in peak tourist seasons: November through March (particularly summer holidays from Christmas to late January), at Easter, and during winter (June to September) in snowy resort towns such as Queenstown and Wanaka.

Motels & Pubs Most towns have low-rise, midrange motels. Even small towns usually have a pub with rooms.

Holiday Parks Ideal if you're camping or touring in a camp-ervan. Choose from unpowered tent sites, simple cabins and en suite units.

Hostels Backpacker hostels include beery, party-prone joints and family-friendly 'flashpackers'.

Hotels Choices range from small-town pubs to slick global-chain operations – with commensurate prices.

B&Bs

Bed and breakfast (B&B) accommodation in NZ pops up in the middle of cities, in rural hamlets and on stretches of isolated coastline, with rooms on offer in everything from sub-urban bungalows to stately manors.

Breakfast may be 'conti-nental' (a standard offering of cereal, toast and tea or coffee, or a heartier version with yoghurt, fruit, home-baked bread or muffins), or a stomach-loading cooked meal (eggs, bacon, sau-sages...though with notice, vegetarians are increasingly being well catered for). Some B&B hosts may also cook dinner for guests and advertise dinner, bed and breakfast (DB&B) packages.

B&B tariffs are typically in the $120 to $200 bracket (per double), though some places cost upwards of $300 per double. Some hosts charge cheeky prices for what is, in essence, a bedroom in their home. Off-street parking is often a bonus in the big cities.

Booking Services

Local visitor information centres around NZ provide reams of local accommoda-tion information, sometimes in the form of folders detail-ing facilities and up-to-date prices; many can also make bookings on your behalf.

Lonely Planet (www.lonely planet.com/new-zealand/hotels) The full range of NZ accommodation, from hostels to hotels.

Automobile Association (www.aa.co.nz/travel) Online accommodation bookings (es-pecially good for motels, B&Bs and holiday parks).

Jasons (www.jasons.co.nz) Long-running travel service with myriad online booking options.

New Zealand Bed & Breakfast (www.bnb.co.nz) The name says it all.

Bed & Breakfast New Zealand (www.bed-and-breakfast.co.nz) B&B and self-contained accom-modation directory.

Rural Holidays NZ (www.ruralholidays.co.nz) Farm and homestay listings across NZ.

Book a Bach (www.booka bach.co.nz) Apartment and holiday-house bookings (and maybe even a bach or two!).

Holiday Houses (www.holiday houses.co.nz) Holiday-house rentals NZ wide.

Price Ranges

The following price ranges refer to a double room with bathroom during high season. Price ranges generally increase by 20% to 25% in Auckland, Wellington and Christchurch. Here you can still find budget accommo-dation at up to $120 per double, but midrange stretches from $120 to $250, with top-end rooms more than $250.

CATEGORY	COST
$	less than $120
$$	$120–$200
$$$	more than $200

New Zealand Apartments

(www.nzapartments.co.nz) Rental listings for upmarket apartments of all sizes.

Camping & Holiday Parks

Campers and campervan drivers converge on NZ's hugely popular 'holiday parks', slumbering in powered and unpowered sites, cheap bunk rooms (dorm rooms), cabins (shared bathroom facilities) and self-contained units (often called motels or tourist flats). Well-equipped communal kitchens, dining areas, games and TV rooms, and playgrounds often feature. In cities, holiday parks are usually a fair way from the action, but in smaller towns they can be impressively central or near lakes, beaches, rivers and forests.

The nightly cost of holiday-park tent sites is usually $15 to $20 per adult, with children charged half price; powered campervan sites can be anything from a couple of dollars more to around the $40 mark. Cabin/unit accommodation normally ranges from $70 to $120 per double. Unless noted otherwise, Lonely Planet lists campsite, campervan site, hut and cabin prices for two people.

Farmstays

Farmstays open the door to the agricultural side of NZ life, with visitors encouraged to get some dirt beneath their fingernails at orchards, and dairy, sheep and cattle farms. Costs can vary widely, with bed and breakfast generally costing $80 to $140. Some farms have separate cottages where you can fix your own food; others offer low-cost, shared, backpacker-style accommodation.

Farm Helpers in NZ (www.fhinz.co.nz) produces a booklet ($25) that lists around 350 NZ farms providing lodging in exchange for four to six hours' work per day.

Pubs, Hotels & Motels

The least expensive form of NZ hotel accommodation is the humble pub. Some are full of character (and characters); others are grotty, ramshackle places that are best avoided (especially by women travelling solo). Check whether there's a band playing the night you're staying – you could be in for a sleepless night. In the cheapest pubs, singles/doubles might cost as little as $45/70 (with a shared bathroom down the hall); $70/90 is more common.

At the top end of the hotel scale are five-star international chains, resort complexes and architecturally splendorous boutique hotels, all of which charge a hefty premium for their mod cons, snappy service and/or historic opulence. We quote 'rack rates' (official advertised rates) for such places, but discounts and special deals often apply.

Book Your Stay Online

For accommodation reviews by Lonely Planet authors, check out http://hotels.lonelyplanet.com/new-zealand. You'll find independent reviews, as well as recommendations on the best places to stay. Best of all, you can book online.

NZ's towns have a glut of nondescript, low-rise motels and 'motor lodges', charging $90 to $200 for double rooms. These tend to be squat structures skulking by highways on the edges of towns. Most are modernish (though decor is often mired in the early 2000s or earlier) and have basic facilities, namely tea- and coffee-making equipment, fridge and TV. Prices vary with standard.

Rental Accommodation

The basic Kiwi holiday home is called a 'bach' (short for 'bachelor', as they were historically used by single men as hunting and fishing hideouts); in Otago and Southland they're known as 'cribs'. These are simple self-contained cottages that can be rented in rural and coastal areas, often in isolated locations, and sometimes include surf, fishing or other outdoor gear rental in the cost. Prices are typically $90 to $180 per night,

Climate

Auckland

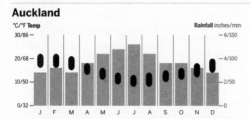

Christchurch

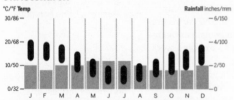

Queenstown

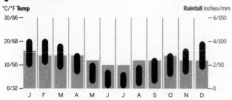

which isn't bad for a whole house or self-contained bungalow. For more upmarket holiday houses, expect to pay anything from $180 to $400 per double.

Customs Regulations

For the low-down on what you can and can't bring into NZ, see the New Zealand Customs Service website (www.customs.govt.nz). Per-person duty-free allowances:

○ Three 1125mL (max) bottles of spirits or liqueur

○ 4.5L of wine or beer

○ 50 cigarettes, or 50g of tobacco or cigars

○ dutiable goods up to the value of $700

It's a good idea to declare any unusual medicines. Tramping gear (boots, tents etc) will be checked and may need to be cleaned before being allowed in. You must declare any plant or animal products (including anything made of wood), and food of any kind. Weapons and firearms are

either prohibited or require a permit and safety testing. Don't take these rules lightly – noncompliance penalties will really hurt your hip pocket.

Electricity

To plug yourself into the electricity supply (230V AC, 50Hz), use a three-pin adaptor (the same as in Australia; different to British three-pin adaptors).

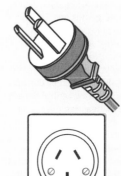

Type I
230V/50Hz

Food

Most eating options are casual walk-ups (pubs, cafes and takeaways) but book top-end restaurants well in advance.

Restaurants Open for dinner and lunch. 'Modern NZ' = locally sourced, top-quality fare with international influences.

Cafes Locally roasted beans, expert baristas, savvy breakfast-to-lunch food and family-friendly.

Takeaways Fish and chips, kebabs, burgers...the big internationals are here, but quality local outfits give them a run for their money.

Pubs & Bars You can get a bite to eat at most Kiwi bars and pubs – from standard stodge to delicately wrought tapas and farmer-sized steaks.

Supermarkets In all sizeable towns – often open until 9pm.

The following price ranges refer to the average price of a main course.

$ less than $15
$$ $15–$35
$$$ more than $35

Health

New Zealand poses minimal health risks to travellers. Diseases such as malaria and typhoid are unheard of, poisonous snakes and other dangerous animals are absent, and there are currently no dangerous insect-borne diseases. The biggest risks to travellers involve exploring the great outdoors: trampers must be clued in on rapid-changing weather and diligent about sharing any plans to visit remote areas, meanwhile drivers must exert extreme caution on NZ's notoriously winding roads.

Before You Go

Health Insurance

Health insurance is essential for all travellers. While health care in NZ is of a high quality and not overly expensive by international standards, considerable costs can be built up and repatriation is pricey.

If you don't have a health insurance plan that covers you for medical expenses incurred overseas, buy a travel insurance policy – see www.lonelyplanet.com/travel-insurance. Find out in advance if your insurance plan will make payments directly to providers or reimburse you later for overseas health expenditures. Check whether your policy covers the activities you're planning to do in NZ (eg rock climbing, winter sports) and whether there's a limit on the number of days of cover for the activity.

Medications

Bring any prescribed medications for your trip in their original, clearly labelled containers. A signed and dated letter from your physician describing your medical conditions and medications (including generic names) and any requisite syringes or needles is also wise.

Recommended Vaccinations

NZ has no vaccination requirements for any traveller, but the World Health Organization recommends that all travellers should

be covered for chickenpox, diphtheria, hepatitis B, measles, mumps, pertussis (whooping cough), polio, rubella, seasonal flu, tetanus and tuberculosis, regardless of their destination. Ask your doctor for an *International Certificate of Vaccination* (or 'the yellow booklet') in which they will list all the vaccinations you've received.

In New Zealand

Availability & Cost of Health Care

New Zealand's public hospitals offer a high standard of care (free for residents). All travellers are covered for medical care resulting from accidents that occur while in NZ (eg motor-vehicle accidents, adventure-activity accidents) by the Accident Compensation Corporation (www.acc.co.nz). Costs incurred due to treatment of a medical illness that occurs while in NZ will only be covered by travel insurance. For more details, see www.health.govt.nz.

The 24-hour **Healthline** (☑0800 611 116) offers health advice throughout NZ (free from local mobile or landlines). Interpreters are available.

Environmental Hazards

NZ's numerous biting insects are an irritation rather than a serious health risk, but hypothermia and drowning are genuine threats.

Hypothermia

Hypothermia, a dangerous drop in body temperature, is a significant risk to travellers in NZ, especially during winter and year-round at altitude. Mountain ranges and/or strong winds produce a high chill factor, which can cause hypothermia even in moderate temperatures. Early signs include the inability to perform fine movements (such as doing up buttons), shivering and a bad case of the 'umbles' (fumbles, mumbles, grumbles, stumbles).

To treat, minimise heat loss: remove wet clothing, add dry clothes with wind- and waterproof layers, and consume carbohydrates and water or warm liquids (not caffeine) to allow shivering to build the internal temperature. In severe hypothermia cases, shivering actually stops; this is a medical emergency requiring rapid evacuation in addition to the above measures.

Surf Beaches

NZ has exceptional surf beaches. The power of the surf can fluctuate as a result of the varying slope of the seabed: rips and undertows are common, and drownings do happen. Check with local surf-lifesaving organisations before jumping in the sea, always heed warning signs at beaches, and be realistic about your own limitations and expertise.

Infectious Diseases

Aside from the same sexually transferred infections that are found worldwide (take normal precautions), giardiasis is the main infectious disease to be aware of when travelling in NZ.

Giardiasis

The giardia parasite is widespread in NZ waterways: drinking untreated water from streams and lakes is not recommended. Using water filters and boiling or treating water with iodine are effective ways of preventing the disease. The parasite can also latch on to swimmers in rivers and lakes (try not to swallow water), or through contact with infected animals. Symptoms consist of diarrhoea, vomiting, stomach cramps, abdominal bloating and wind. Effective treatment is available (tinidazole or metronidazole).

Pharmaceuticals

Over-the-counter medications are widely available in NZ through private chemists (pharmacies). These include painkillers, antihistamines, skincare products and sunscreen. Some medications, such as antibiotics, are only available via a prescription obtained from a general practitioner. Some varieties of the contraceptive pill can be bought at pharmacies without a prescription (provided the woman has been prescribed the pill within the last three years). If you take regular medications, bring an adequate supply and details of the generic name, as brand names differ country to country.

Tap Water

Tap water throughout New Zealand is generally safe to drink and public taps with nondrinkable water tend to be labelled as such. However, water quality has faced pollution challenges in some places. Very occasionally, a warning may be issued that tap water must be boiled – your accommodation should inform you if this happens.

Insurance

° A watertight travel-insurance policy covering theft, loss and medical problems is essential. Some policies specifically exclude designated 'dangerous activities', such as scuba diving, bungy jumping, white-water rafting, skiing and even tramping. If you plan on doing any of these things (a distinct possibility in NZ!), make sure your policy covers you fully.

° It's worth mentioning that under NZ law, you cannot sue for personal injury (other than exemplary damages). Instead, the country's Accident Compensation Corporation (www.acc.co.nz) administers an accident compensation scheme that provides accident insurance for NZ residents and visitors to the country, regardless of fault. This scheme, however, does not negate the necessity for your own comprehensive travel-insurance policy, as it doesn't cover you for such things as income loss, treatment at home or ongoing illness.

○ Consider a policy that pays doctors or hospitals directly, rather than you paying on the spot and claiming later. If you have to claim later, keep all documentation. Some policies ask you to call (reverse charges) to a centre in your home country where an immediate assessment of your problem is made. Check that the policy covers ambulances and emergency medical evacuations by air.

○ Worldwide travel insurance is available at www. lonelyplanet.com/travel-insurance. You can buy, extend and claim online anytime – even if you're already on the road.

Internet Access

Getting online in NZ is easy in all but remote locales. Expect abundant wi-fi in cafes and accommodation in big towns and cities, but thrifty download limits elsewhere.

Wi-fi & Internet Service Providers

Wi-fi You'll be able to find wi-fi access around the country, from hotel rooms to pub beer gardens to hostel dorms. Usually you have to be a guest or customer to log in; you'll be issued with an access code. Sometimes it's free, sometimes there's a charge, often there's a limit on time or data.

Hotspots The country's main telecommunications company is Spark New Zealand (www.spark.co.nz), which has more than 1000 wireless hotspots around the country. You can purchase prepaid access cards or a prepaid number from the login page at any wireless hotspot using your credit card. See Spark's website for hotspot listings.

Equipment & ISPs If you've brought your tablet or laptop, consider buying a prepay USB modem (aka a 'dongle') with a local SIM card: both Spark and Vodafone (www.vodafone.co.nz) sell these from around $50.

Legal Matters

If you are questioned or arrested by police, it's your right to ask why, to refrain from making a statement, and to consult a lawyer in private.

Plans are brewing for a referendum on whether personal use of cannabis should be decriminalised, but at the time of writing it was still illegal. Anyone caught carrying this or other illicit drugs will have the book thrown at them.

Drink-driving is a serious offence and remains a significant problem in NZ. The legal blood alcohol limit is 0.05% for drivers aged 20 years and over, and zero for those under 20.

LGBTIQ+ Travellers

The gay tourism industry in NZ isn't as high profile as it is in some other developed nations, but LGBT communities are prominent in Auckland and Wellington, with myriad support organisations across both islands. NZ has progressive laws protecting human rights: same-sex marriage and adoption by same-sex couples were legalised in 2013, while the legal minimum age for sex between consenting persons is 16. Generally speaking, Kiwis are fairly relaxed and accepting about gender fluidity, but that's not to say that homophobia doesn't exist. Rural communities tend to be more conservative; here public displays of affection should probably be avoided.

Resources

There are loads of websites dedicated to gay and lesbian travel in NZ. Gay Tourism New Zealand (www.gaytourismnewzealand.com) is a starting point, with links to various sites. Other worthwhile websites:

○ www.gaynz.net.nz

○ www.lesbian.net.nz

○ www.gaystay.co.nz

Check out the nationwide monthly magazine *express* (www.gayexpress.co.nz) for the latest happenings, reviews and listings on the NZ gay scene. New Zealand Awaits (www.newzealand awaits.com) is a local operator specialising in tours serving LGBT travellers.

Festivals & Events

Auckland Pride Festival (www. aucklandpridefestival.org. nz) Two-and-a-bit weeks of rainbow-hued celebrations in February.

Big Gay Out (www.biggayout. co.nz) Part of the Auckland Pride Festival in February, this flagship day features live music and 'Mr Gay New Zealand'.

Gay Ski Week (www. gayskiweekqt.com) Annual Queenstown snow-fest in August/September.

Maps

New Zealand's **Automobile Association** (AA; ☎0800 500 444; www.aa.co.nz/travel) produces excellent city, town, regional, island and highway maps, available from its local offices. The AA also produces a detailed *New Zealand Road Atlas*. Other reliable countrywide atlases, available from visitor information centres and bookshops, are published by Hema and KiwiMaps.

Land Information New Zealand (www.linz.govt.nz) publishes several exhaustive map series, including street, country and holiday maps, national park and forest park maps, and topographical trampers' maps. Scan the larger bookshops, or try the nearest DOC office or visitor information centre for topo maps.

Online, log onto AA Maps (www.aamaps.co.nz) or Wises (www.wises.co.nz) to pinpoint exact NZ addresses.

Money

ATMs & Eftpos

Branches of the country's major banks across both islands have ATMs, but you won't find them everywhere (eg not in small towns).

Many NZ businesses use Eftpos (electronic funds transfer at point of sale), allowing you to use your bank card (credit or debit) to make direct purchases and often withdraw cash as well. Eftpos is available practically everywhere: just like at an ATM, you'll need a PIN number.

Credit & Debit Cards

Credit cards (Visa, Master-Card) are widely accepted for everything from a hostel bed to a bungy jump, and are pretty much essential for car hire. Credit cards can also be used for over-the-counter cash advances at banks and from ATMs, but be aware that such transactions incur charges. Diners Club and American Express cards are not as widely accepted.

Debit cards enable you to draw money directly from your home bank account using ATMs, banks or Eftpos facilities. Any card connected to the international banking network (Cirrus, Maestro, Visa Plus and Eurocard) should work with your PIN. Fees will vary depending on your home bank; check before you leave. Alternatively, companies such as Travelex offer debit cards with set withdrawal fees and a balance you can top up from your personal bank account while on the road.

Currency

New Zealand's currency is the NZ dollar, comprising 100 cents. There are 10c, 20c, 50c, $1 and $2 coins, and $5, $10, $20, $50 and $100 notes. Prices are often still marked in single cents and then rounded to the nearest 10c when you hand over your money.

Money Changers

Changing foreign currency (and to a lesser extent old-fashioned travellers cheques) is usually no problem at NZ banks or at licensed money changers (eg Travelex) in major tourist areas, cities and airports.

Taxes & Refunds

The Goods and Services Tax (GST) is a flat 15% tax on all domestic goods and services. NZ prices listed by Lonely Planet include GST. There's no GST refund available when you leave NZ.

Tipping

Tipping is completely optional in NZ.

Restaurants The total on your bill is all you need to pay (though sometimes a service charge is factored in). If you like, reward good service with 5% to 10%.

Taxis If you round up your fare, don't be surprised if the driver hands back your change.

Guides Your kayaking guide or tour group leader will happily accept tips; up to $10 is fine.

Opening Hours

Opening hours vary seasonally depending on where you are. Most places close on Christmas Day and Good Friday.

Banks 9am to 4.30pm Monday to Friday, some also 9am to noon Saturday

Cafes 7am to 4pm

Post Offices 8.30am to 5pm Monday to Friday; larger branches also 9.30am to noon Saturday

Pubs & Bars noon to late ('late' varies by region, and by day)

Restaurants noon to 2.30pm and 6.30pm to 9pm

Shops & Businesses 9am to 5.30pm Monday to Friday and 9am to noon or 5pm Saturday

Supermarkets 8am to 7pm, often 9pm or later in cities

Practicalities

Newspapers Check out Auckland's *New Zealand Herald* (www.nzherald.co.nz), Wellington's *Dominion Post* (www.stuff.co.nz/dominion-post) or Christchurch's *The Press* (www.stuff.co.nz/the-press).

TV Watch one of the national government-owned TV stations – including TVNZ 1, TVNZ 2, Māori TV or the 100% Māori-language Te Reo.

Radio Tune in to Radio New Zealand (www.radionz.co.nz) for news, current affairs, classical and jazz. Radio Hauraki (www.hauraki.co.nz) cranks out rock.

DVDs Kiwi DVDs are encoded for Region 4, which includes Australia, the Pacific, Mexico, Central America, the Caribbean and South America.

Smoking Smoking on public transport and in restaurants, cafes, bars and pubs is banned.

Weights & Measures NZ uses the metric system.

Public Holidays

New Zealand's main public holidays:

New Year 1 and 2 January

Waitangi Day 6 February

Easter Good Friday and Easter Monday; March/April

Anzac Day 25 April

Queen's Birthday First Monday in June

Labour Day Fourth Monday in October

Christmas Day 25 December

Boxing Day 26 December

In addition, each NZ province has its own anniversary-day holiday. The dates of these provincial holidays vary: when they fall on Friday to Sunday, they're usually observed the following Monday; if they fall on Tuesday to Thursday, they're held on the preceding Monday. To see an up-to-date list of provincial anniversaries during the year you travel, see www.govt.nz/browse/work/public-holidays-and-work/public-holidays-and-anniversary-dates.

School Holidays

The Christmas holiday season, from mid-December to late January, is part of the summer school vacation: expect transport and accommodation to book out in advance, and queues at tourist attractions. There are three shorter school-holiday periods during the year: from mid- to late April, early to mid-July, and late September to mid-October. For exact dates, see the Ministry of Education website (www.education.govt.nz).

Safe Travel

New Zealand is no more dangerous than other developed countries, but exert normal safety precautions, especially after dark on city streets and in remote areas.

○ Kiwi roads are often made hazardous by map-distracted tourists, wide-cornering campervans and traffic-ignorant sheep.

○ Major fault lines run the length of NZ, causing occasional earthquakes.

○ Avoid leaving valuables in vehicles: theft is a problem, even in remote areas.

○ NZ's climate is unpredictable: hypothermia is a risk in high-altitude areas.

○ At the beach, beware of rips and undertows, which can drag swimmers out to sea.

Government Travel Advice

The following government websites offer travel advisories and information on current hotspots:

Australian Department of Foreign Affairs & Trade (www.smarttraveller.gov.au)

British Foreign & Commonwealth Office (www.gov. uk/fco)

Foreign Affairs, Trade & Development Canada (www. international.gc.ca)

Dutch Ministry of Foreign Affairs (www.government. nl/ministries/ministry-of-foreign-affairs)

German Federal Foreign Office (www.auswaertiges-amt.de)

Japanese Ministry of Foreign Affairs (www.mofa. go.jp)

US Department of State (www.travel.state.gov)

○ NZ's sandflies are an itchy annoyance. Use repellent in coastal and lakeside areas.

Telephone

New Zealand uses regional two-digit area codes for long-distance calls, which can be made from any payphone. If you're making a local call (ie to someone else in the same town), you don't need to dial the area code. But if you're dialling within a region (even if it's to a nearby town with the same area code), you do have to dial the area code.

To make international calls from NZ (which is possible on payphones), you need to dial the international access code 00, then the country code and the area code (without the initial '0'). So for a London number, for example, you'd dial 00-44-20, then the number. If dialling NZ from overseas, the country code is 64, followed by the appropriate area code minus the initial '0'.

Mobile Phones

Most NZ mobile phone numbers are preceded by the prefix 021, 022 or 027. Mobile phone coverage is good in cities and towns and most parts of the North Island, but can be patchy away from urban centres on the South Island.

If you want to bring your own phone and use a pre-paid service with a local SIM card (rather than pay for expensive global roaming on your home network), Vodafone (www.vodafone. co.nz) is a practical option. Any Vodafone shop (in most major towns) will set you up with a NZ Travel SIM and a phone number (from around $30; valid for 30, 60 or 90 days). Top-ups can be purchased at newsagents, post offices and petrol stations all over the country.

Phone Hire New Zealand (www.phonehirenz.com) rents out mobiles, modems and GPS systems (from $3/10/7 per day).

Payphones

Local calls from payphones cost $1 for the first 15 minutes, and $0.20 per minute thereafter, though coin-operated payphones are scarce (and if you do find one, chances are the coin slot will be gummed up); you'll generally need a phonecard. Calls to mobile phones attract higher rates.

Premium-Rate & Toll-Free Calls

Numbers starting with 0900 charge upwards of $1 per minute (more from mobiles). These numbers cannot be dialled from payphones, and sometimes not from prepaid mobile phones.

Toll-free numbers in NZ have the prefix 0800 or 0508 and can be called from anywhere in the country, though they may not be accessible from certain areas or from mobile phones. Numbers beginning with 0508, 0800 or 0900 cannot be dialled from outside NZ.

Phonecards

New Zealand has a wide range of phonecards available, which can be bought at hostels, newsagencies and post offices for a fixed-dollar value (usually $5, $10, $20 and $50). These can be used with any public or private phone by dialling a toll-free access number and then the PIN number on the card. Shop around – rates vary from company to company.

Time

New Zealand is 12 hours ahead of GMT/UTC and two hours ahead of Australian Eastern Standard Time. The

Chathams are 45 minutes ahead of NZ's main islands.

In summer, NZ observes daylight saving time, where clocks are wound forward by one hour on the last Sunday in September; clocks are wound back on the first Sunday of the following April.

Toilets

Toilets in NZ are sit-down Western style. Public toilets are plentiful, and are usually reasonably clean with working locks and plenty of toilet paper.

See www.toiletmap.co.nz for public toilet locations around the country.

Tourist Information

The website for the official national tourism body, Tourism New Zealand (www.newzealand.com), is an excellent place for pre-trip research. The site has information in several languages, including German, Spanish, French, Chinese and Japanese.

Princes Wharf i-SITE (☑09-365 9914; www.aucklandnz.com; Princes Wharf; ⊗9am-5pm) Auckland's main official information centre.

Auckland International Airport i-SITE (☑09-365 9925; www.aucklandnz.com;

International Arrivals Hall; ⊗6.30am-10.30pm)

Christchurch i-SITE (☑03-379 9629; www.christchurchnz.com; Arts Centre, 28 Worcester Blvd; ⊗8.30am-5pm)

Christchurch Airport i-SITE (☑03-741 3980; www.christchurchnz.com; International Arrivals Hall; ⊗8am-6pm)

Queenstown i-SITE (☑03-442 4100; www.queenstownisite.co.nz; cnr Shotover & Camp Sts; ⊗8.30am-8pm)

Local Tourist Offices

Almost every Kiwi city or town seems to have a visitor information centre. The bigger centres stand united within the outstanding i-SITE network (www.newzealand.com/travel/i-sites) – more than 80 info centres affiliated with Tourism New Zealand. i-SITEs have trained staff, information on local activities and attractions, and free brochures and maps. Staff can also book activities, transport and accommodation.

Bear in mind that some information centres only promote accommodation and tour operators who are paying members of the local tourist association, and that sometimes staff aren't supposed to recommend one activity or accommodation provider over another.

There's also a network of Department of Conservation (DOC; www.doc.govt.nz) visitor centres to help you plan outdoor activities and make bookings (particularly for tramping trails and huts). DOC visitor centres – in national parks, regional centres and major cities – usually also have displays on local flora and fauna.

Travellers with Disabilities

Kiwi accommodation generally caters fairly well for travellers with disabilities, with most hostels, hotels and motels equipped with one or two wheelchair-accessible rooms. (B&Bs aren't required to have accessible rooms.) Many tourist attractions similarly provide wheelchair access, with wheelchairs often available. Most i-SITE visitor centres can advise on suitable attractions in the locality.

Tour operators with accessible vehicles operate from most major centres. Key cities are also serviced by 'kneeling' buses (buses that hydraulically stoop down to kerb level to allow easy access), and many taxi companies offer wheelchair-accessible vans. Large car-hire firms (Avis, Hertz etc) provide cars with hand controls at no extra charge (but advance notice is required). Air New Zealand is also very well equipped to accommodate travellers in wheelchairs.

Download Lonely Planet's free Accessible Travel guides from http://lptravel.to/AccessibleTravel.

Activities

Out and about, the DOC has been hard at work improving access to short walking trails (and some of the longer ones). Tracks that are wheelchair accessible are categorised as 'easy access short walks'; the Cape Reinga Lighthouse Walk and Milford Foreshore Walk are two prime examples.

If cold-weather activity is more your thing, see Snow Sports NZ's page on adaptive winter sports: www.snowsports.co.nz/get-involved/adaptive-snow-sports.

Resources

Access4All (www.access4all.co.nz) Listings of accessible accommodation and activities around New Zealand.

Firstport (http://firstport.co.nz) Includes a high-level overview on transport in NZ, including mobility taxis and accessible public transport.

Mobility Parking (www.mobilityparking.org.nz) Apply for an overseas visitor mobility parking permit ($35 for 12 months) and have it posted to you before you even reach NZ.

Visas

Citizens of 60 countries, including Australia, the UK, the US and most EU countries, don't need visas for New Zealand (length-of-stay allowances vary). See www.immigration.govt.nz.

Visa application forms are available from NZ diplomatic missions overseas, travel agents and **Immigration New Zealand** (☎09-914 4100, 0508 558 855; www.immigration.govt.nz). Immigration New Zealand has more than 25 offices overseas, including the US, UK and Australia; consult the website.

Women Travellers

New Zealand is generally a very safe place for female travellers, although the usual sensible precautions apply (for both sexes): avoid walking alone at night; never hitchhike alone; and if you're out on the town, have a plan on how to get back to your accommodation safely. Sexual harassment is not a widely reported problem in NZ, but of course that doesn't mean it doesn't happen. See www.womentravel.co.nz for tours aimed at solo women.

Transport

Getting There & Away

New Zealand is a long way from almost everywhere – most travellers jet in from afar. Flights, cars and tours can be booked online at lonelyplanet.com/bookings.

Entering the Country

Disembarkation in New Zealand is generally a straightforward affair, with only the usual customs declarations and luggage-carousel scramble to endure. Under the Orwellian title of 'Advance Passenger Screening', documents that used to be checked after you touched down in NZ (passport, visa etc) are now checked before you board your flight – make sure all your documentation is in order so that your check-in is stress-free.

Air

New Zealand's abundance of year-round activities means that airports here are busy most of the time: if you want to fly at a particularly popular time of year (eg over the Christmas period), book well in advance.

The high season for flights into NZ is during summer (December to February), with slightly less of a premium on fares over the shoulder months (October/November and March/April). The low season generally tallies with the winter months (June to August), though this is still a busy time for airlines ferrying ski bunnies and powder hounds.

Departure tax is included in the price of a ticket.

Climate Change & Travel

Every form of transport that relies on carbon-based fuel generates CO_2, the main cause of human-induced climate change. Modern travel is dependent on aeroplanes, which might use less fuel per kilometre per person than most cars but travel much greater distances. The altitude at which aircraft emit gases (including CO_2) and particles also contributes to their climate change impact. Many websites offer 'carbon calculators' that allow people to estimate the carbon emissions generated by their journey and, for those who wish to do so, to offset the impact of the greenhouse gases emitted with contributions to portfolios of climate-friendly initiatives throughout the world. Lonely Planet offsets the carbon footprint of all staff and author travel.

Airlines Flying to & from New Zealand

New Zealand's international carrier is Air New Zealand (www.airnewzealand.co.nz), which flies to runways across Europe, North America, eastern Asia, Australia and the Pacific, and has an extensive network across NZ.

Winging in with direct flights from Australia, Virgin Australia (www.virginaustralia.com), Qantas (www.qantas.com.au), Jetstar (www.jetstar.com) and Air New Zealand are the key players.

Joining Air New Zealand from North America, other operators include Air Canada (www.aircanada.com) and American Airlines (www.aa.com) – the latter has direct flights from Los Angeles to Auckland.

From Europe, the options are a little broader, with British Airways (www.britishairways.com),

Lufthansa (www.lufthansa.com) and Virgin Atlantic (www.virginatlantic.com) entering the fray. Flights go via major Middle Eastern or Asian airports. Several other airlines stop in NZ on broader round-the-world routes.

From Asia and the Pacific there are myriad options, with direct flights from China, Japan, Singapore, Malaysia, Thailand and Pacific Island nations.

Airports

A number of NZ airports handle international flights, with Auckland receiving the most traffic:

Auckland Airport (AKL; ☎09-275 0789; www.aucklandairport.co.nz; Ray Emery Dr, Mangere)

Christchurch Airport (CHC; ☎03-358 5029; www.christchurchairport.co.nz; 30 Durey Rd)

Dunedin Airport (DUD; ☎03-486 2879; www.dnairport.co.nz; 25 Miller Rd, Momona; ☎)

Queenstown Airport (ZQN; ☑03-450 9031; www.queens townairport.co.nz; Sir Henry Wrigley Dr, Frankton)

Wellington Airport (WLG; ☑04-385 5100; www.welling tonairport.co.nz; Stewart Duff Dr, Rongotai)

Note that Hamilton, Rotorua and Palmerston North airports are capable of handling direct international arrivals and departures, but are not currently doing so.

Sea

Cruise Ship If you're travelling from Australia and content with a slow pace, try P&O (www. pocruises.com.au) and Princess (www.princess.com) for cruises to New Zealand.

Cargo Ship If you don't need luxury, a berth on a cargo ship or freighter to/from New Zealand is a quirky way to go. Freighter Expeditions (www. freighterexpeditions.com.au) offers cruises to New Zealand from Singapore (49 days return) and Antwerp in Belgium (32 days one way).

Yacht It is possible (though by no means straightforward) to make your way between NZ, Australia and the Pacific islands by crewing on a yacht. Try asking around at harbours, marinas, and yacht and sailing clubs. Popular yachting harbours in NZ include the Bay of Islands and Whangarei (both in Northland), Auckland and Wellington. March and April are the best months to look for boats heading to Australia. From Fiji, October to November is a peak departure season to beat the cyclones that soon follow in that neck of the woods.

Getting Around

Air

Those who have limited time to get between NZ's attractions can make the most of a widespread (and very reliable and safe) network of intra- and inter-island flights.

Airlines in New Zealand

The country's major domestic carrier, Air New Zealand, has an aerial network covering most of the country, often operating under the Air New Zealand Link moniker on less popular routes. Australia-based Jetstar also flies between main urban areas. Between them, these two airlines carry the vast majority of domestic passengers in NZ. Beyond this, several small-scale regional operators provide essential transport services to outlying islands, such as Great Barrier Island in the Hauraki Gulf, to Stewart Island and the Chathams. There are also plenty of scenic- and charter-flight operators around NZ, not listed here. Operators:

Air Chathams (☑0800 580 127; www.airchathams. co.nz) Services to the remote Chatham Islands from Wellington, Christchurch and Auckland. Auckland–Whakatane flights also available.

Air New Zealand (☑0800 737 000; www.airnewzealand.co.nz) Offers flights between 20-plus domestic destinations, plus myriad overseas hubs.

Air2there.com (☑0800 777 000; www.air2there.com) Connects destinations across Cook Strait, including Paraparaumu, Wellington, Nelson and Blenheim.

Barrier Air (☑0800 900 600; www.barrierair.kiwi) Flies the skies over Great Barrier Island, Auckland and Kaitaia (and seasonally, Tauranga and Whitianga).

FlyMySky (☑0800 222 123; www.flymysky.co.nz) At least three flights daily from Auckland to Great Barrier Island.

Golden Bay Air (☑0800 588 885; www.goldenbayair.co.nz) Flies regularly to Takaka in Golden Bay from Wellington and Nelson. Also connects to Karamea for Heaphy Track trampers.

Jetstar (☑0800 800 995; www.jetstar.com) Joins the dots between key tourism centres: Auckland, Wellington, Christchurch, Dunedin, Queenstown, Nelson, Napier, New Plymouth and Palmerston North.

Sounds Air (☑0800 505 005; www.soundsair.co.nz) Numerous flights daily between Picton and Wellington, plus flights from Wellington to Blenheim, Nelson, Westport and Taupo. Also flies Blenheim to Christchurch, Kaikoura, Paraparaumu and Napier, and Nelson to Paraparaumu.

Stewart Island Flights (☑03-218 9129; www.stewartisland flights.co.nz) Flies between Invercargill and Stewart Island three times daily.

Sunair (☎ 0800 786 247; www. sunair.co.nz) Flies to Whitianga from Ardmore (near Auckland), Great Barrier Island and Tauranga, plus numerous other North Island connections between Hamilton, Rotorua, Gisborne and Whakatane.

Air Passes

Available exclusively to travellers from the USA or Canada who have bought an Air New Zealand fare to NZ from the USA or Canada, Australia or the Pacific Islands, Air New Zealand offers the good-value New Zealand Explorer Pass (www.airnewzealand.com/explorer-pass). The pass lets you fly between up to 37 destinations in New Zealand, Australia and the South Pacific islands (including Norfolk Island, Tonga, New Caledonia, Samoa, Vanuatu, Tahiti, Fiji, Niue and the Cook Islands). Fares are broken down into four discounted, distance-based zones: zone one flights start at US$99 (eg Auckland to Wellington); zone two from US$129 (eg Auckland to Queenstown); zone three from US$214 (eg Wellington to Sydney); and zone four from US$295 (eg Tahiti to Auckland). You can buy the pass before you travel, or after you arrive in NZ.

Bicycle

Touring cyclists proliferate in NZ, particularly over summer. The country is clean, green and relatively uncrowded, and has lots of cheap accommodation (including camping) and abundant fresh water. The roads are generally in good nick, and the climate is usually not too hot or cold. Road traffic is the biggest danger: trucks overtaking too close to cyclists are a particular threat. Bikes and cycling gear are readily available to rent or buy in the main centres, and bicycle-repair shops are common.

By law all cyclists must wear an approved safety helmet (or risk a fine); it's also vital to have good reflective safety clothing. Cyclists who use public transport will find that major bus lines and trains only take bicycles on a 'space available' basis (in cities, usually outside rush hour) and may charge up to $10. Some of the smaller shuttle bus companies, on the other hand, make sure they have storage space for bikes, which they carry for a surcharge.

If importing your own bike or transporting it by plane within NZ, check with the relevant airline for costs and the degree of dismantling and packing required.

See www.nzta.govt.nz/walking-cycling-and-public-transport for more bike safety and legal tips, and the New Zealand Cycle Trail (Nga Haerenga; www.nzcycletrail.com) – a network of 22 'Great Rides' across NZ.

Hire

Rates offered by most outfits for renting road or mountain bikes are usually around $20 per hour to $60 per day. Longer-term rentals may be available by negotiation. You can often hire bikes from your accommodation (hostels, holiday parks etc), or rent more reputable machines from bike shops in the larger towns.

Boat

New Zealand may be an island nation but there's virtually no long-distance water transport around the country. Obvious exceptions include the boat services between Auckland and various islands in the Hauraki Gulf, the inter-island ferries that cross the Cook Strait between Wellington and Picton, and the passenger ferry that negotiates Foveaux Strait between Bluff and the town of Oban on Stewart Island.

If you're cashed-up, consider the cruise liners that chug around the NZ coastline as part of broader South Pacific itineraries: P&O Cruises (www.pocruises.com.au) is a major player.

Bus

Bus travel in NZ is easy-going and well organised, with services transporting you to the far reaches of both islands (including the start/end of various walking tracks)...but it can be expensive, tedious and time-consuming.

NZ's main bus company is **InterCity** (www.intercity.co.nz), which can drive you to just about anywhere on the North and South Islands. **Naked Bus** (📱09-979 1616; https://naked bus.com) has similar routes and remains the main competition. Both bus lines offer fares as low as $1(!). InterCity also has a South Island sightseeing arm called **Newmans Coach Lines** (www.newmanscoach. co.nz), travelling between Queenstown, Christchurch and the West Coast glaciers.

Privately run shuttle buses can transport travellers to some trailheads or collect them from the end point of a tramp; advance booking essential.

Seat Classes & Smoking

There are no allocated economy or luxury classes on NZ buses (very democratic), and smoking on the bus is a definite no-no.

Naked Bus has a sleeper class on overnight services between Auckland and Wellington (stopping at Hamilton and Palmerston North) where you can lie flat in a 1.8m-long bed (bring a sleeping bag, pillowcase and maybe earplugs). See http://nakedbus.com/nz/home/sleeper-bus for details.

Reservations

Over summer (December to February), school holidays and public holidays, book well in advance on popular routes (a week or two if possible). At other times a day or two ahead is usually fine. The best prices are generally available

online, booked a few weeks in advance.

Bus Passes

If you're covering a lot of ground, both InterCity and Naked Bus offer bus passes (respectively, priced by hours and number of trips). This can be cheaper than paying as you go, but do the maths before buying and note that you'll be locked into using one network. Passes are usually valid for 12 months.

On fares other than bus passes, InterCity offers a discount of around 10% for YHA, ISIC, HI, Nomads, BBH or VIP backpacker card holders. Senior discounts only apply for NZ citizens.

Nationwide Passes

Flexipass A hop-on/hop-off InterCity pass, allowing travel to pretty much anywhere in NZ, in any direction, including the Interislander ferry across Cook Strait. The pass is purchased in blocks of travel time: minimum 15 hours ($125), maximum 60 hours ($459). The average cost of each block becomes cheaper the more hours you buy. You can top up the pass if you need more time.

Aotearoa Explorer, Tiki Tour & Island Loop Hop-on/hop-off, fixed-itinerary nationwide passes offered by InterCity. These passes link up tourist hotspots and cost $775 to $1140. Passes with a narrower scope (eg West Coast or Southern Alps) are also offered. See www.intercity. co.nz/bus-pass/travelpass for details.

Naked Passport (www.naked passport.com) A Naked Bus pass that allows you to buy trips in blocks of five, which you can add to any time, and book each trip as needed. Five/15/20 trips cost $159/269/439.

North Island Passes

InterCity offers six hop-on/hop-off, fixed-itinerary North Island bus passes, from short $125 runs between Auckland and Paihia, to $405 trips from Auckland to Wellington via the big sights in between. See www. intercity.co.nz/bus-pass/travelpass for details.

South Island Passes

On the South Island, InterCity offers six hop-on/hop-off, fixed-itinerary passes, from $125 runs along the West Coast between Picton and Queenstown, to a $549 loop via Christchurch, Queenstown and the West Coast glaciers. See www. intercity.co.nz/bus-pass/travelpass for details.

Shuttle Buses

As well as InterCity and Naked Bus, regional shuttle buses fill in the gaps between the smaller towns. Operators include the following (see www.tourism. net.nz/transport/bus-and-coach-services for a complete list), offering regular scheduled services and/or bus tours and charters:

Abel Tasman Travel (www.abel tasmantravel.co.nz) Traverses the roads between Nelson, Motueka, Golden Bay and Abel Tasman National Park.

Atomic Shuttles (www.atomic travel.co.nz) Has services throughout the South Island, including to Christchurch, Dunedin, Invercargill, Picton, Nelson, Greymouth, Hokitika, Queenstown and Wanaka.

Catch-a-Bus South (www. catchabussouth.co.nz) Inver-cargill and Bluff to Dunedin and Queenstown.

Cook Connection (www.cook connect.co.nz) Triangulates between Mt Cook, Twizel and Lake Tekapo.

East West Coaches (www. eastwestcoaches.co.nz) Offers a service between Christchurch and Westport via Lewis Pass.

Go Kiwi Shuttles (www.go-kiwi.co.nz) Links Auckland with Whitianga on the Coromandel Peninsula daily.

Hanmer Connection (www. hanmerconnection.co.nz) Daily services between Hanmer Springs and Christchurch.

Headfirst Travel (www.trav-elheadfirst.com) Does a loop from Rotorua to Waitomo (with an option to finish in Auckland).

Manabus (www.manabus.com) Runs in both directions daily between Auckland and Wel-lington via Hamilton, Rotorua, Taupo and Palmerston North. Also runs to Tauranga, Paihia and Napier. Some services operated by Naked Bus.

Tracknet (www.tracknet. net) Summer track transport (Milford, Hollyford, Routeburn, Kepler) with Queenstown, Te Anau and Invercargill connections.

Trek Express (www.trekex press.co.nz) Shuttle services to all tramping tracks in the top half of the South Island

(eg Heaphy, Abel Tasman, Old Ghost Road).

West Coast Shuttle (www. westcoastshuttle.co.nz) Daily bus from Greymouth to Christchurch and back.

Car & Motorcycle

The best way to explore NZ in depth is to have your own wheels. It's easy to hire cars and campervans, though it's worth noting that fuel costs can be eye-watering. Alternatively, if you're in NZ for a few months, you might consider buying your own vehicle.

Automobile Association (AA)

New Zealand's **Automobile Association** (AA; ☑0800 500 444; www.aa.co.nz/travel) provides emergency break-down services, distance calculators and accommo-dation guides (from holiday parks to motels and B&Bs).

Members of overseas automobile associations should bring their mem-bership cards – many of these bodies have reciprocal agreements with the AA.

Driving Licences

International visitors to NZ can use their home country driving licence – if your licence isn't in English, it's a good idea to carry a certified translation with you. Alternatively, use an International Driving Permit (IDP), which will usually be issued on the spot (valid for 12 months) by your home country's automobile association.

Fuel

Fuel (petrol, aka gasoline) is available from service stations across NZ: unless you're cruising around in something from the 1970s, you'll be filling up with 'unleaded', or LPG (gas). LPG is not always stocked by rural suppliers; if you're on gas, it's safer to have dual-fuel capability. Aside from remote locations like Milford Sound and Mt Cook, petrol prices don't vary much from place to place: per-litre costs at the time of research were hovering above \$2.

Hire

Campervan

Check your rear-view mirror on any far-flung NZ road and you'll probably see a shiny white campervan (aka mobile home, motor home, RV) packed with liberated travellers, mountain bikes and portable barbecues cruising along behind you.

Most towns of any size have a campground or holi-day park with powered sites (where you can plug your vehicle in) for around \$35 per night. There are also 250-plus vehicle-accessible Department of Conserva-tion (DOC; www.doc.govt. nz) campsites around NZ, priced up to \$21 per adult. Weekly campsite passes for rental campervans slice up to 50% off the price of stays in DOC campgrounds; check the website for info.

You can hire campervans from dozens of companies.

Prices vary with season, vehicle size and length of rental, and it pays to book months in advance.

A small van for two people typically has a minikitchen and foldout dining table, the latter transforming into a double bed when dinner is done and dusted. Larger 'superior' two-berth vans include shower and toilet. Four- to six-berth campervans are the size of trucks (and similarly sluggish) and, besides the extra space, usually contain a toilet and shower.

Over summer, rates offered by the main rental firms for two-/four-/six-berth vans booked three months in advance start at around $120/150/230 per day (though they rise much higher, depending on model) for a rental of two weeks or more. Rates drop to $60/75/100 per day during winter.

Major operators:

Apollo (☑0800 113 131, 09-889 2976; www.apollocamper.co.nz)

Britz (☑09-255 3910, 0800 081 032; www.britz.co.nz) **Also does** 'Britz Bikes' (add a mountain or city bike from $12 per day).

Maui (☑09-255 3910, 0800 688 558; www.maui-rentals. com)

Wilderness Motorhomes (☑09-282 3606; www.wilder ness.co.nz)

Car

Competition between car-hire companies in NZ is torrid, particularly in the big cities and Picton. Remember that if you want to travel far, you need unlimited kilometres. Some (but not all) companies require drivers to be at least 21 years old – ask around.

International car-hire firms don't generally allow you to take their vehicles between islands on the Cook Strait ferries. Instead, you leave your car at either Wellington or Picton terminal and pick up another car once you've crossed the strait. This saves you paying to transport a vehicle on the ferries, and is a pain-free exercise. However, some local car-hire firms (such as Apex) are fine with you taking your rental vehicle on the ferry and will even book your ferry ticket for you.

International Rental Companies

The big multinational companies have offices in most major cities, towns and airports. Firms sometimes offer one-way rentals (eg collect a car in Auckland, leave it in Wellington), but there are usually restrictions and fees.

The major companies offer a choice of either unlimited kilometres, or 100km (or so) per day free, plus so many cents per subsequent kilometre. Daily rates in main cities typically start at around $40 per day for a compact, late-model, Japanese car, and from $70 for medium-sized cars (including GST, unlimited kilometres and insurance).

Avis (☑0800 655 111, 09-526 2847; www.avis.co.nz)

Budget (☑09-529 7788, 0800 283 438; www.budget.co.nz)

Europcar (☑0800 800 115; www.europcar.co.nz)

Hertz (☑0800 654 321; www. hertz.co.nz)

Thrifty (☑03-359 2721, 0800 737 070; www.thrifty.co.nz)

Local Rental Companies

Local rental firms proliferate. These are almost always cheaper than the big boys – sometimes half the price – but the cheap rates may come with serious restrictions: vehicles are often older, depots might be further away from airports/ city centres, and with less formality sometimes comes a less protective legal structure for renters.

Rentals from local firms start at around $30 or $40 per day for the smallest option. It's cheaper if you rent for a week or more, and there are often low-season and weekend discounts.

Affordable, independent operators with national networks:

a2b Car Rentals (☑0800 545 000, 09-254 4397; www.a2b-car-rental.co.nz)

Ace Rental Cars (☑0800 502 277, 09-303 3112; www.ace rentalcars.co.nz)

Apex Rentals (☑03-595 2315, 0800 500 660; www.apex rentals.co.nz)

Ezi Car Rental (☑0800 545 000, 09-254 4397; www.ezicar rental.co.nz)

Go Rentals (☑0800 467 368, 09-974 1598; www.gorentals. co.nz)

Omega Rental Cars (📞09-377 5573, 0800 525 210; www. omegarentalcars.com)

Pegasus Rental Cars (📞0800 803 580; www.rentalcars.co.nz)

Transfercar (📞09-630 7533; www.transfercar.co.nz) Relocation specialists with massive money-saving deals on one-way car rental.

Motorcycle

Born to be wild? NZ has great terrain for motorcycle touring, despite the fickle weather in some regions. Most of the country's motorcycle-hire shops are in Auckland and Christchurch, where you can hire anything from a little 50cc moped (aka nifty-fifty) to a throbbing 750cc touring motorcycle and beyond. Recommended operators (who also run guided tours) offer rates around $100 per day:

New Zealand Motorcycle Rentals & Tours (📞09-486 2472; www.nzbike.com)

Te Waipounamu Motorcycle Tours (📞03-372 3537; www. motorcycle-hire.co.nz)

Insurance

Rather than risk paying out wads of cash if you have an accident, you can take out your own comprehensive insurance policy, or (the usual option) pay an additional fee per day to the rental company to reduce your excess. This brings the amount you must pay in the event of an accident down from around $1500 or $2000 to around $200 or $300. Smaller operators offering cheap rates often have a compulsory insurance excess, taken as a credit-card bond, of around $900.

Many insurance agreements won't cover the cost of damage to glass (including the windscreen) or tyres, and insurance coverage is often invalidated on beaches and certain rough (4WD) unsealed roads – read the fine print.

See www.acc.co.nz for info on NZ's Accident Compensation Corporation insurance scheme (fault-free personal injury insurance).

Road Hazards

There's an unusually high percentage of international drivers involved in road accidents in NZ – something like 30% of accidents involve a nonlocal driver. Kiwi traffic is usually pretty light, but it's easy to get stuck behind a slow-moving truck or campervan – pack plenty of patience, and know your road rules before you get behind the wheel. There are also lots of slow wiggly roads, one-way bridges and plenty of gravel roads, all of which require a more cautious driving approach. And watch out for sheep!

To check road conditions call 📞0800 444 449 or see www.nzta.govt.nz/traffic.

Road Rules

○ Kiwis drive on the left-hand side of the road; cars are right-hand drive. Give way to the right at intersections.

○ All vehicle occupants must wear a seatbelt or risk a fine. Small children must be belted into approved safety seats.

○ Always carry your licence when driving. Drink-driving is a serious offence and remains a significant problem in NZ, despite widespread campaigns and severe penalties. The legal blood alcohol limit is 0.05% for drivers aged over 20, and 0% (zero) for those under 20.

○ At single-lane bridges (of which there are a surprisingly large number), a smaller red arrow pointing in your direction of travel means that *you* give way.

○ Speed limits on the open road are generally 100km/h; in built-up areas the limit is usually 50km/h. Speed cameras and radars are used extensively.

○ Be aware that not all rail crossings have barriers or alarms. Approach slowly and look both ways.

○ Don't pass other cars when the centre line is yellow.

○ It's illegal to drive while using a mobile phone.

Local Transport

Bus, Train & Tram

New Zealand's larger cities have extensive bus services but, with a few honourable exceptions, they are mainly daytime, weekday operations; weekend services can be infrequent or nonexistent. Negotiating inner-city

Auckland is made easier by Link buses; Hamilton has a free city-centre loop bus; Christchurch has city buses and the historic tramway. Most main cities have late-night buses for boozy Friday and Saturday nights. Don't expect local bus services in more remote areas.

The only cities with decent local train services are Auckland and Wellington, with four and five suburban routes respectively.

Taxi

The main cities have plenty of taxis and even small towns may have a local service. Taxis are metered, and generally reliable and trustworthy.

Train

New Zealand train travel is all about the journey, not about getting anywhere in a hurry. **Great Journeys of New Zealand** (☑0800 872 467, 04-495 0775; www.great journeysofnz.co.nz) operates four routes, listed below. It's best to reserve online or by phone; reservations can be made directly through Great Journeys of New Zealand (operated by KiwiRail), or at most train stations, travel agents and visitor information centres. Cheaper fares appear if you book online within NZ. All services are for day travel (no sleeper services).

Capital Connection Weekday commuter service between Palmerston North and Wellington.

Coastal Pacific Track damage during the 2016 earthquakes put this scenic Christchurch–Picton route out of action, but when we went to press it was estimated to return in late 2018.

Northern Explorer Between Auckland and Wellington: southbound on Mondays, Thursdays and Saturdays; northbound on Tuesdays, Fridays and Sundays.

TranzAlpine Over the Southern Alps between Christchurch and Greymouth – one of the world's most famous train rides.

Train Passes

A Scenic Journeys Rail Pass allows unlimited travel on all of its rail services, including passage on the Wellington–Picton Interislander ferry. There are two types of pass, both requiring you to book your seats a minimum of 24 hours before you want to travel. Both have discounts for kids.

Fixed Pass Limited duration fares for one/two/three weeks, costing $629/729/829 per adult.

Freedom Pass Affords you travel on a certain number of days over a 12-month period; a three-/seven-/10-day pass costs $439/969/1299.

Language

New Zealand has three official languages: English, Māori and NZ sign language. Although English is what you'll usually hear, Māori has been making a comeback. You can use English to speak to anyone in New Zealand, but there are some occasions when knowing a small amount of Māori is useful, such as when visiting a *marae*, where often only Māori is spoken. Some knowledge of Māori will also help you interpret the many Māori place names you'll come across.

Kiwi English

Like the people of other English-speaking countries in the world, New Zealanders have their own, unique way of speaking the language. The flattening of vowels is the most distinctive feature of Kiwi pronunciation. For example, in Kiwi English, 'fish and chips' sounds more like 'fush and chups'. On the North Island sentences often have 'eh!' attached to the end. In the far south a rolled 'r' is common, which is a holdover from that region's Scottish heritage – it's especially noticeable in Southland.

Māori

The Māori have a vividly chronicled history, recorded in songs and chants that dramatically recall the migration to New Zealand from Polynesia as well as other important events. Early missionaries were the first to record the language in a written form using only 15 letters of the English alphabet.

Māori is closely related to other Polynesian languages such as Hawaiian, Tahitian and Cook Islands Māori. In fact, New Zealand Māori and Hawaiian are quite similar, even though more than 7000km separates Honolulu and Auckland.

The Māori language was never dead – it was always used in Māori ceremonies – but over time familiarity with it was definitely on the decline. Fortunately, recent years have seen a revival of interest in it, and this forms an integral part of the renaissance of *Māoritanga* (Māori culture). Many Māori people who had heard the language spoken on the *marae* for years but had not used it in their day-to-day lives, are now studying it and speaking it fluently. Māori is taught in schools throughout New Zealand, some TV programs and news reports are broadcast in it, and many English place names are being renamed in Māori. Even government departments have been given Māori names: for example, the Inland Revenue Department is also known as Te Tari Taake (the last word is actually *take*, which means 'levy', but the department has chosen to stress the long 'a' by spelling it 'aa').

In many places, Māori have come together to provide instruction in their language and culture to young children; the idea is for them to grow up speaking both Māori and English, and to develop a familiarity with Māori tradition. It's a matter of some pride to have fluency in the language. On some *marae* only Māori can be spoken.

Pronunciation

Māori is a fluid, poetic language and surprisingly easy to pronounce once you remember to split each word (some can be amazingly long) into separate syllables. Each syllable ends in a vowel. There are no 'silent' letters.

Most consonants in Māori – h, k, m, n, p, t and w – are pronounced much the same as in English. The Māori r is a flapped sound (not rolled) with the tongue near the front of the mouth. It's closer to the English 'l' in pronunciation.

The ng is pronounced as in the English words 'singing' or 'running', and can be used at the beginning of words as well as at the end. To practise, just say 'ing' over and over, then isolate the 'ng' part of it.

The letters wh, when occuring together, are generally pronounced as a soft English 'f'. This pronunciation is used in many place names in New Zealand, such as

Whakataneand Whakapapa (all pronounced as if they begin with a soft 'f'). There is some local variation: in the region around the Whanganui River, for example, *wh* is pronounced as in the English word 'when'.

The correct pronunciation of the vowels is very important. The examples below are a rough guideline – it helps to listen carefully to someone who speaks the language well. Each vowel has both a long and a short sound, with long vowels often denoted by a line over the letter or a double vowel. We have not indicated long and short vowel forms in this book.

Vowels

a	as in 'large', with no 'r' sound
e	as in 'get'
i	as in 'marine'
o	as in 'pork'
u	as the 'oo' in 'moon'

Vowel Combinations

ae, ai	as the 'y' in 'sky'
ao, au	as the 'ow' in 'how'
ea	as in 'bear'
ei	as in 'vein'
eo	as 'eh-oh'
eu	as 'eh-oo'
ia	as in the name 'Ian'
ie	as the 'ye' in 'yet'
io	as the 'ye o' in 'ye old'
iu	as the 'ue' in 'cue'
oa	as in 'roar'
oe	as in 'toe'
oi	as in 'toil'
ou	as the 'ow' in 'how'
ua	as the 'ewe' in 'fewer'

Greetings & Small Talk

Māori greetings are becoming increasingly popular – don't be surprised if you're greeted with *Kia ora*.

Welcome!	*Haere mai!*
Hello./Good luck./ Good health.	*Kia ora.*
Hello. *(to one person)*	*Tena koe.*
Hello. *(to two people)*	*Tena korua.*
Hello. *(to three or more people)*	*Tena koutou.*
Goodbye. *(to person staying)*	*E noho ra.*
Goodbye. *(to person leaving)*	*Haere ra.*
How are you? *(to one person)*	*Kei te pehea koe?*
How are you? *(to two people)*	*Kei te pehea korua?*
How are you? *(to or three more people)*	*Kei te pehea koutou?*
Very well, thanks./ That's fine.	*Kei te pai.*

Māori Geographical Terms

The following words form part of many Māori place names in New Zealand, and indicate the meaning of these place names. For example: Waikaremoana is the Sea *(moana)* of Rippling *(kare)* Waters *(wai)*, and Rotorua means the Second *(rua)* Lake *(roto)*.

a – of
ana – cave
ara – way, path or road
awa – river or valley
heke – descend
hiku – end; tail
hine – girl; daughter
ika – fish
iti – small
kahurangi – treasured possession; special greenstone
kai – food
kainga – village
kaka – parrot
kare – rippling
kati – shut or close
koura – crayfish
makariri – cold
manga – stream or tributary
manu – bird
maunga – mountain
moana – sea or lake
moko – tattoo
motu – island
mutu – finished; ended; over

nga – the (plural)

noa – ordinary; not *tapu*

nui – big or great

nuku – distance

o – of, place of...

one – beach, sand or mud

pa – fortified village

papa – large blue-grey mudstone

pipi – common edible bivalve

pohatu – stone

poto – short

pouri – sad; dark; gloomy

puke – hill

puna – spring; hole; fountain

rangi – sky; heavens

raro – north

rei – cherished possession

roa – long

roto – lake

rua – hole in the ground; two

runga – above

tahuna – beach; sandbank

tane – man

tangata – people

tapu – sacred, forbidden or taboo

tata – close to; dash against; twin islands

tawaha – entrance or opening

tawahi – the other side (of a river or lake)

te – the (singular)

tonga – south

ure – male genitals

uru – west

waha – broken

wahine – woman

wai – water

waingaro – lost; waters that disappear in certain seasons

waka – canoe

wera – burnt or warm; floating

wero – challenge

whaka... – to act as ...

whanau – family

whanga – harbour, bay or inlet

whare – house

whenua – land or country

whiti – east

GLOSSARY

Following is a list of abbreviations, 'Kiwi English', Māori and slang terms used in this book and which you may hear in New Zealand.

All Blacks – NZ's revered national rugby union team

Anzac – Australia and New Zealand Army Corps

Aoraki – Māori name for Mt Cook, meaning 'Cloud Piercer'

Aotearoa – Māori name for NZ, most often translated as 'Land of the Long White Cloud'

aroha – love

bach – holiday home (pronounced 'batch'); see also crib

bro – literally 'brother'; usually meaning mate

BYO – 'bring your own' (usually applies to alcohol at a restaurant or cafe)

choice/chur – fantastic; great

crib – the name for a bach in Otago and Southland

DOC – Department of Conservation (or Te Papa Atawhai); government department that administers national parks, tracks and huts

eh? – roughly translates as 'don't you agree?'

farmstay – accommodation on a Kiwi farm

football – rugby, either union or league; occasionally soccer

Great Walks – set of nine popular tramping tracks within NZ

greenstone – jade; *pounamu*

haka – any dance, but usually a war dance

hangi – oven whereby food is steamed in baskets over embers in a hole; a Māori feast

hapu – subtribe or smaller tribal grouping

Hawaiki – original homeland of the Māori

hei tiki – carved, stylised human figure worn around the neck; also called a *tiki*

home-stay – accommodation in a family house

hongi – Māori greeting; the pressing of fore-heads and noses, and sharing of life breath

hui – gathering; meeting

i-SITE – information centre

iwi – large tribal grouping with common lineage back to the original migration from *Hawaiki*; people; tribe

jandals – contraction of 'Japanese sandals'; flip-flops; thongs; usually rubber footwear

kauri – native pine

kia ora – hello

Kiwi – New Zealander; an adjective to mean anything relating to NZ

kiwi – flightless, nocturnal brown bird with a long beak

Kiwiana – things uniquely connected to NZ life and culture, especially from bygone years

kiwifruit – small, succulent fruit with fuzzy brown skin and juicy green flesh; aka Chinese gooseberry or zespri

kumara – Polynesian sweet potato, a Māori staple food

Kupe – early Polynesian navigator from *Hawaiki*, credited with the discovery of the islands that are now NZ

mana – spiritual quality of a person or object; authority or prestige

Māori – indigenous people of NZ

Māoritanga – things Māori, ie Māori culture

marae – sacred ground in front of the Māori meeting house; more commonly used to refer to the entire complex of buildings

Maui – figure in Māori (Polynesian) mythology

mauri – life force/principle

moa – large, extinct flightless bird

moko – tattoo; usually refers to facial tattoos

nga – the (plural); see also *te*

ngai/ngati – literally, 'the people of' or 'the descendants of'; tribe (pronounced 'kai' on the South Island)

pa – fortified Māori village, usually on a hilltop

Pakeha – Māori for a white or European person

Pasifika – Pacific Island culture

paua – abalone; iridescent paua shell is often used in jewellery

pavlova – meringue cake topped with cream and kiwifruit

PI – Pacific Islander

poi – ball of woven flax

pounamu – Māori name for greenstone

powhiri – traditional Māori welcome onto a *marae*

rip – dangerously strong current running away from the shore at a beach

Roaring Forties – the ocean between 40° and 50° south, known for very strong winds

silver fern – symbol worn by the All Blacks and other national sportsfolk on their jerseys; the national netball team is called the Silver Ferns

sweet, sweet as – all-purpose term like choice; fantastic, great

tapu – strong force in Māori life, with numerous meanings; in its simplest form it means sacred, forbidden, taboo

te – the (singular); see also *nga*

te reo – literally 'the language'; the Māori language

tiki – short for *hei tiki*

tiki tour – scenic tour

tramp – bushwalk; trek; hike

tuatara – prehistoric reptile dating back to the age of dinosaurs

tui – native parson bird

wahine – woman

wai – water

wairua – spirit

Waitangi – short way of referring to the Treaty of Waitangi

waka – canoe

Behind the Scenes

Acknowledgements

Climate map data adapted from Peel MC, Finlayson BL & McMahon TA (2007) 'Updated World Map of the Köppen-Geiger Climate Classification', *Hydrology and Earth System Sciences*, 11, 1633–44.

This Book

This 2nd edition of Lonely Planet's *Best of New Zealand* guidebook was curated by Charles Rawlings-Way and researched and written by Brett Atkinson, Andrew Bain, Peter Dragicevich, Samantha Forge, Anita Isalska and Sofia Levin. The previous edition was written by Charles, Brett and Peter, along with Sarah Bennett and Lee Slater. This guidebook was produced by the following:

Destination Editor Tasmin Waby

Senior Product Editor Kate Chapman

Product Editor Kathryn Rowan

Senior Cartographer Diana von Holdt

Book Designer Clara Monitto

Assisting Editors Janet Austin, Katie Connolly, Monique Perrin

Cartographer Julie Dodkins

Cover Researcher Naomi Parker

Thanks to Franziska Duge, Sandie Kestell, Kate Mathews, Rachel Rawling, Angela Tinson

Send Us Your Feedback

We love to hear from travellers – your comments keep us on our toes and help make our books better. Our well-travelled team reads every word on what you loved or loathed about this book. Although we cannot reply individually to postal submissions, we always guarantee that your feedback goes straight to the appropriate authors, in time for the next edition. Each person who sends us information is thanked in the next edition, the most useful submissions are rewarded with a selection of digital PDF chapters.

Visit lonelyplanet.com/contact to submit your updates and suggestions or to ask for help. Our award-winning website also features inspirational travel stories, news and discussions.

Note: We may edit, reproduce and incorporate your comments in Lonely Planet products such as guidebooks, websites and digital products, so let us know if you don't want your comments reproduced or your name acknowledged. For a copy of our privacy policy visit lonelyplanet.com/privacy.

Index

O

Symbols & Map Key

Look for these symbols to quickly identify listings:

◎ Sights

✪ Activities

❸ Courses

◉ Tours

✪ Festivals & Events

✖ Eating

☕ Drinking

✪ Entertainment

🔒 Shopping

ℹ Information & Transport

These symbols and abbreviations give vital information for each listing:

🍃 Sustainable or green recommendation

FREE No payment required

🕿 Telephone number

🕓 Opening hours

🅿 Parking

🚭 Nonsmoking

❄ Air-conditioning

@ Internet access

🛜 Wi-fi access

🏊 Swimming pool

🚌 Bus

🛥 Ferry

🚊 Tram

🚆 Train

📖 English-language menu

🥦 Vegetarian selection

👫 Family-friendly

Find your best experiences with these Great For... icons.

🖼 Art & Culture

🏖 Beaches

💰 Budget

☕ Cafe/Coffee

🚲 Cycling

▶ Detour

🍷 Drinking

🎟 Entertainment

🎆 Events

👪 Family Travel

🍽 Food & Drink

📖 History

💬 Local Life

🐦 Nature & Wildlife

📷 Photo Op

🔭 Scenery

🛍 Shopping

🧳 Short Trip

🏀 Sport

🥾 Walking

❄ Winter Travel

Sights

🏖 Beach
🐦 Bird Sanctuary
☸ Buddhist
🏰 Castle/Palace
✝ Christian
☯ Confucian
🕉 Hindu
☪ Islamic
卍 Jain
✡ Jewish
❶ Monument
🏛 Museum/Gallery/Historic Building
🏚 Ruin
⛩ Shinto
☬ Sikh
☯ Taoist
🍇 Winery/Vineyard
🐾 Zoo/Wildlife Sanctuary
◎ Other Sight

Points of Interest

🏄 Bodysurfing
⛺ Camping
☕ Cafe
🛶 Canoeing/Kayaking
● Course/Tour
🤿 Diving
🍸 Drinking & Nightlife
✖ Eating
🎭 Entertainment
♨ Sento Hot Baths/Onsen
🛍 Shopping
🎿 Skiing
🛏 Sleeping
🤿 Snorkelling
🏄 Surfing
🏊 Swimming/Pool
🚶 Walking
🏄 Windsurfing
❋ Other Activity

Information

$ Bank
📧 Embassy/Consulate
➕ Hospital/Medical
@ Internet
👮 Police
✉ Post Office
📞 Telephone
🚻 Toilet
ℹ Tourist Information
● Other Information

Geographic

🏖 Beach
⊢ Gate
🛖 Hut/Shelter
🗼 Lighthouse
🔭 Lookout
▲ Mountain/Volcano
🌴 Oasis
🌳 Park
)(Pass
🧺 Picnic Area
💧 Waterfall

Transport

✈ Airport
Ⓑ BART station
✖ Border crossing
Ⓣ Boston T station
🚌 Bus
🚡 Cable car/Funicular
🚲 Cycling
⛴ Ferry
Ⓜ Metro/MRT station
🚝 Monorail
🅿 Parking
⛽ Petrol station
Ⓢ Subway/S-Bahn/Skytrain station
🚕 Taxi
🚉 Train station/Railway
🚊 Tram
⊖ Tube Station
Ⓤ Underground/U-Bahn station
● Other Transport

Peter Dragicevich

After a successful career in niche newspaper and magazine publishing, both in his native New Zealand and in Australia, Peter finally gave into Kiwi wanderlust, giving up staff jobs to chase his diverse roots around much of Europe. Over the last decade he's written dozens of guidebooks for Lonely Planet on an oddly disparate collection of countries, all of which he's come to love. He once again calls Auckland his home – although his current nomadic existence means he's often elsewhere.

Samantha Forge

Samantha became hooked on travel at the age of 17, when she arrived in London with an over-stuffed backpack and a copy of LP's *Europe on a Shoestring*. After a stint in Paris, she moved back to Australia to work as an editor in LP's Melbourne office. Eventually, however, her wanderlust got the better of her, and she now works as a freelance writer and editor.

Anita Isalska

Anita is a travel journalist, editor and copywriter whose work for Lonely Planet has taken her from Greek beach towns to Malaysian jungles. After several merry years as an in-house editor and writer – with a few of them in Lonely Planet's London office – Anita now works freelance between the UK, Australia and any Balkan guesthouse with a good wi-fi connection. Anita writes about travel, food and culture for a host of websites and magazines. Read her stuff on www.anitaisalska.com.

Sofia Levin

Sofia is a Melbourne-based journalist with an insatiable appetite for food and travel. She is a regular contributor to Lonely Planet, Fairfax newspapers and a range of magazines. When she's not travelling, Sofia runs Word Salad – a social media and copywriting business established in 2012 – and spreads smiles with her Insta-famous toy poodle, @lifeofjinkee. Follow her adventures at @sofiaklevin.

Our Story

A beat-up old car, a few dollars in the pocket and a sense of adventure. In 1972 that's all Tony and Maureen Wheeler needed for the trip of a lifetime – across Europe and Asia overland to Australia. It took several months, and at the end – broke but inspired – they sat at their kitchen table writing and stapling together their first travel guide, *Across Asia on the Cheap*. Within a week they'd sold 1500 copies. Lonely Planet was born.

Today, Lonely Planet has offices in Franklin, London, Melbourne, Oakland, Dublin, Beijing and Delhi, with more than 600 staff and writers. We share Tony's belief that 'a great guidebook should do three things: inform, educate and amuse'.

Our Writers

Charles Rawlings-Way

Charles is a veteran travel, food and music writer who has penned 30-something titles for Lonely Planet – including guides to Singapore, Tonga, Toronto, Sydney, Tasmania, New Zealand, the South Pacific and Australia – and numerous articles. After dabbling in the dark arts of architecture, cartography, project management and busking for some years, Charles hit the road for LP in 2005 and hasn't stopped travelling since.

Brett Atkinson

Brett is based in Auckland but is frequently on the road for Lonely Planet. He's a full-time travel and food writer and is featured regularly on the Lonely Planet website, and in newspapers, magazines and websites across New Zealand and Australia. Craft beer and street food are Brett's favourite reasons to explore places. Since becoming a Lonely Planet author in 2005, Brett has covered areas as diverse as Vietnam, Sri Lanka, the Czech Republic, Morocco, California and the South Pacific.

Andrew Bain

Andrew's writing and photography feature in magazines and newspapers around the world, and his writing has won multiple awards, including best adventure story and best Australian story (three times) from the Australian Society of Travel Writers. He was formerly commissioning editor of Lonely Planet's outdoor adventure series of titles, and is the author of *Headwinds*, the story of his 20,000-km cycling journey around Australia, and Lonely Planet's *A Year of Adventures*. His musings can be found at www.adventurebeforeavarice.com.

--- More Writers ---

STAY IN TOUCH LONELYPLANET.COM/CONTACT

AUSTRALIA The Malt Store, Level 3, 551 Swanston St, Carlton, Victoria 3053
☏ 03 8379 8000, fax 03 8379 8111

IRELAND Digital Depot, Roe Lane (off Thomas St), Digital Hub, Dublin 8, D08 TCV4

USA 124 Linden Street, Oakland, CA 94607
☏ 510 250 6400, toll free 800 275 8555, fax 510 893 8572

UK 240 Blackfriars Road, London SE1 8NW
☏ 020 3771 5100, fax 020 3771 5101

 twitter.com/lonelyplanet
 facebook.com/lonelyplanet
 instagram.com/lonelyplanet
 youtube.com/lonelyplanet
 lonelyplanet.com/newsletter